KU-411-958

STEPHEN BURGEN

Your Mother's Tongue

A BOOK OF EUROPEAN INVECTIVE

INDIGO

First published in Great Britain 1996
by Victor Gollancz

This Indigo edition published 1997
Indigo is an imprint of the Cassell Group
Wellington House, 125 Strand, London WC2R 0BB

© Stephen Burgen 1996

The right of Stephen Burgen to be identified as author
of this work has been asserted by him in accordance with
the Copyright, Designs and Patents Act, 1988.

A catalogue record for this book is
available from the British Library.

ISBN 0 575 40090 0

Page 34: extract from *Treason Against God* by Leonard W. Levy
© 1981, reproduced by kind permission of Schocken Books;
page 56: extract from *Glitz* by Elmore Leonard and page
143: extract from *Farewell My Lovely* by Raymond Chandler
reproduced by kind permission of Penguin Books Ltd; pages
181–2: extract from *The Gypsies* by Angus Fraser
reproduced by kind permission of Blackwell Publishers.

Printed in Great Britain by
Guernsey Press Co. Ltd,
Guernsey, Channel Isles

All rights reserved. No part of this publication may be
reproduced or transmitted in any form or by any means,
electronic or mechanical including photocopying,
recording or any information storage or retrieval system,
without prior permission in writing from the publishers.

This book is sold subject to the condition that it shall not,
by way of trade or otherwise, be lent, resold, hired out, or
otherwise circulated without the publisher's prior consent
in any form of binding or cover other than that in which it
is published and without a similar condition including this
condition being imposed on the subsequent purchaser.

97 98 99   10 9 8 7 6 5 4 3 2 1

Your Mother's Tongue

Stephen Burgen is a journalist on *The Times*, and has contributed articles on language to the *Guardian* and the *Independent*. He lives in south London.

Contents

For Doodie,
who gave me the word

Acknowledgements

I've never understood that old dictum about leaving the best wine till last, as by then you'd be too drunk to appreciate it. Nor do I buy that last-but-not-least tradition of author's acknowledgements whereby the person who plainly has endured the most during the writing of the book is relegated to the end. So, best wine first, thanks to Sarah Davison for everything. I could drink a case of you.

For reading all or part of the manuscript and for their advice and corrections I am greatly indebted to Teresa Coral Albert, David Altheer, Ann Brady, Sue Herrod, Mary Kerrigan, Helen Knox, Jeremy Morton, Vassilis Nastos and Steffen Runki. Thanks also to Vicki Harris, Mike Petty and Viv Redman at Gollancz and to my agent David O'Leary.

Isaac Newton said modestly, 'If I have seen further it is by standing on the shoulders of giants.' For my part, if I've seen anything at all, it's been by plying strangers with drink and urging them to talk dirty. This book attempts to come to grips with or at least touch upon the vernacular of twenty-one European tongues: Catalan, Corsican, Danish, Dutch, English, Euskera, Finnish, Flemish, French, Gallego, German, Greek, Irish, Italian, Pied-Noir, Portuguese, Romani, Spanish, Swedish, Welsh and Yiddish. It could not have been written without the help and encouragement of many people. Heartfelt thanks to:

Máire ní Aighleart, Vicky Anning, Denis Archdeacon, Will Atkins, Francisco Bello Landeira, Marta Berraondo Lahuerta,

Hannele Branch, The British Library, Arnold, Daniel and Jennie Burgen, Miguel Carbonell, Reme Castrejón Puyo, Alice Cescatti, Laurent Cescatti, Penelope Christoffel, Máire ní Chuinn, Mary Davison, Caterina De Felice, Laoise De Paor, Corinne Descamps-Merlino, Nils Erik Enkvist, Giovanni Ferri, Hans-Jürgen Förster, Sue and Thanasis Frentzos, Haldo Gibson, Frank Gephardt, Seosaimhín ní Gloinn, Lina Goncalves, Julian Green, Helene Stenkjar Iversen, Ceri Jones, Raimo Jussila, Donald Kenrick, Martin Kømmler, Pierre Lanfranchi, Pãola Lopes, Kathryn Lowrie, Piet Lüthi, Philip Lyman at Gotham Book Mart (New York), Uinsionn Mac Dubhghaill, Brendan Mac Lua, Tomás Mac Stiofáin, Clarence Major, Marcos Matos, Kari Nahkola, Mary O'Carroll, Liám O'Choinléain, Pádraig O'Conchóir, Maria Palma Castillón, Heikki Paunonen, Juan Rossell Carol, George Roubicek, Ingrid Scherf, Ivana, Alfredo and Francesca Schiaffella, Strand Books (New York), Ulf Teleman, David Thomas, Alex Tapaccos, TSB Booksearch, Rosa Vázquez, Charo Vivas Sabido, Mariano Vivas Sabido, Christina Wegener, Saskia Wesnigk, Lex Wolf, Graham Wood and Wordsworth Books (Clapham).

1 ★ Babel Talk

America is God's crucible, the great melting pot where
all the races of Europe are melting and re-forming.

Israel Zangwill, *The Melting Pot*. 1908

Europe isn't America, so don't talk to us about melting pots.
Here we like to nourish our differences and pamper our prejudices. We fatten our resentment to keep the wolf from the
door – in case it gets out. Take the Cerdagne, for example.
The where? La Cerdagne, La Cerdanya. Some time during the
1980s I rented a house in the Cerdagne, an area that I naively
took to be in the French Pyrenees. The house was owned by
an elderly man with an accent that could split logs who, after
showing me where the woodpile and fusebox were, proceeded
to explain that this was not in fact France but a part of
Catalonia.

He related with some venom, as though it was something
that had happened only the other day, how the Cerdagne –
that is to say, the Cerdanya – had been ceded to France as
part of a sordid political deal. He had no time for the French
and resented the fact that he had to speak their language in
addition to his native Catalan. The man was by no means
stupid, nor a nutcase, nor was he making any of this up. The
Cerdanya had been part of the great Catalo-Aragonese empire
that in the fifteenth century encompassed Sicily and Greece at
a time when, next to Arabic, Catalan was perhaps the most
widely spoken language on the Mediterranean shore. And the
Cerdanya, or at least the part that is now in France, had indeed

been ceded as part of a sordid deal when the Spanish king Felipe IV, who was a Habsburg, and Louis XIV signed the Peace of the Pyrenees. But this betrayal, which this affable old man was relating with such feeling, took place in 1659.

This is the Europe we are seeking to unify, a patchwork of Cerdagnes, where we don't forgive and forget and let bygones be bygones. In the circumstances, nothing is more laughable than the constant bleating of Little Englanders and their fellow Europhobes about how our national identities are about to be swallowed up into some amorphous 'Euroness'. It's difficult to imagine a more improbable scenario. If European identity was so perishable, then the peoples who have been colonized or absorbed into Europe's nation-states – the Irish, Corsicans, Basques, Bretons and Finns, to name only a few – would have lost theirs long ago. Heaven knows, they've been given every encouragement. But it's not the European way to let sleeping dogs lie, because history teaches us that the dog will wake – or be woken, more likely – and it will wake up hungry. The recent wars in what was briefly called Yugoslavia demonstrated the European ethos at its worst: think small, forget nothing, forgive no one, and never sign anything unless there's a gun at your head.

It's not that we don't settle our differences, more that we never resolve them. As the poet Yeats said of the Irish, there is 'more substance in our enmities than in our love'. This is the dead weight of history on Europe's back, though also what keeps the place interesting. Unfortunately, through force of habit, we've tended to settle things the old-fashioned way, by killing each other. But sooner or later the killing stops and one or more party has to sign a paper in which they make an act of contrition for all the misery they've caused. At the same time they grudgingly renounce their claim to whatever disputed valley or riverbank the blood has been shed over. As a rule, we like to use these treaty signings as an opportunity to put some one-horse town on the map – Ghent, Utrecht, Versailles, Yalta, Maastricht, for instance.

However, the big one was in Rome in 1957, when the foundations of the new Europe were laid. Not that it was a new idea. The poet Dante proposed a Europe united under one sovereign back in the fourteenth century and in the years since the idea has been espoused by such diverse Europeans as Kant and Rousseau, Garibaldi and Metternich. At the end of the Second World War even the British warmed to the idea of a European federation, not that Britain would join, goodness no; Britain was a world power and had bigger fish to fry. In 1951 a Foreign Office paper concluded: 'Owing to her position as a world power the United Kingdom cannot join the integration movement.' At least not until 1972 when, suitably abject, and after Ted Heath had licked Georges Pompidou's *bottes* to the requisite high shine, Britain's application to join was grudgingly accepted.

And now we're all going to mend our bad old ways; no more wars, no more pogroms, no inquisitions. In the new Europe *le rosbif* will lie down with the frog and kraut shall speak – nicely – unto wop. We shall no longer settle our differences on the fields of Picardie or on the banks of the Ebro, but in the marbled halls of Brussels and Strasbourg, where amendments will be the only casualties and lunch the heaviest weapon.

Somehow this harmony is to be achieved in the absence of a common language. De Gaulle famously remarked of France: '*Comment voulez-vous gouverner un pays qui a deux cent quarante-six variétés de fromage?*' ('How can you expect to govern a country that has 246 varieties of cheese?') But, whatever the French believe, the issue of European identity doesn't revolve around cheese, it revolves around language. Not only do we not have a common language but, *merci quand même*, we don't want one either. Babel is our hometown and we like it just fine. All right, flags are at issue, too, and national holidays and the colour of police uniforms. But at root it's about language. We are what we speak.

The European Union recognizes among its fifteen members eleven official languages. All directives, discussion documents, reports of working parties and so on issued by the Union are made available in these eleven languages. As a consequence, the work of its five thousand translators and interpreters absorbs one-third of the European Commission's administrative budget. But eleven is only scratching the surface; Brussels acknowledges at least fifteen others and a European Union stretching from the Atlantic to the Urals would encompass fifty or more tongues. The British Isles embrace four distinct languages (English, Welsh, Irish and Gaelic), France has five (French, Breton, Occitan, Provençal and Corsican), while in Spain a quarter of the population speak either Gallego, Euskera (the Basque tongue) or Catalan in addition to Castilian Spanish. Indeed Catalan is spoken by six million people, more than either Danish or Finnish.

Swedish has equal status with Finnish in Finland, while Belgium is divided between three language communities – French, Flemish and German – in addition to the officially bilingual (French/Flemish) city of Brussels. So sensitive is the language issue in Belgium that the census never asks people to state their first language, and the distribution and proportion of the various language communities is a state secret lest it fuel border disputes. In Greece there is also the question of the Vlach dialect, which is not a written language, and the Slavic dialect spoken in Macedonia. As for Italy, the state has accorded official status to a dozen languages as diverse as German, Greek, Catalan, Slovenian and Provençal, on top of which Italians speak a further dozen or so dialects, some of which are almost mutually unintelligible. Italian, a Florentine dialect that at the time of unification in 1861 was spoken by less than 10 per cent of the population, is the linguistic string that loosely binds Italy into nationhood. Italy bears out the writer Max Weinreich's dictum that 'A language is a dialect with an army and navy.'

However, amid the clamour for the right to be educated in Sardinian or to watch Welsh TV, it should be borne in mind that the largest numbers of minority language speakers in countries such as France and Britain are not the inheritors of ancient Celtic or Latin tongues but native Urdu, Hindi, Arabic, Yoruba and Hausa speakers. A recent report showed that London schoolchildren shared between them over two hundred mother tongues. Behold tomorrow's sleeping dogs.

If Europe has a lingua franca it's English, spoken worldwide by perhaps a billion people, and the second language of choice of the majority (83 per cent) of European secondary school students, as compared to 32 per cent who study French and 16 per cent German. But while English appears to be taking the corridors of Brussels by stealth – though not if France has anything to do with it – there's no reason to believe that it or any other language is about to become a transnational European tongue. If language had anything to do with common sense we'd all be speaking Esperanto. But it hasn't; language is about being human, and particular languages are about being particular humans.

Consider the Basques: the common sense thing for a person growing up in, say, San Sebastian would be to master the 'national' language, Castilian Spanish, the third most widely spoken language in the world, and be done with it. That would be the sensible thing. But in reality what happens is that people from San Sebastian and elsewhere in the Basque country – or Euskadi, to give it its proper name – insist, rather forcefully, on their right to speak Euskera, a language only slightly more difficult to learn than Martian.

Euskera isn't an Indo-European language, a family of 132 diverse but related tongues that range from German and French to Irish and Russian. It doesn't belong to any other family either; it stands all by itself and, as a result, no matter how many languages you speak none of them will be of any help whatsoever when it comes to learning Euskera. The most likely explanation for this linguistic isolation is that the Basques were not among those waves of people who tramped muttering and squabbling out of the Caucasus and northern India to become in due course the peoples of Europe. The Basques, it's believed, were already here, snuggled up in the Bay of Biscay, and may have been here longer than any of us. Which is a good enough reason, if you're growing up in San Sebastian, or Donostia, to give it its Basque name, to insist on your right to speak Euskera. Not the sensible thing, no, but most definitely the human thing. Naturally the Basques learn Spanish and often French as well; they're not idiots.

This diversity is what makes the project of European union such a challenge. The people of Europe have clung to their cultural identities, their cuisines, and above all to their languages, in the face of every inducement, including persecution, exile and genocide. It hardly seems credible, therefore, that the Maastricht or any other treaty is going to achieve what neither Charlemagne, Cromwell, Napoleon, Hitler, Franco or Stalin managed, that is, to stuff all these babbling, mulish genii into some monocultural bottle.

This diversity doesn't mean that we can't all get along together. To do so, however, some of us are going to have to make a bit more effort to learn each other's languages, and when we do we shall have to come to grips with the vernacular, the everyday workhorse words we use to intensify our phrases, bemoan our fate and condemn or provoke our fellow citizens. The vernacular is where cultural attitudes settle and condense, a rich residue of language that often defies analysis. Cursing and swearing is in essence a small set of words orbiting around an even smaller set of taboos surrounding God, family, sex, and some bodily functions. However, like pop music, which has concocted a seemingly inexhaustible variety of recipes from the same basic ingredients, slang has a great capacity to refresh itself without ever draining the glass. When Humpty-Dumpty tells Alice: 'When I use a word, it means just what I choose it to mean, neither more nor less,' she retorts: 'The question is whether you *can* make words mean so many different things.' Well, when it comes to the vernacular, yes you can, you can make them mean whatever you damn well please.

For all our differences and for all they're heartfelt, Europeans have much in common; above all a set of values, prejudices, superstitions and taboos based on Judaeo-Christian – and to a lesser extent Islamic – custom and morality. You'd think, therefore, that when it came to breaking these taboos, we'd all go about it in much the same way and to more or less the same extent. Far from it. For example, a Swede will have little problem getting through the day without calling anyone or thing a 'prick', and an entire lifetime without comparing either God or the Mother of God to a pig, feats that the average Italian would find virtually impossible. On the other hand the Italian would be baffled that the Swedes regard *fitta* (cunt) as an unutterably nasty word when *figa*, its Italian counterpart, has no negative connotations and is used to compliment both women and men on their looks, their clothes or their cars. Likewise, if the Italian tried to enrage the Swede by calling him a cuckold, the latter – in common with other northern Europeans – would probably reach for a dictionary. But if the roles were reversed the Italian – or any southern European man – would more likely reach for his knife.

In 1649 the British parliament introduced the death penalty for swearing at one's parents, a statute which, were it revived today, would wipe out an entire generation. Since the turn of the century, and especially since the 1960s, swearing has

become increasingly widespread and acceptable, commonplace in the street and at work as well as on television. It's
almost de rigueur in serious literature, while in the cinema subtitlers and dubbers grapple with the foul-mouthed vérités of
modern dialogue. Women of all social classes have taken to
swearing and in some countries, notably France, women insult
men more than vice versa.

This shift in attitude holds good right across Europe – not
that swearing has an equal place in every European country.
One can only conjecture as to why, although it's plainly
another manifestation of a general easing of social constraints.
On the one hand this can be seen as just another stage of a
cycle. Taking the example of Britain: the Elizabethans liked to
curse, the Puritans put a stop to it; then came the foul-mouthed
period of the Restoration but by the middle of the eighteenth
century cursing was frowned on again. Then came the new
puritanism of the Victorians upon whose tight lips even
innocuous words such as breast became unspeakable.

This latest upsurge in 'bad language' is a post-war phenomenon, the work of the so-called 'baby boomers', who were
underwhelmed by the moral authority of the generation that
had brought them Auschwitz, Hiroshima and the Cold War,
a mood captured by the line in Allen Ginsberg's poem
'America': 'Go fuck yourself with your atom bomb'. A few
years later the Sixties radical Abbie Hoffman signalled the
decline of sexual taboos with the comment: 'Work is the only
dirty four-letter word in the language' – the sort of thing
people only say during an economic boom.

For the purposes of this book, when I say, for example,
that 'the Portuguese say' it should be understood that in general this refers to a Portuguese born after 1945 as, right across
the national and social spectrum, the previous generation was
considerably more restrained in its speech. Naturally, I also
recognize that in any culture, some people swear much more

than others, and some do so hardly at all. But if vulgarity can have a mean, then that is what this book represents. No attempt is made here to judge whether this general loosening of tongues is a good or a bad thing for society, the individual or freedom of speech. But 'bad language' – both its quantity and quality – is very revealing of cultural attitudes.

As we shall see, with the exception of the British Isles, the Protestant north swears and curses less and with less imagination than the Catholic and Orthodox south, although this generalization would have to be revised should Poland, Russia and the Baltic states join the Union. Nor do we use the same words or harp on the same taboos and, even when we do, often they mean quite different things. Furthermore, some cultures have adopted portmanteau swearwords, words that are in constant use, signifying anything and nothing. For English speakers the word is 'fuck', for Italians it's *cazzo* (prick), for Greeks *malakas* (wanker), and so on. We do not, in more senses than one, speak the same language.

Aside from England's conflict with the Irish and Madrid's with the Basques, Europeans among the current EU member states have not taken up arms against each other for an unprecedented fifty years. Not because we've forgotten our differences, that's not our style, but we're trying really hard not to kill each other over them, nor over farm subsidies or fishing quotas or whose head should appear on the new European banknotes. What follows is a grand tour of anger, exasperation, prejudice, irony, loathing and wit as expressed in twenty-one of the languages spoken in the present European Union. We're going to try to get along, but we won't be rushed and we won't be coerced. And anyone who tries to strong-arm us into anything is going to feel the rough side of the European tongue.

2 ★ Do You Eat With That Mouth?

> You taught me language; and my profit on't
> Is, I know how to curse.
>
> Caliban, *The Tempest*

What's the point of swearing? People are quick to condemn 'bad language', or *la langue verte* (green language) as the French call it, but what exactly is it and what's it for? In the famous 1971 *Oz* obscenity trial, three editors of an 'alternative' magazine were prosecuted by the British Crown on charges which included conspiracy to corrupt public morals and contravening the Obscene Publications Act. The prosecution opened by claiming that the magazine promoted homosexuality and lesbianism, implicitly the outer limits of obscenity, and in its concluding remarks six weeks later said: 'It is up to you, ladies and gentlemen of the jury, to set the moral standard by which we shall continue to live.' During those six weeks the court tried to arrive at a definition of obscenity. When the jury asked the judge for assistance in this matter he angrily told them that obscenity meant anything that was 'repulsive, filthy, loathsome, indecent or lewd or any of these'. But that's the dictionary, not the legal, definition, for which reason the convictions on the main charges were shortly overturned. The law defines obscenity as anything that might 'deprave or corrupt'.

But whatever the law says, twenty-five years on from the *Oz* trial we're no closer to a working definition. For example, nearly everyone would agree that 'cunt' is 'bad language', but that 'vagina' isn't. That is, unless you happen to be a London

Underground executive. London Underground banned the contraceptive ads put out by Marie Stopes International because the text included the apparently offensive word 'vagina'. And only a few weeks earlier a public outcry forced America Online, the biggest US commercial online service, to restore the word 'breast' which it had banished in a bid to keep the Internet 'obscenity-free'. Both events occurred in 1995, proof that the spirit of puritanism is far from dead. The Puritans themselves set to work in 1606 with a law that banned public performances of works that jestingly or profanely used the name of 'God, or of Jesus Christ, or the Holy Ghost, or of the Trinity'. Then in 1642 they stopped pussyfooting around and banned theatre altogether, confirming H. L. Mencken's definition of puritanism as 'the haunting fear that someone, somewhere, may be happy'.

This book deals with invective, insults and maledictions, a relatively small neighbourhood in the sprawling logopolis of slang. Slang, a word of English but uncertain origin, has been borrowed into languages as diverse as German and Italian which had presumably lacked a slang word for slang. But slang is enormous, endless. Every occupation and activity has its own body of slang. You could fill a large volume with British Army slang and half of it would be out of date by the time it went to press. A book on black street talk would be largely *passé* as soon as it was written.

What we're dealing with here is cursing and swearing, of which there are three fundamental forms: expletives and exclamations; curses; and everyday 'bad language'. With expletives and exclamations, the sort of things you say when you slam your finger in a drawer, or when your number comes up in the lottery, catharsis is the name of the game, whether you shout Damn!, Ouch! or Jesus, Mary and Joseph! There's a wide range of such utterances, but in European terms Shit! is practically universal. Then there are curses, distinct from run-of-the-mill swearing because with a curse you wish harm on someone, even if the harm may not befall them for many years, as for example in the Yiddish curse *Zolst farliren aleh tseyner achitz eynm, un dos zol dir vey ton!* (May you lose all your teeth but one and that should ache!).

Cursing, therefore, is part of a longer game, which may partly explain why it has died out in our impatient age. The other reason, no doubt, is the decline in the belief in God or other powers that could be invoked to cause harm to others. In the next chapter we shall examine how, over the past one hundred years, the tendency to swear *by* – for which religious belief is a prerequisite – has given way to a tendency to swear *at*. In grammatical terms this represents a shift from the subjunctive 'May you be fucked' (cursing) to the imperative 'Fuck you' (swearing). Whether the overall demise of the subjunctive in English parallels a decline in religious belief would make a fascinating study, perhaps even a TV mini-series.

The distinction between cursing and swearing was nicely made three hundred years ago by John Bunyan in his morality tale *The Life and Death of Mr Badman*. 'Swearing,' he says,

> 'hath immediately to do with the name of God, and it calls upon him to be witness to the truth of what is said; that is, if they that swear, swear by him. Some, indeed, swear by idols, as by the mass, by our lady, by the saints, beasts, birds and other creatures; but the usual way of our profane ones in England is to swear by God, Christ, faith, and the like. But, however, or by whatever they swear, cursing is distinguished from swearing thus. To curse, to curse profanely, is to sentence another or ourself, for or to evil; or to wish that some evil might happen to the person or thing under the curse unjustly.'

Cursing is not something most of us do any more but the tradition is very much alive in Irish, Romani and Yiddish. The

Spanish occasionally spit out some baroque curse such as *Así te tragues un pavo y todas las plumas se conviertan en cuchillas de afeitar* (May all your turkey's feathers turn into razor blades) but this is fairly unusual. Gypsy curses such as *Ja and o beng* (Go to the devil) were once much feared and are still quite common. Jews are superstitious about mentioning death or wishing it upon others, and also avoid mentioning either God or the devil, a fear that is turned on its head in the hyperbolic 'May God strike me down if there's one word of a lie' that is a trademark of Jewish banter. Despite this superstition there are some powerful curses in Yiddish such as *A mise meshinne af dir!* (A horrible death to you!), or *In d'rerd arayn!* (Into the ground!). *Zol dir chapn a chalerye!* (May you catch cholera!) harks back to earlier times and is redolent of the unusual Dutch custom of insulting people by suggesting that they're afflicted with diseases. *Kankerleir* (cancer carrier), *teringleir* (TB carrier) and *aidsleir* (Aids carrier) are all common insults in Holland. The nearest equivalent is the Greek description of a prostitute as a *siphiliàra* (syphilis carrier). As a rule, however, of all the taboos, those surrounding death and disease are invoked least in popular speech.

Europe's cursing capital is Ireland, where a combination of Catholicism and more ancient mythologies have kept superstition alive. (Interestingly, the Irish word *guíodóreacht* means both 'praying' and 'cursing'.) One of the oldest maledictory rituals in Ireland involves the use of 'cursing stones'. In one custom, water-rounded stones were collected and heaped in the form of a peat fire. The person laying the curse knelt before the stones and cursed their intended victim, always ending the ritual with the words 'until these stones go on fire'. The curser then hid the stones, each with a separate curse, in an inaccessible place. There are also a number of 'public' cursing stones in Ireland, notably the eleven stones known as St Bridget's Stone at Killinagh in Co. Cavan.

Irish curses take many forms, the most basic of which is *Mallacht Dé ort* (The curse of God on you). Then there are a number that involve choking and drowning. A terrible curse on a fisherman, for example, is *Bás múch ort* (May you die by smothering, i.e. drowning) or, more euphemistically, *Bás na bpisín chugat* (The death of kittens to you). On the other hand there's *Go dtachta an diabhal thú, a chonúis* (May the devil choke you, o slovenly useless person) or the chilling *Marbhfháisc ort* (The death-knot on you), a reference to the custom of tying a corpse's jaws shut.

But one of the worst must be *Mallacht Chromaill ort* (The curse of Cromwell on you). The English like to think of Cromwell as some kind of republican hero, but he didn't like the Irish and loathed Catholics, and the feeling was mutual. Cromwell committed what can only be called genocide in Ireland, banishing the entire population to the beautiful but barren western province of Connacht and transporting the Catholic clergy and many others to the Caribbean, mostly to Barbados, where they were among the first slaves and thanks to whom so many Afro-Caribbean men are called Desmond. On Montserrat in the Leeward Islands, Irish was the lingua franca until the end of the eighteenth century. Three hundred years later the curse of Cromwell is not to be taken lightly. In common with other Europeans, the Irish don't forget those who have wronged them, and they have more to remember than most. They certainly haven't forgotten old Ironsides.

In Ireland, as elsewhere, swearing of a more personal kind has taken precedence over curses. The primary functions of swearing are to deliver direct insults such as 'You bastard!', and to intensify speech, as in 'It's bloody useless'. But there are also people for whom swearing forms an essential part of the rhythm of speech. As we shall see, for English speakers this typically results in a grammar and syntax underpinned by the word 'fuck'. Many English speakers are so dependent on 'fuck' to pilot them across the choppy straits of a five-word phrase that without it they are left mouthing soundlessly like a fish caught high and dry by the tide. In other languages, Spanish for example, this habit of speech can result in more elaborate forms such as *Estoy hasta los cojones de este jodido hijo de puta* (I'm fed up to the bollocks with this fucked-up son of a whore).

Swearing is by no means a universal trait. The Japanese, for example, scarcely ever resort to swearing. Japanese is such an inflected language that it is possible to insult someone simply by choosing a part of speech inappropriate to the relationship. For example, it is enough to use a form of 'you' unbefitting someone's station in order to convey one's contempt. Sexual swearing is practically unknown to either the Japanese or the Mohawks. Closer to home, Germans, Belgians, Danes and Swedes swear relatively little. The Finns, however, are pretty robust swearers, a habit they may have picked up from their Russian neighbours or, more likely, as an expression of their chagrin at being ruled by the Swedes for six hundred years, which is long enough for anyone.

Unlike their northern neighbours, the English are notoriously attached to bad language. One hundred and fifty years ago William Hazlitt remarked, 'The English (it must be owned) are rather a foul-mouthed nation.' The Irish and Scots are, if anything, even worse and it was in Scotland that the first attempts were made to outlaw swearing. In 1551 the Scots parliament passed an Act outlawing profanity and introduced a scale of fines, increased under a further Act in 1609, to punish offenders. In England the Puritans, not satisfied with the Act they had passed in 1606, introduced another in 1623 outlawing all swearing on pain of a one shilling fine or, for non-payers, a spell in the stocks. However, lest anyone doubt that the milk of human kindness still ran in their Christian veins, they ruled that children under twelve wouldn't have to endure the stocks and were to be let off with a light whipping. Finally in 1649 – and Tory Home Secretaries anxious for a standing ovation at party conference take note – they invoked the ultimate sanction, the death penalty, for children who swore at their parents.

All this puritanical nonsense came to an abrupt and vulgar end with the restoration to the throne of the foul-mouthed Charles II, who devoted his 25-year reign to ravishing as many of his subjects as possible, as though making up for time lost under Cromwellian austerity. When it came to swearing, Charles II followed in the footsteps of Elizabeth I, of whom it was said that 'she never spared an oath in public speech or private conversation when she thought it added energy to either'.

The English proclivity for strong talk is not new. John Bunyan commented that his fictitious Mr Badman 'counted it a glory to swear and curse, and it was as natural to him as to eat, and drink, and sleep'. Two hundred years earlier Dan Michel, a monk from Canterbury, complained that 'some are so evil taught that they can say nothing without swearing', and in the same century the Dominican John Bromyard campaigned for Britain to follow the French example and have swearers put in stocks, their faces branded and tongues slit. Or better still, he said, apply the Sicilian model and cut their tongues out altogether. Elsewhere in Europe Maximilian I, the Holy Roman Emperor who presided over the Habsburg empire, issued 'The Edict Against Blasphemers' in 1495, although apparently to little effect. More recently Mussolini tried to stamp out swearing in Italy. Notices appeared on trains, buses and in other public places with the words: *Non bestemmiare per l'onore d'Italia* (For Italy's honour, do not swear). But this campaign made little impact. It seems you can't keep a bad word down.

The problem with trying to understand the vernacular,

especially someone else's, is that the cultural meanings tend to outweigh the literal ones. Take the word 'bastard'. For what it's worth, it derives from *fils de bast*, son of a packsaddle, which was just one of many euphemisms such as 'born on the wrong side of the blanket', the only difference being that this one stuck. There are worse epithets; William the Conqueror, before he conquered, was known as 'William the Bastard'. Bastards will be examined in greater detail later; for now suffice to say that this popular and durable epithet can be nuanced across a scale ranging from 'a bit of a bastard' to 'a right bastard' to 'a total bastard', all of which is as literally inexact as it is, depending on context, culturally precise. But at no time does it mean 'born out of wedlock'. Of the various insulting sobriquets, 'bastard' is one of the mildest and is used in a jocular or affectionate way almost as often as it's used to wound. In English, that is; it's no laughing matter in Italian.

This is why it's a mistake to ask, 'How do you say bastard in Italian?' because, in a cultural sense, these things don't translate. The question should be, 'How do Italians insult each other?' For the record, the word in Italian is *bastardo* and it's a dire insult. It's also *bastardo* in Spanish but you hardly ever hear it, not because it's not an insult – it's every bit as bad as it is in Italy – but because Spaniards prefer to say *hijo de puta* (son of a whore), which is just another way of calling someone a bastard. The Italians say this, too (*figlio di puttana*), but it's not as bad as calling someone a *bastardo*. It's just a matter of taste. And, as has been noted, although a man from Stockholm probably doesn't like his wife stepping out on him any more than a Florentine does, calling the former a cuckold is culturally meaningless while to the latter it's a grave insult. Just what upsets men from different cultures is discussed at length in a later chapter, which should furnish anyone who enjoys getting their head kicked in with the means of provoking men to violence from one end of the Union to the other.

A primary function of 'bad language' is to intensify speech and almost any word will answer this need, so long as the word is in some way freighted with a taboo. The German preference is for 'damn' which acts as an intensifier much as it does in English in expressions such as *verdammte Scheiße* (damned shit) while the Finns and Swedes generally use respectively *perkeleen* or *jävla*, both meaning 'devilish'. The Spanish call upon the much-abused *puta* (whore) in phrases such as *no tengo ni puta idea* (I haven't got a fucking clue) whereas in Greek you can intensify almost any noun by sticking *palio* (old) in front of it, so that *kariola* (slut) is still more insulting when rendered as *paliokariola*. (The literal meaning of *paliokariola* is 'old king-size bed'.) In French you can choose from *vachement* (cow-ish) to *foutrement* (fucking) to *sacré* (sacred), although the latter is passing out of fashion.

In English, of course, the favourites are 'bloody' and 'fucking' and, in the US, 'motherfucking'. The question of the lineage of bloody, a word that has passed in and out of respectability, has provoked much debate. Etymologists have produced numerous theories, the most popular and improbable of which is that it's a contraction of 'by our lady'. Shakespeare uses 'bloody' and 'by'r lady' in the same act of *Titus Andronicus* and it's difficult to see why, if one was a euphemism, he would use both. Other theories suggest it derives from the Old English *bloidhe*, meaning 'rather', that it's a contraction of 'God's blood', that it refers either to menstruation or dysentery, that British soldiers picked it up from the Russian *bludi* (dirty) in the Crimean War, or that it derives simply from blood's powerful life and death associations. In French it exists in forms such as *critique sanglante* (scathing criticism) or *Bon sang de bon Dieu!* (Bloody hell!) while the German *blutig* is used in much the same way as in English.

'Bloody' illustrates one of the fundamentals of swearing, that a 'bad' word can still punch its vernacular weight long after it has shed its literal meaning. Even people who never swear will surprise themselves with a 'damn' or 'shit' when they hit their thumb with a hammer; sometimes 'ouch' simply isn't cathartic enough. It's as though the pain needs to be balanced or eased by a word that's equally strong, plosive and ideally monosyllabic. This is not a time for an imaginative turn of phrase and everyone reaches for their standbys: the German for *Verdammt!* (Dammit!), the Swede for *Jävlar!* (Devils!) or *Himmel och pannkaka!* (Heaven and pancakes!), the Dane for *Av for satan!* (Oh, Satan!), the Spaniard ¡*Hostia!* (Sacred host!), the Greek *Yamòto!* (Fuck it!) and the Portuguese *Caralho!* (Prick!) or the more acceptable euphemism *Caramba!*, immortalized in such peerless songs as Doris Day's 'Caramba! It's the samba, the one dance I can't do.'

It's when it comes to expressing surprise or disbelief that our cultural roots really start to show, especially if we think someone's pulling our leg or, if we're Spanish, pulling our hair. So while the French are content to shout *Merde!* (Shit!) or *Putain!* (Whore!) if you tread on their toes, they're more likely to say *Et ta soeur!* (And your sister!) if you try to pull the wool over their eyes. The pragmatic Germans would say *Du spinnst wohl!* (You must be crazy!), and the more opaque Danes are inclined, when taken by surprise, to exclaim *Vildt fedt!* (Wild fat!).

Inevitably, things start to get out of hand around the Mediterranean, whose peoples take far more delight in fantastical and robust figures of speech than the more measured northerners. An Italian, for example, may express surprise with *Madonna!* or *Merda!* (Shit!) or *Cazzo!* (Prick!) but will give vent to disbelief with such gems as *Alla faccia del cazzo!* (To the prick face!). Likewise a Portuguese, who is not above responding to an improbable piece of news with *Puta que pariu!* (The whore that bore you!) or *Vai t'a pôr num porco!* (Go fuck a pig!), or a Greek with *Yamó tin poutana mu!* (I fuck my whore!). In Spain there's an unselfconscious earthiness, often combined with sentimentality, that surprises those who cling to the stereotype of a repressed, priest-ridden people. Tell a Spaniard a tall story and as likely as not they'll retort ¡Cojón de mi corazón! (My precious bollock!) or ¡El coño de tu hermana! (Your sister's cunt!). Now, let's be honest, no one's ever going to say that in Esperanto.

Insults are meant to provoke or disparage but not, as a rule, to wound. This is why insults tend not to be true, or at least not demonstrably so. When you lean out of the car window and shout 'Wanker!' at the guy who's just nicked your parking space it's insulting but – as you neither know nor care to know anything about this stranger's habits – it's more or less meaningless; offensive, yes, but not unkind. Name-calling – calling someone 'kike' or 'nigger' – is a different matter because, pejoratives aside, it's 'true'. As an insult, 'wanker' is a figure of speech, as are most of the common insults. But there's nothing figurative about being black or Jewish and as insults these epithets call on a real prejudice, on a real history of persecution and are designed to wound. It's noticeable that dominant social groups have far more pejoratives for the oppressed than vice versa. White people, for example, have devised twice as many sobriquets for blacks as blacks have for whites.

Jews may choose to call other Jews kikes, and black people often call each other nigger, but that's their business. It's one dimension of what anthropologists call the 'joking relationship', a universal human trait. In 1991, after studying the archives on all the world's documented cultures in search of human universals, the anthropologist Donald E. Brown published his findings. In a list that ranged from a love of gossip, the manufacture of tools, mourning the dead to a preference for having sex in private, he included 'humorous insult'. He showed that there is a universal human tendency to express kinship or intimacy by breaking verbal taboos. It's part of friendship's shorthand, in which men friends call each other 'bastard' and women call their friends 'bitch' with impunity. We all do it, reinforcing a bond and following some unspoken code of behaviour of which we are unaware until someone with whom we don't share such a bond oversteps the bounds of our intimacy.

It's a tricky, sometimes dangerous business. You see men do it as they get to know each other better, trying it on, seeing how far they can go, like dogs sniffing each other's arses. And not everyone plays by the same rules; an Englishman who doesn't balk at a matey 'bastard' may well bristle if called a 'cunt'. A woman who doesn't mind if her friends call her 'bitch' might find 'slut' too much to take. Then there are the things that no one can say. For example, probably the worst insult for a Spanish woman is *puta* (whore) and for a man *hijo de puta* (son of a whore). But while men, especially in the southern province of Andalusia, might affectionately call each other *hijo de puta*, there is no context or relationship in which it's acceptable, pally or witty to call a woman a *puta*. Indeed, in Spain you can call just about anything a whore, anything at all, except a woman.

Some people, the Irish, for example, and people from Belfast in particular, revel in a sort of mutual banter where the participants sail as close to the wind with their insults as they dare, backing off a little if things go too far, only to resume for another round. Belfast people have a very low threshold for pretentiousness, and anyone putting on airs find themselves unceremoniously stripped bare in the cutting wit of a good 'slagging'. In a number of cultures humorous insults take on a ritual form. The insults follow a set pattern, sometimes in rhyme, in a ritual that was common among the Vikings, widespread in Scotland until the sixteenth century and still practised today by Turkish boys, Mexicans and young black males in the US.

In Old English and Norse texts this practice is known as
flyting, meaning 'to chide or scold' and in its most developed
form the 'opponents' improvised verses in which they accused
each other of anything from cowardice to homosexuality to
incest. In Scotland William Dunbar, the sixteenth-century
Franciscan friar and poet whose vulgarity is thought to have
provoked the anti-swearing legislation cited earlier, composed
the 'Flyting of Dunbar and Kennedy' which contained such
exchanges as *Wan fukkit funling* (ill-conceived foundling), which
is met by *Cuntbitten crawdon* (pox-smitten coward). Scottish clerics aren't what they used to be, it seems. Elsewhere young
men play games in which they ritually insult each other's
mothers and other female relatives as a test of both verbal
skills and self-discipline. As with other forms of swearing, it's
an essential element of these exchanges that what is said isn't
true.

In other contexts, however, young children, untamed by
social convention and uninhibited in their cruelty, don't hesitate to use 'true' insults. Any child who is fat or pimply or
wears glasses is guaranteed to be saddled with the schoolyard
monicker of 'fatty', 'spotty' or 'four-eyes'. But in time we
learn that, whatever we say behind their backs, we don't insult
people to their faces, at least we don't insult them with the
truth. For example, every language has scathing expressions
to describe a complete bore, but they are practically never said
to their face. It's one thing to say of someone that they're 'as
exciting as watching paper yellow' but it would be extraordi-
narily rude to say it to them.

Exposing or condemning a person as a murderer or child
abuser is not the province of invective either, even though
these acts are every bit as taboo as having sex with your
mother. Behind the insult 'motherfucker' lies the assumption
that it isn't true, that the person in question has never actually
had sex with his mother. But call someone 'murderer' and

everyone's going to look up and say, 'Why? Who'd he kill?' Murderer is a word we take at face value. Life can be murder, maybe you could murder a pizza or a song, but murderers are as yet real people who murder other real people, not metaphors.

But before we started calling people bastards and mother-fuckers, we called on God to curse them, and cursed God for our own accursed fate. Religion may not have the hold on the European mind that it did, but the Judaeo-Christian tradition lies at the root of all of our most important taboos. And not just the taboo on blasphemy. An outsider could be forgiven for thinking that the Church has been more preoccupied with regulating sexual behaviour than with how to lead a good life in the sight of God. The Church's utterances could easily lead to the conclusion that, when it comes to sainthood and sexuality, the one precludes the other. Indeed, the topic on which Christianity, Judaism and Islam can all agree is sex: they don't like it. They don't much like women either, whom they consider both unclean and a regrettable diversion on man's path to righteousness. As for homosexuals, well, they can go straight to hell.

Sexual taboos have given rise to more 'bad language' than any others. But the oldest taboo that we know of is the one against taking the name of God in vain. So, in the name of the father, let's take an impious look at blasphemy.

3 ★ *As God Is My Judge*

Blasphemy is a litmus test of the standards a society feels
it must enforce to preserve its unity, its peace, its morality
and above all its salvation.

Leonard W. Levy, *Treason Against God*. 1981

These days we don't bother God with our petitions the way
we used to and scarcely anyone invokes His name with any
passion except during an orgasm. We don't even have to swear
an oath in God's name to testify in court as we can now choose
to take a secular oath. But right across Europe blasphemy, the
taking of God's name in vain, was until the 1870s the worst
kind of swearing, worse than personal insults, and in the main
it was blasphemy that the Puritan legislators had sought to
stamp out. Dante, no shrinking violet when it came to obscenity, had no time for blasphemers whom he condemned to the
seventh circle of hell along with murderers and suicides.

In ancient Greece and Rome invoking the gods as witnesses
was proof of one's sincerity. For the ancient Greeks, impiety
and blasphemy were one and the same. Anaxagoras, who
impiously said the gods were myths and that the moving force
of life was something he called nous or mind, was probably
the first person to be jailed for his beliefs, the proto-heretic.
That was around 450 BC and it was shortly afterwards that,
following his trial on charges of impiety, Socrates was forced
to drink the hemlock. Up until a hundred years ago, reinforcing one's word with the phrase 'as God is my witness' was
more than a figure of speech. Using God's name frivolously

undermined His authority and righteousness. In 1680 John Bunyan complained that,

> 'to swear is to call God to witness; and to swear to a lie is to call God to witness that lie is true . . . this kind of swearing is put in with lying, and killing, and stealing, and committing adultery and therefore must not go unpunished.'

Two hundred and fifty years later T. S. Eliot reproached 'a world in which blasphemy is impossible', that is, one in which nothing is held sacred and, it follows, nothing is profane. The question is this: if you don't fear God, how can anyone take you at your word? As Lucius says to Aaron in *Titus Andronicus*: 'Who should I swear by? Thou believest no god: / That granted, how canst thou believe an oath?'

There's a scene in the film *The Godfather* where the Mafia boss Vito Corleone, who is unquestionably a good Catholic, has to convince some fellow dons − and fellow Catholics − that he can be taken at his word. Plainly 'as God is my witness' wouldn't do the trick as God had already witnessed considerable mayhem on Don Corleone's part without feeling it necessary to intervene. So he takes what is in effect a secular oath and vows 'on the heads of my grandchildren' that he will keep his word. This does the trick; Italians have always been big on family.

Fast forward to July 1977. In Memphis a post-mortem examination is uncovering the bloated pharmacopoeia that a few days earlier had been Elvis Presley. In London, meanwhile, the editor of the magazine *Gay News* is being convicted of blasphemy. His crime was to have published 'The Love That Dares to Speak Its Name', a poem by the writer and academic James Kirkup in which a gay Roman centurion mourns the death of his lover, Jesus, on the cross. What shocked some people most was not the suggestion that the beloved

Saviour might have been a faggot but that, in a Britain that was teetering godlessly on its platform soles, blasphemy was still a crime. *Gay News* was fined £1,000 and its editor, on top of a £500 fine, received a nine-month suspended jail sentence, although the latter was dropped on appeal. Mary Whitehouse, the moral crusader who brought the case, declared after the verdict, 'It's been a great day for the country. A line has at last been drawn.'

In Britain it's still possible to bring a civil action for blasphemy, though only if it's the Christian God who has been blasphemed: you may say what you like about Allah, the Prophet, Krishna or the unnameable Jewish deity, although Tehran's *fatwa* against the writer Salman Rushdie for his alleged blaspheming of the Prophet has given the concept of international law an added dimension. It's also a warning to those European countries with large Muslim populations – France and Britain in particular – that there are still those among their citizens who take religion and blasphemy very seriously indeed. Recently India's cricket captain, Mohammed Azharuddin, was forced to reconsider a sponsorship deal with the American sports shoe company Reebok after clerics argued that the names of the prophet Mohammed, and Azhar, one of Allah's ninety-nine names, would be defiled if the cricketer allowed his autograph to appear on something as lowly as a shoe.

As science advanced, faith retreated and blasphemy began to lose its sting, but the strength of its taboo varies enormously across the European vernacular. Broadly speaking, in the mainly Protestant north, blasphemy is unremarkable and mostly passes unremarked; few blaspheme with any passion or imagination and it is the most socially acceptable form of 'bad language'. However, it's worth noting that a report on swearing on television published by the Broadcasting Standards Council in June 1996 recorded that 38 per cent of complaints concerned swearing with a religious connotation. In the same week a separate poll found that 46 per cent of Britons don't believe that God exists. In Germany and Scandinavia, presumably following Luther's satanic obsessions, the devil is invoked at least as often as God or Christ. In the mainly Catholic south, people blaspheme constantly and elaborately, mostly about Christ and the Virgin, rarely about the devil, but it remains socially unacceptable, something you wouldn't do at home. The exception is Portugal, where blasphemy is very rare and very much frowned upon. The mixing of the sacred and the profane – 'I shit on the cross' and suchlike – which is typical of Spanish, French and Italian blasphemy, is unheard of in Portugal. One can only speculate whether this is due to the country's isolation or in some part to the fact that Portuguese Catholicism triumphed over Islam two hundred years before the Spanish *reconquista*. Eastern Orthodox Greece falls somewhere between the Protestant north and the Catholic south; they blaspheme somewhat less than Catholics and frequently invoke the devil, but blasphemy doesn't carry quite such a strong taboo.

In Belgium the Flemings stack up their blasphemy for greater effect. Thus the three common outbursts *Godverdomme!* (God damn!), *Nondedjuë!* (In the name of God!) and *Miljaardedjuë!* (Millions of gods!) can, if circumstances dictate, all be rolled together as *Godvermiljaardenondedjuë!* However, it is rare in northern Europe to hear anything more than an exclamatory *Gott im Himmel!* or Sweet Jesus!, so it comes as something of a surprise to hear a southern Catholic say ¡*Em cago en les cinc llagues de Crist!* (I shit on the five wounds of Christ!), as they do in Catalonia, or *Madonna puttana!* (Madonna the whore!), as Italians do. In Galicia, the Celtic and conservative north-western province of Spain, however, blasphemy remains the most taboo form of swearing.

In Italy, while an inadvertent *cazzo* (prick) or *puttana* (whore) might be overlooked in polite company, *Porco Dio!* (Pig God!) would probably not, and even those who swear continually, as many Italians do, frequently avoid such expressions. In Latin *porcus* also denoted a woman's sex, which would account for the heavy taboo on such outwardly childish Italian utterances as *porco Dio* and *porca Madonna*. Why the link between *porcus* (pig) and the female genitals? *Porcellana* (little sow), from which we derive the word porcelain, was the name given to the Cypraea family of shells and in particular to *Cypraea moneta*, the cowrie shell, which is shaped like a pig's back. But turn the shell over and its ventral side bears a striking resemblance to a woman's sexual parts, hence the sexual association with pigs. It's unlikely that many Italians have taken this curious etymological journey, they just know not to say *porco Dio*. That's taboos for you.

But I digress, and not for the last time. In theory the secular north would curse God day and night while the God-fearing south would rather die than blaspheme, but in fact the opposite is true. However, the vigour and quantity of blasphemy in Catholic countries is more a measure of the strength of Catholic anti-clericalism – especially in Spain and Italy – than of any hostility towards the Creator, and its taboo is likewise indicative of the Church's power. The Church of Rome, itself a landowner on a grand scale, has not been a conspicuous champion of the poor and has given its blessing to all manner of social hierarchies. The wretched of the earth have had many more reasons to fear than love a clergy that grew fat at the landlord's table while it pacified its flock with promises of pie in the sky.

We're not talking metaphorical fat here, either. Many Italian restaurants offer dishes described as *strozzapreti*. Linguini strozzapreti, for example, means 'enough linguini to choke a priest', implying that the serving is generous enough even to satisfy the greed of the clergy. And when a Spaniard remarks that someone *vive como un cura* (lives like a priest), they mean they live very well indeed. As the saying goes: *Los curas son las únicas personas a quienes todo el mundo llama padre, menos sus hijos, que los llaman tíos* (Priests are the only people whom everyone calls father, except their sons who call them uncle). Such colloquialisms don't signal a grovelling respect for men of the cloth. Similarly, the Spanish and especially the Catalans have found it necessary, even purgative, to burn down churches and murder priests on a regular, almost cyclical basis. Four thousand priests, two thousand monks and three hundred nuns were killed during the Spanish Civil War. This doesn't necessarily imply a loss of faith, but while it is true that sometimes the churches were attacked because they were soft targets and in some areas often the only symbols of the establishment on which the poor could vent their rage, it shows that, at least in times of crisis, the Church was seen as a wing of the State.

Cursing God was a way of cursing the forces that claimed they were the agents of God's will, but in the final analysis it's about politics, not religion. Ireland is, in the main, a Catholic country but anti-clericalism is mild compared to Spain or Italy, and when it comes to the style and quantity of blasphemy, the Irish belong in the northern European camp. It seems reasonable to assume that this is because Britain not only colonized Ireland but also persecuted the Irish for being Catholics. As a result, Catholicism and the Church, rather than being the pillars of the status quo that they were in most of Europe, became synonymous with political subversion and the national struggle. In the long run this has benefited the Church, which has retained in Ireland a role in the affairs of state and the power to impose Catholic morality through constitutional means that it has all but lost in the rest of Catholic Europe.

The Church made a point of blurring the distinction between offending God and offending Rome but the original taboo on taking the Lord's name in vain reflects

– notwithstanding the old rhyme about sticks and stones –
the ancient and universal fear of the power of names. The
injunction against naming the deity has echoes in societies
where it is forbidden to name the dead, or cultures where
people are given one secret and sacred name which must not
be uttered and another for everyday use. When Moses receives
the Ten Commandments on Mount Sinai God tells him:

> 'Thou shalt not take the name of the Lord thy God in
> vain; for the Lord will not hold him guiltless that taketh
> his name in vain.' Exodus 20: 7.

During this encounter the Almighty sounds like He's already
had it up to here with His earthly likenesses and is having
second thoughts about choosing the Jews to be His people.
They never seem to do as He tells them, they're forever
kvetching about one thing or another, and keep slipping back
into their bad old idolatrous ways. Moses is the only one
who's prepared to take Him at His word without arguing the
toss.

Right from the start the offence of blasphemy carried the
most severe punishment. When Moses is later asked to deal
with a blasphemer he asks God, to whom he alone has a direct
line, for a ruling. The Almighty is unequivocal:

> 'Bring forth him that has cursed . . . and let all that
> heard him lay their hand upon his head, and let all the
> congregation stone him . . . he that blasphemeth the
> name of the Lord, he shall surely be put to death.'
> Leviticus 24: 13–16.

The Old Testament has little more to say on the subject,
despite many references to a reversion to idolatry on the part
of the Chosen, but it resurfaces in the New Testament when
Stephen is stoned to death for 'blasphemous words against
Moses and God'. Up to a point Jews solved the blasphemy

problem by making the deity unnameable, represented only by YHVH, the tetragrammaton, rendered by some as Yahweh or Jehovah and meaning roughly 'I am who I am', or 'the essence of His being', but considered both unpronounceable and unspeakable and for which the Hebrew *adonai* (my Lord) has stood in. But even the fear of God can't stop the irony from seeping out, as in the Yiddish saying, *Mit Got tor men zich nit shpilen — ershtns tor men nit, un tsveytns lozt er nit* (We'd better not fool around with God; in the first place, we mustn't, and in the second he doesn't let us). Jews have also wryly observed that *Az Got zol voynen af der erd, voltn im di mentshn di fenster oysgeshlogn* (If God lived on earth, people would break his windows).

For Christians the resistance to naming God — which is technically not a blasphemy in itself — seems to have come in with the Reformation, which is when euphemisms such as 'zounds' (God's wounds), apparently a favourite of Elizabeth I, "struth' (God's truth), 'by George' (by God) and *sacré bleu* (sacré Dieu) start to make their appearance. Before long the northern English 'by gum' or the cockney 'gorblimey' had become part of the language, as had 'doggone' and such Hollywoodisms as 'land sakes!' in America. It had long been common practice, however, to swear by God's bones or God's fish or even by God's eyelids to which were added similar but secular oaths such as 'by my beard', 'by my faith' and 'by this hand'.

Religious euphemisms and nonsense words remain commonplace. In Wales, where blasphemy retains much of its taboo, Welsh speakers will say the meaningless *Brensiach* for *Brenin Mawr* (literally, God, great king) or *Duwcs* for *Duw* (God). The Irish oath *Dár fia* (By the deer) or the Swedish *Järnvägar!* (Railways!, a euphemism for the similar sounding *djävul*, devils) serve the same purpose while in Spain the common exclamation ¡*Hostia!* (Holy sacrament!) is often replaced by ¡*Ostras!* (Oysters!). *Hostia*, as we shall see, can mean practically anything in colloquial Spanish, and boasts more entries in Spanish slang dictionaries than any other word apart from *cojón* (testicle) and the evergreen *culo* (bum).

By the early Middle Ages the Catholic Church, determined to plait the heterodox Christian sects into a single orthodoxy, had made blasphemy (an offence against God) and heresy (an offence against the Church) synonymous and they remained inseparable for hundreds of years. The distinction between, on the one hand, the fear of God, and on the other a natural reluctance to be burnt at the stake, more or less disappeared until the seventeenth century.

One consequence of this blurring of the line between God and His ministry was that the majority of those thousands who perished on the rack or at the stake were either utterly innocent or utterly devout. But however devoutly they believed in God or followed Christ, heretics were persecuted and destroyed because their beliefs differed from those of the Church. St Thomas Aquinas argued in the thirteenth century that heretics 'can be put to death ... even if they do not corrupt others, for they are blasphemers against God, because they observe a false faith'. The Church's war against heresy produced a populace terrified of attracting the attention of the ecclesiastical authorities through behaviour or remarks that might be construed as heretical. This equation of the Catholic church with order is reflected in the French vernacular use of *catholique* to mean 'fine, in good order', or *ce n'est pas très catholique*, meaning 'it's a bit fishy'.

Even Aquinas admitted that God cannot be harmed by blasphemy, as He's above that sort of thing. However, blasphemy – for which read heresy – might annoy Him, and when God is vexed He tends to overreact, visiting such things as plagues and famines on those who have caused the irritation. The founding fathers of the church, St Augustine and St Ambrose in particular, argued therefore that, as society could not afford to appear soft on blasphemers, the State had a duty to punish heretics in order to protect its citizens from the wrath of God. Thus divine and temporal authority became one: the iron fist in the mailed glove.

Outside Spain, which until the late fifteenth century was still to a considerable extent a Muslim country, those who suffered most from the Church's drive for conformity were Christians, as only a Christian could be a heretic. Gypsies, although they tend to adopt the religion of the host country, were often persecuted as Heiden (heathen) in Germany and the Low Countries; Tzigan, or gitanes, the name by which they became widely known, is from the Greek tsingani, meaning heathen. But it was left to the Muslims and Jews to assume the semi-official role of Europe's blasphemers, the one because they followed the false prophet Mohammed and the other because they refused to recognize the – in Jewish eyes – false prophet, Jesus. The Jews were further condemned for that supreme blasphemy: the crucifixion. Christians have always held them responsible, although it seems more probable that Jesus was executed by the Romans for declaring himself king of the Jews, an act of treason under Roman law. Furthermore, crucifixion was a Roman and not a Jewish custom, but one shouldn't let the facts get in the way of a good libel. The pejorative use of 'Jew' continues to carry – with all its other baggage – the unspoken 'Christ killer'.

Although Islam was their real target, the crusades were bad news for Jews as well. The holy warriors, impatient to encounter Muslim infidels during the long journey east, murdered any Jews they encountered en route to the Holy Land. As the Abbé Pierre of Cluny said during the second crusade, which began in 1147:

'What is the good of going to the end of the world, at great loss of men and money, to fight the Saracens, when

we permit among us other infidels a thousand times
more guilty towards Christ than the Mohammedans.'

Where there is God there is the devil, and the further north
one goes in Europe the more curses invoke the devil and the
fewer references there are to Christ or the Virgin, although
the Greeks frequently say *Sto thiaolo!* (Go to the devil!), often
accompanied by a five-fingered gesture, sometimes in the general direction of hell. This is quite a powerful curse, though
not such strong talk as the heavily taboo *Yamó to Christó sou*
(Fuck your Christ) or *Yamó tin Panayía sou* (Fuck your mother
of God). As a way of avoiding taking the Lord's name in vain
Greeks often say *Yamó ton antichristó* (Fuck your antichrist). The
Portuguese also invoke the devil and to ward off misfortune
say *Que o diabo seja surdo, cego e mudo!* (May the devil be deaf,
blind and dumb!). Germans say *Scher dich zum Teufel* (Go to the
devil), as we would say 'Go to hell!', or *Pfui Teufel!* as a way of
saying 'Yuck!' at something disgusting. Gypsies don't use oaths
concerning God or Christ but many Romani curses invoke the
devil, such as *Te hal to o beng* (May the devil eat you up).

The Danes exclaim *Av for fanden!* (The devil!) or *Av for satan!*
although the latter is also rendered euphemistically *Av for Søren!*
(Søren is a common boy's name), a sort of Danish *what the
dickens*, not that blasphemy is any big deal in Denmark. In
Swedish *fan* is one of various words for devil and the most
common intensifier is *jävla* (devilish), derived from *djävul*, producing demonic sentences such as this: *Jag tog sågfan för att såga
ner björk-djäveln och då gick bladhelvetet* (I took the saw-devil to saw
down the birch-Satan and the blade-hell broke). The Finns
are fairly devilish, too, and invoke Satan far more often than
his counterpart, indeed, speaking of the devil is stronger talk
in Finland than calling on God. The Finns include in their
repertoire the exclamation: *Saatanan perkeleen vittu!* (Satan's devil's
cunt!).

The Prince of Darkness must not, however, be raised to the same level as the Prince of Peace; such dualism is heresy, the Manichean heresy to be precise, and it was to destroy such heretics that the first Inquisition was instigated by the Synod of Toulouse in 1229. By now the distinction between blasphemy and heresy had all but disappeared and the taboo was reinforced as the Inquisition threw its considerable secular weight behind the divine prohibition. Initially the job of the Inquisition was to stamp out heretical sects such as the Albigensians or Cathars who had grown up around the southern French towns of Albi and Toulouse. They believed that life was a struggle between the forces of light and darkness and Satan, not God, was running the earthly show, a belief for which they were slaughtered and had their lands confiscated, a pattern that would persist throughout the Middle Ages. Inquisitorial justice was fairly rough. When Arnold Amalric, a papal legate overseeing operations, was asked what to do when it wasn't clear if a suspect was an Albigensian heretic or a good, God-fearing Catholic, he declared: 'Kill them all. God will know which are his.' It was enlightened jurisprudence of precisely this sort that discouraged people in the Middle Ages from shooting their mouths off in a manner that might attract the attention of the church authorities.

Both Church and State quickly acquired a taste for the inquisitorial style and when Pope Innocent IV authorized the use of torture in 1252, a more or less constant supply of heretics was guaranteed. This after all was the era of such forensic wheezes as trial by drowning, an investigative method through which suspects could only prove their innocence by dying. A disinclination to confess under torture, rather than implying innocence, merely raised the suspicion that the suspect's heresy was so advanced they would rather die on the rack than admit it. Presented with a choice between confession or being tortured to death, people soon realized that an early confession followed by a slightly less protracted death at the stake or on the wheel was as near as they were going to get to a quiet life. As a result, there was no shortage of heretics and no pressure on the busy Inquisitors to retire until they finally hung up their thumbscrews in 1834.

The Inquisition operated mainly in southern France and northern Italy, but in 1478 Sextus IV authorized the establishment of the Spanish Inquisition, headed by the Grand Inquisitor, Tomás de Torquemada, a Dominican monk whose name, rather appositely in one so fond of fires, contains the past participle of *quemar*, the verb 'to burn'. Estimates of how many perished in Torquemada's *autos-da-fé* range from 2,000 to 30,000, with the lower figure thought to be the more accurate. Most of his victims were Marranos (converted Jews) and Moriscos (converted Muslims) who were suspected of practising their faiths in secret. Torquemada, who was born Jewish, was himself a *converto*, and all the more zealous for it. Later, when he had tired of the smell of burning flesh, Torquemada concentrated his energies on furthering Spain's own 'final solution' – the expulsion of all the country's 200,000 Jews in 1492 and, with the fall of Islamic Spain at Granada that same year, the forced conversion of the Muslims. The year 1492 is better remembered, of course, as the year in which either coincidentally or as a diversionary tactic to keep all this religious persecution out of the headlines, Columbus announced that he'd found the back door to India, although it later turned out to be Haiti.

Part of this forced conversion of Muslims would have involved the converts imbibing the symbolic blood and body of Christ. The Eucharist or host is central to the Catholic Mass, so central that in 1995 the Vatican decreed that sufferers of coeliac disease – an allergy to gluten, a necessary ingredient of the host according to Rome – were not eligible as candidates for the priesthood. The word for the holy sacrament (*hostie*, *ostia*) may be heard occasionally as an exclamation in France and Italy (though not Portugal) and as *sakra* in Catholic Bavaria. In Italian it sometimes means 'nothing' – *non ho capito un'ostia* (I didn't understand a thing) – and the Corsican expression *manghja Diu è caca Diavuli* (she eats God, i.e. the host, and shits the devil) suggests someone so wicked they transmute even the symbolic body of Christ into evil. But no one gets as much mileage out of these little wafers as the Spanish.

¡*Hostia!* is probably the most commonly heard Spanish exclamation, approximating roughly to Wow! or Bloody hell! As an exclamation it can be fortified to express extra disbelief or amazement as ¡*Hostia puta!* or ¡*Hostia santa!* (whore's or saint's host) or anger as ¡*Hostias en vinagre!* (Hosts in vinegar!). On the other hand an *hostia* can be a smack in the face or a dent in your car, and to go *a toda hostia* is to go at top speed, as it is if you *sales cagando hostias* (set off shitting hosts). If something is *de la hostia* it's terrific but someone who is *de mala hostia* is either in a bad mood or means you no good. There are many more, or as a Spaniard might say, *y toda la hostia* (et cetera). But even so, just as Italians don't say *Porco Dio!* at home, ¡*Hostia!* is less acceptable at many Spanish dinner tables than even ¡*Joder!* (Fuck!).

History has been punctuated by many violent epochs and many brutal regimes but the medieval appetite for blood seemed insatiable. Those who fell foul of the double-headed axe of Church and State suffered the most terrible punishments, and none more terribly than those accused of heresy. God might be merciful, but not the Church, whose drive to corner the God-fearing market seemed to have become entangled with a most un-Christian hunger for sacrificial victims. It wasn't just that so many people had confessions tortured out of them. Often they were driven to confess heresies and crimes of such dreadfulness that they could rarely expect the relief of execution – even of the flames – without first having their tongues ripped out, their eyes gouged and their flesh picked to pieces with red hot tongs. Anyone who imagines the nightmare world depicted in the paintings of Hieronymus Bosch is the work of a deranged mind is mistaken; even a cursory reading of the Middle Ages reveals Bosch to be a social realist.

By the late fifteenth century the Inquisition had extended its brief and, in addition to heresy, was trying people for sorcery, alchemy and what it deemed unacceptable sexual practices. (Aquinas had helpfully provided a list of unnatural sexual vices. These were, in descending order of iniquity: sodomy, fellatio, cunnilingus, pederasty and masturbation.) The Inquisition had also opened offices in Sicily (1517) and The Netherlands (1522) where by the end of the century it had murdered eighteen thousand people in a bid to stop Protestantism catching on. The Inquisition was effectively extended to England when parliament passed De Haeretico Comburendo (On the Burning of Heretics), a piece of legislation which neglected to define heresy, thus giving the Church a free hand. But by then a new craze was about to sweep Europe: the witch hunt.

Throughout Europe, 'witch' is a pejorative for a woman and continues to imply malevolence, if not actual sorcery. It was those nice Swiss people who kicked off the season with the first witch hunt in 1427 and who also staged the last legal execution for witchcraft in 1782. In between, at least 500,000 people were burnt at the stake as witches, more than 80 per cent of them women. Some have put the number as high as nine million but even the lower figure dwarfs the number put to death for heresy. The witch hunts of the fifteenth and sixteenth centuries consolidated the power of both Church and State at a time when feudalism was in decline, the centralized authority of Rome was under threat and the peasantry was on the brink of revolt against the corruption and cruelty of its secular and ecclesiastical masters.

Perhaps the most famous woman to be condemned as both a heretic and a witch was the nineteen-year-old Joan of Arc, who is sometimes credited with coining the term *les goddams* for the English, and was burnt by them at Rouen in May 1431. After perusing her CV for almost five hundred years, the Vatican finally made her a saint in 1920. In Britain the last execution for blasphemy took place in 1697, but the death penalty for witchcraft was retained until 1736. However, in October 1995 the *Guardian* reported that Rochester Cathedral had withdrawn an invitation to Tony Grist, an ex-priest, to speak at an ecumenical conference, because he claimed to be a witch. His wife, Aileen, protested: 'We run a coven which is very active on the religious side of witchcraft rather than physical spellcraft. We don't go in for human sacrifice. Most witches are vegetarian.' All of which is somewhat dispiriting, rather like alcohol-free lager.

Witch hunts proved very useful. As well as assuaging the bloodlust and misogyny of a power-crazed clergy, they served to distract and terrify the poor, who were persuaded to see their misfortunes as the product of supernatural powers from which the Church and nobility were offering them tangible protection. But it was virtually impossible for a woman to protect herself from the charge of witchcraft. For example, wet dreams were said to be the result of a nocturnal visit by a *succubus*, or female spirit, so a woman could find herself accused of sorcery because a man, especially a man of the cloth, had dreamt about her. In one case in 1593 a woman found herself in hot water after her husband had discovered her clitoris. Any pleasure this discovery might have given her was short-lived as he jumped to the glaringly obvious conclusion that this 'little lump of flesh, in a manner sticking out as if it had been a teat, to the length of half an inch' must be the devil's teat. She was duly convicted for witchcraft.

A witch might also put a *gramarye* on a man, a highly

specialized spell which made him imagine that his penis had, well, disappeared. This was a very tough charge to beat, as even if the defendant could prove beyond reasonable doubt that the plaintiff's apparatus remained in situ, she was still unable to shake his conviction that it was not. The Dominicans Heinrich Kramer and Jacobus Sprenger, whose pamphlet *Malleus Maleficarum* (Witches' Hammer) launched the witch hunts in 1487, explained the man's predicament as arising because 'some glamour was cast over him so that he could see or touch nothing but his smooth body'. And that is how the word lives on in English, as 'glamour', the Scottish variant of *gramarye*, meaning a magic spell, introduced into mainstream English via Sir Walter Scott's poem of 1805, 'The Lay of the Last Minstrel'. A fifteenth-century woman would not be flattered, therefore, if told she was bewitching or glamorous as the slightest suspicion of involvement in witchcraft – and inevitably the accusation was often made simply to settle old scores – led to torture, the inevitable confession and a horrible death. So up until 1700, to call a woman a witch was to condemn her to almost certain death.

Any hope that the Reformation would usher in an era of greater religious tolerance was short-lived. Aided by the printing press, the emerging Protestants made the Bible available to all who could read or listen. The new faith taught the supremacy of the Bible over hierarchies and priests and offered God's grace directly to individuals; not that this intimacy shook the prohibition on taking God's name in vain.

But this bypassing of the religious hierarchy shouldn't be interpreted as populist or democratic. Nor did it take Martin Luther long to learn what the Catholic church had known for centuries: that you don't make it big in the divinity business by pinning your colours to the underdogs. When the Peasants' War of 1525 broke out Luther condemned it and the peasants as blasphemous and took the side of the nobility, even though they slaughtered 100,000 wretches in the course of reminding them of their proper place in the order of things. The peasants, he said, 'take up the sword without God's authorisation' and to support them 'would be the same as to blaspheme God, and to throw God out of heaven'. The swords of the gentry, by implication, had been authorised by the deity. Luther disliked the word heretic as that was what he was called by the Catholics, and we have him to thank for reviving the word blasphemer. Nowadays this word seems almost quaint, but on the lips of a Scottish or Northern Irish Presbyterian preacher it still retains the authentic whiff of hellfire and disembowelment.

The purpose of this brief tour of some of Christianity's bloodier landscapes is to emphasize that the force of the taboo on blasphemy derived as much from the fear of a hideous death at the hands of a merciless Church as from the dread of eternal damnation meted out by a vengeful god. This didn't change overnight; well into the 1970s small Spanish towns and villages still displayed signs warning of the fines levied on blasphemers. Elsewhere in Europe swearing became more widespread and acceptable in the 1960s, but the trend didn't really take hold in Spain until after the death of Franco in 1975, and blasphemy – though common there – still carries a strong taboo.

God is one thing, the Church another, and the apparent hypocrisy of European Catholics in developing a rich vein of blasphemy while imposing strict social restrictions on its usage is understandable in the context of anti-clericalism. Anti-clericalism is an act of defiance by a God-fearing peasantry – the most extreme expressions come from rural areas – against a clergy that sanctified poverty and the status quo that sustained it during the thousand years it took the Church to fasten its grip on European life. When a Catalan says *Em cago en els collons del Pare Sant* (I shit on the Pope's balls) it's plain their beef is not with the Almighty but with His earthly representatives, although when they say *Em cago en Déu en la creu en el fuster que la fen i en el fill de puta que va plantar el pi!* (I shit on God, on the cross and on the carpenter who made it and on the son of a whore who planted the pine!) one wonders whether perhaps the speaker had some bad experiences as an altar boy.

Just as you don't have to go to synagogue to be a Jew, you don't have to believe in papal infallibility to be a Catholic. Take Italy; better still, take Bologna. In Bologna they vote Communist and when they speak of *andare in chiesa* (going to church) they mean going to a bar, but this doesn't mean they're not Catholics. Like most Italians, they cross themselves whenever they need a little luck and many will marry in church and have their children baptized. English Catholics are Catholics by conviction; for an Italian being Catholic is just something that comes with the territory, like mozzarella or organized crime; you don't have to believe all or even anything the Church says. The Pope can say, as he recently did, that in the afterlife we will retain our male and female sexual characteristics but won't – you've guessed it – have any sex and the majority of Italians, and Catholics elsewhere, will laugh as loud as anyone else. Furthermore, the Pope can take to the balcony of St Peter's to denounce the evils of contraception and abortion but the fact remains that Italy, headquarters of the Church of Rome, has the lowest birth rate in Europe, with God-fearing Spain running a close second. People are stupid, but not that stupid.

In most of Britain blasphemy counts for little these days. But the English are widely regarded as being among the most foul-mouthed people on earth and it's plain that the modern English-speaker's tendency to construct their entire discourse around every possible form of the word 'fuck' has supplanted an earlier, blasphemous turn of speech. The medieval friar John Waldeby voiced a common complaint when he wrote:

If one comes into the market place or the tavern where these infernal dogs, that is to say, the swearers are, one will find Christ's blood held at so small a price and in such little reverence among them that scarcely a single word will escape their lips − be it true or false − without mention by name of the blood of Christ in an oath along with it . . . and not only Christ's blood, but all the members of Christ.

In English nowadays mention of the Redeemer is restricted to 'For Christ's sake!', 'Christ Almighty!', 'Sweet Jesus!' and the American 'Jesus H. Christ!', but the sort of swearing that so distressed Friar Waldeby persists in southern Europe. Italians will say *Cristo morto!* or *Cristo nudo!* (Christ dead or naked), *Sangue di Dio!* (Blood of God!), or *Dio prete!* (Priest of a God!), or *Bestia Dio!* (Beast of a God!), but such expressions would not be used in the presence of older or religious people, or in most Italian homes − not even the more modern *Cazzo di Buddha!* (Buddha's prick!) − nor are they likely to be heard on radio or television or in polite conversation. Sometimes the blasphemy can be 'softened' by being more expansive and elaborate, as in the Parma dialect expression *Dio scapà da lett senza scarpi!* (God escaped from bed without shoes!), or the Florentine *Madonna damigiana con tutti i santi dentro e Dio per tappo!* (The Madonna demijohn with all the saints inside and God for a cork!), an expression that can be heard − in so far as anyone says such things at all − verbatim in Catalan.

In Spain, the Catalans have a reputation for being skinflints and they themselves have a blasphemous but widely used expression which describes a tightfisted person as *Mes agarrat que les nansses de Sant Cristo* (Tighter than Christ's grip on the nails). And however much blasphemy is frowned upon in Spain, the national appetite for extravagant speech and gothic imagery cannot be suppressed and bursts out in such oaths as

¡Me cago en los veinticuatro cojones de los apóstoles de Jesús! (I shit on the twenty-four balls of Christ's apostles!).

In old-fashioned French sacrer, 'to sacred', meant to swear and sacré is still much used, as in sacré nom de Dieu (often euphemistically rendered as sacré nom d'un chien), or c'est un sacré lapin (he's a great guy, literally a sacred rabbit). The Spanish for the sacristy, the part of a church where the sacred vessels are kept, is a sacristía, but a man who tiene la sacristía abierta (has an open sacristy) has left his flies undone.

In most of Europe blasphemy began to lose its power during the latter half of the nineteenth century as the Church's authority was shaken by liberalism and the rise of science. It may not have been his intention, but Luther's famous retort to his accusers: 'Here I stand, I can do no other,' presaged the Enlightenment's espousal of freedom of conscience. If one could assert, as Luther did, the right to worship God as one thought fit, then one also had the right not to worship Him at all. Liberty began to be valued not as a quality of something else but as an end and a virtue in itself, and once the right to be irreligious had been won, the demand soon followed for the separation of Church and State. Pope Pius IX deplored universal suffrage as a 'horrible plague', an attitude that no doubt reinforced the conviction of Léon Gambetta, a founder of the French republic, that 'it is rare for a Catholic to be a patriot'. Even the Church couldn't hold back the tide, though not for lack of trying, and its power began gradually and then rapidly to decline. In twentieth-century Europe only in Ireland, Portugal and Franco's Spain would the hand of God continue to fit the glove of government so snugly.

Not that secular ideas were encouraged among the lower orders. Voltaire, who discouraged talk of atheism in front of the servants, said, 'I want my lawyer, tailor, valets, even my wife, to believe in God; I think that if they do I shall be robbed less and cheated less.' But through the proliferation of newspapers, the new gospel of Marx and Darwin, Charles Fourier, Robert Owen and John Stuart Mill began to trickle down to the masses packed into the squalid hell of the new Jerusalem.

Science couldn't prove that miracles didn't happen and for the most part didn't try; but it sowed doubts and de facto called into question the veracity of the Bible as a historical record. The Church had never left any room for doubt that the Bible was the word of God, but scientific theories of creation inevitably raised questions about the existence or at least the nature of the deity. However laughable people found the hypothesis that we might be descended from the apes, it was scarcely more absurd than the claim that an omniscient being, toying with the idea of a beast fashioned in His own likeness, had knocked us up in an afternoon.

Something else that began to change was the use of invective. We've seen that during the latter half of the nineteenth century the majority of Europeans, who for centuries had been swearing by, began swearing at. Henceforth all forms of swearing would become increasingly direct, independent of divine intervention, and the art of insult would grow more personal, strumming with tireless invention on the same three chords: parentage, sex and excrement. From now on women would be bitches, sluts and whores, and from their loins would issue sons of bitches, little shits and complete bastards; arseholes, dickheads and poofters. For five hundred years the French had called the English les goddams; by the 1960s they had earned a new epithet – les fuckoffs. God was well dead.

4 ★ *A Final Word*

> '. . . I bet him a hundred bucks he couldn't go the whole
> trip, from wherever we were at the time all the way to
> San Juan without saying "fuck" in one form or another
> at least once . . . He could barely speak. He'd start to say
> something and there'd be a long pause, like he was learn-
> ing a foreign language. Finally he said, "Fuck it," and
> handed me a hundred-dollar bill.'
>
> Elmore Leonard, *Glitz*

God took one look at Babel and said, 'Let us go down, and
there confound their language, that they may not understand
one another's speech.' Since then the nearest we've come to
having a common language was Latin, but as a popular tongue
that soon splintered into the mutually unintelligible Romance
languages. Now English is the closest thing to an international
language. At the time of the Norman conquest in 1066 English
could muster barely 1.5 million speakers; now there are perhaps a billion. It owes much of its spread to British imperial-
ism, spurred on by the need for a lingua franca in the
post-colonial era. India, for example, encompasses 845 languages and dialects, but for lack of a common tongue the
constitution of 1950 that enshrines Hindi as the national language was written in English. However, it's the world's love
affair with all things American that over the past fifty years
has driven the English language into every corner of the globe.

English is an open language, it borrows freely and unselfconsciously whatever it fancies from wherever it finds it. And
almost from the start it's shown a passion for simplicity, stripping away unnecessary parts of speech, insouciantly casting

aside grammar and shamelessly flouting its own rules. For example, the seven simple tenses of a typical French or Spanish verb run to forty-two parts; English has learnt to get by with three. By the twelfth century English had shed noun cases, replacing this cumbersome structure with a simple set of prepositions – to, from, with, and so on – that could be applied universally.

As for gender, surely one of speech's most useless encumbrances, leading to such idiocies as the male sexual organs being a feminine noun and vice versa in some languages, English ditched it for all but the distinction between male and female creatures at around the same time that it abandoned noun declensions. And good riddance. Surely even the Académie Française, that champion of linguistic purity, doesn't have a rational explanation for why un *carburateur* (carburettor) is masculine and une *bougie d'allumage* (spark plug) feminine. Over the past hundred and fifty years English has also dropped the formalities of the thee/thou, tu/vous forms of address in favour of the more democratic 'you'. This drive towards simplification continues to the point where, since the end of the First World War, it has been demonstrated that English discourse can be boiled down to a single word: 'fuck'.

It's said that OK is the most widely known word – if it is a word – in the world, but 'fuck' must come a close second. From Rio to Riyadh young men who cannot ask the time in English but have studied the complete works of Rambo can effortlessly strike tough guy poses, curl their lips and utter 'Fuck you' with complete self-assurance. And 'fuck' has been adopted by Danes, Finns and Swedes whose own word rather unimaginatively refers only to the sex act and has no metaphorical uses. So any Dane who wants to 'talk the talk' is driven to employ such alien constructions as *Fuck-man huor er det mørkt* (Fucking hell, man, it's dark in here). In Finland someone even brought out a magazine entitled simply *Fuck*.

We've seen that *les goddams* gave way in the 1960s to *les fuckoffs*. This is only to be expected, as all over the English-speaking world there are people whose speech, if you removed the fucks, would hardly be joined-up talking at all, but just a sorry bunch of indefinite articles hanging round an out of work subordinate clause. The scenario described by Elmore Leonard at the beginning of this chapter is a familiar one. Listen to a post-match TV interview with a footballer, or to a policeman giving evidence in court. Constrained by the know-ledge that they can't say 'fuck' in court or in a broadcast interview, their speech becomes stilted, halting, robbed of its natural cadence. Deprived of their fucking map, they feel their way across an alien vocabulary and stumble into grammatical holes from which there's no escape.

'Fuck' is the English word *par excellence*, enlisted to serve as any and every part of speech. Is there any other language in which it is possible to construct a sentence such as, 'Fuck me, I'm fucked if I fucking know what to fucking do, the fucking fucker's fucking fucked up and fucked off,' which, while it is semantic rubbish, is capable of being understood? Elegant it is not; granted, it comes up a little short in the nuance depart-ment, but it is, in context, perfectly intelligible to any native English speaker. 'Fuck' is the distillate of a millennium of English evolution, of a language rooted in German, Norse and French, and heavily laced with Latin, a magpie language that nonchalantly picks up whatever words take its fancy, from sources as diverse as Urdu, Portuguese and Algonquin. But it all boils down to 'fuck'. In any British or American town centre you will find people who, to use the clinical term, have completely lost their marbles. They pass their days locked in interminable harangues with invisible interlocutors, harangues that are constructed almost exclusively around the various parts and participles of 'fuck'.

And yet this little word of uncertain origin has only achieved its dominant position since the turn of the century, although it's been in use since about 1500. Prior to that it had lain fallow for over a thousand years, during which time it seems to have been supplanted by the distinctly rustic 'swive'. As is often the case with taboo words, its etymology is much disputed. The Oxford English Dictionary retreats behind a cautious 'origin unknown'. Others derive it from the German *ficken* and Middle Dutch *fokken*, meaning to strike, which relate to the Indo-European root word *peik*, meaning enmity. The possible Latin roots put forward are *pungere* and *pugil* as in pugilist, or *futuere*, allegedly related to *battuere*, to strike. Faced with an etymology of such unremitting wham bam thank you ma'am it would be heartening to come across a theory that 'fuck' derives from the Gaelic for 'is this good for you, darling?' or the Old High Frisian for 'let's take it nice and slow, sugar lips'. Sadly not; when it comes to fucking, etymologists seem to favour the rough end of the pineapple, as they say in Australia.

Its first appearance in print was in 1503 in a work by the Scottish poet William Dunbar, the vulgar friar whom we met earlier, but in common with its often close associate 'cunt', it was deemed unworthy of a place in mainstream dictionaries until 1965. In 1882 it made an unscheduled appearance in a parliamentary report in The Times, which contained the line: 'The Speaker then said he felt inclined for a bit of fucking.' The paper has never recovered from this insertion, thought to be the work of a mischievous or disgruntled compositor, and even after 'fuck' was decriminalized in 1960, following the Lady Chatterley trial, it declined to use it, although the euphemistic 'footling' continues to find its way into print. Exactly one hundred years after The Times' embarrassing slip, in 1982 the House of Commons banned 'fuck' as unparliamentary language.

Shakespeare wasn't one to pass up the chance of a *jeu de*

mots, least of all if it presented the opportunity for a little smut. Take the scene in *Henry V* where Katharine, the French princess, is trying to learn English from her maid, who is also French. To Katharine's enquiry, '*Comment appelez-vous le pied et la robe?*' ('How do you say foot and gown?') the maid replies, to her mistress's horror, 'De foot, *madame; et* de coun.' Apart from the more obvious 'de coun', Shakespeare knew perfectly well that *foutre* is French for fuck and used it in several plays. D. H. Lawrence, who used 'fuck' thirty times in *Lady Chatterley's Lover* (cunt and balls scored respectively fourteen and thirteen times), was one of the first to show that the word packed such great literary potential, or at least potential for literary notoriety. In 1960, more than thirty years after Lawrence wrote it, Penguin Books published an unexpurgated version of *Lady Chatterley's Lover* and the ensuing prosecution for obscenity – which the Crown lost – would in 1980 be referred to by the *News of the World* as 'the trial that ushered in the permissive society'.

Thereafter this little word would guide many a writer on to the fast track to celebrity. Philip Larkin is often cited as Britain's finest post-war poet, but the only lines anyone seems to remember are, 'They fuck you up, your mum and dad. / They may not mean to, but they do.' In 1994 James Kelman won the Booker Prize with *How Late It Was, How Late*, a 374-page novel that included four thousand uses of the word 'fuck'. As Cole Porter wrote, 'Good authors, too, who once knew better words, now only use four-letter words, writing prose – anything goes.' At least Kelman showed more mettle than Norman Mailer whose *The Naked and the Dead*, published in 1948, resorted to the euphemism 'fug', an evasion that got what it deserved when Mailer was introduced to the actress Tallulah Bankhead and she quipped, 'Oh, you're the man who doesn't know how to spell fuck.'

Another famous trial over this difficult little word went all the way to the US Supreme Court. In 1968, during the Vietnam war, a Los Angeles man was convicted of disturbing the peace for wearing a jacket with the slogan 'Fuck the draft'. He appealed, claiming an infringement of his right to free speech guaranteed under the First Amendment. The Supreme Court overturned the conviction as unconstitutional censorship, Justice Harlan making a name for himself with the ruling that, however offensive the word, 'it is nevertheless often true that one man's vulgarity is another's lyric'.

The first accounts of 'fuck' being used in English as the portmanteau word it has become today are of British soldiers returning from the First World War trenches who displayed the now common trait of using fuck every other fucking word. Wars and armies are great innovators and scatterers of slang and there is no reason to doubt that the twentieth-century love affair with fuck began among British and US servicemen in France. However, they had not yet developed the knack, especially common in Ireland, of making verbal sandwiches by inserting fuck into the middle of words, exemplified by such turns of speech as 'yer man Irwin made an absofuckinglutely diafuckingbolical hash of that fucking free kick, so he did'.

Although it's much used in the Antipodes, 'bloody' remains the most popular adjective there, where it is sometimes known as 'the great Australian adjective', often as a companion to that other word beloved of antipodeans, 'bastard'. However, we do have Australia to thank for the unequivocal 'fuckwit' and for the retort, often used by women in response to unwanted male attention: 'Why don't you stick your dick in your ear and fuck some sense into yourself?'

Despite their unquenchable enthusiasm for this word, people in the British Isles have yet to adopt it as a personal noun the way they have in America, where it is possible to call someone 'a fuck'. There's a scene in the film *A Fish Called Wanda* in which Kevin Kline, exasperated by John Cleese's air of unshakeable superiority, says to him, 'You pompous, stuck-up, snot-nosed, English, giant, twerp, scumbag, fuck-face, dickhead, asshole!' to which Cleese replies smugly, 'How very interesting. You are a true vulgarian, aren't you?' A view that Kline seems to confirm with the retort, 'You're the vulgarian, you fuck.' Calling someone 'a fuck' has so far been resisted by British aficionados, perhaps because it lacks the impact of 'cunt', a word that rarely crosses the lips of even the most foul-mouthed American. While the peculiarly satisfying Americanism 'shut the fuck up' has made the crossing, the other variation that has yet to take off on this side of the Atlantic is 'motherfucker', well-known in Britain through cinema and rap music.

Of African-American origin, motherfucker appears to have been in use as a derogatory or playful epithet for a person since 1790 but, strangely, has only been used to describe objects or situations since the 1950s. As an adjective, 'motherfucking' signifies much the same as 'fucking', but as a noun it is more nuanced: a 'sorry motherfucker' is pitiful, a 'bad motherfucker' is admirable, 'mad as a motherfucker' is very mad indeed. Black America has made a huge contribution to popular speech – imagine life without being 'cool' or having 'the blues', for example – but motherfucker has become so overused that the black vernacular sometimes seems in danger of painting its motherfucking ass into a bit of a motherfucking corner.

Hollywood has always hated writers, or 'word-men' as they are disparagingly known. But thanks to 'method' acting and a fashion for improvised dialogue it's now often possible to dispense with them altogether. All the director needs to do is explain the action and motive of each scene to the actors. The actors then proceed to improvise a dialogue around the words 'asshole', 'fuck' and 'motherfucker', modulating the dramatic impact by leavening their speech with post-modern enigmas such as 'and', 'but' and 'dunno'. If it's a 'black' movie the core vocabulary can be augmented by regular use of the term 'nigger' and, more or less at random, the phrase 'know what I'm sayin'?'. The script isn't always improvised, however, and no doubt there is an art to writing dialogue that goes, 'Get your motherfuckin' ass in here, motherfucker.' 'Fuck you, you dickless fuck. This motherfucker ain't going nowhere. Know what I'm sayin'?' One can only assume that it was to protect his integrity as a screenwriter that I was refused permission to quote from the screenplay of Quentin Tarantino's *Pulp Fiction*, a prime example of the genre.

Films such as *Pulp Fiction* or Spike Lee's *Do The Right Thing*, which ride heavily on the American vernacular and are well up to quota on motherfuckers, are a nightmare when it comes to producing a dubbed or subtitled version. Faced with this challenge the German translator, armed with relatively tame and unimaginative slang, renders motherfucker as *Arschloch* (arsehole), the keystone of German vulgarity. The Spanish translator, somewhat better equipped, opts for *hijo de puta* (son of a whore). *Arschloch* is wheeled out again as the translation of 'fucker', while Spanish elaborates on the theme with *algún jodido hijo de puta* (some fucked son of a whore). 'Fucked up' is covered by the other German portmanteau *Scheiße* as *so eine Scheiße* (what a shit) whereas Spanish can call on the variant *guarrado*, roughly 'pigged-up'. But ultimately it doesn't really work, and a dialogue so drenched in the vernacular is beyond translation. You can translate 'it's a motherfucking fact of life' into *es un jodido hecho de la vida*, but that doesn't mean it's something a Spaniard would actually say. The difficulties involved in translating vernacular are one reason − the other is lack of money − why many subtitlers merely render the sense and leave the rest to the imagination. With dubbing, of course, there is the added problem of lipsynch. Sometimes even the title defeats the translators. The French film *Gazon Maudit*, literally 'cursed pubic triangle', was released in English as French Twist.

Many English speakers, to whom the word 'fuck' is almost as vital as oxygen, find it hard to believe that there are people on this earth who can get by without it, but they do. In Germany, for example, while a particularly vulgar German might use *ficken* to describe the sex act it is not generally used metaphorically, any more than it is in Scandinavia. One assumes that the liberated, free-loving, anything-goes Swedes have no need to resort to such language as the Swedish psyche has been swept clean of taboos. On the other hand, maybe they're just too uptight.

Anyway, back to Germany. The German equivalents of 'fuck off' – and these are both very strong talk indeed, much stronger than in English – are *Leck mich am Arsch!* (Lick my arse!) and *Verpiß dich!* (Piss off!) while *Verfick dich!* (Fuck off!) is less common. *Fick dich doch selbst* is Germany's contribution to the almost pan-European challenge to go fuck yourself. A few examples of how others say it are *Vaffanculo!* (Italian), *Va te faire enculer!* (French), ¡*Métetelo en el culo!* (Spanish) or *Vai tomar no cu!* (Portuguese), *Ai yamísou!* (Greek) and *Gabh suas ort fhéin* (Irish).

In German you can also tell someone to get lost by saying *Spritz ab!* (Ejaculate!), a strange exhortation, but then this is the nation which describes an orgasm as *höchste Wallung* (maximum bubbling). At least it's less alarming than the Finnish proposition that you *Vedä vittu päähäs!* (Go pull a cunt over your head!). *Ficken* isn't normally used to intensify speech, a role fulfilled by *verdammt* (damn), and as a rule Germans, who are among the least foul-mouthed of Europeans, use *Arsch*, *Arschloch* and *Scheiße* where English uses 'fuck'. So 'Fuck him!' is rendered *Der kann mich doch am Arsch lecken* (He can lick my arse), while *Ich scheiß' was auf seine Meinung* (I shit on his opinion) is the German equivalent of 'Fuck what he thinks!'. *Der hat keine Scheiß Ahnung davon* amounts to 'He knows fuck all about it'.

This harping on arses has been transplanted into American English in forms such as 'It's your ass' and 'Get your ass out of there'.

In the north of Portugal, and especially in Porto, whose citizens are notoriously foul-mouthed, people lace their speech and in some cases every sentence with *foda-se* (fuck it). One wonders whether this reflects the city's close association with the English, who dominate the port wine business. But the language that comes nearest to the English use of 'fuck' is French, although somehow the French found themselves in the potentially embarrassing position of having a verb *baiser* which means both to kiss and to fuck. To avoid confusion most people use *embrasser* as the kiss word and *baiser* is probably best avoided unless you're very sure of your ground. As is often the case with French, in its different guises the same word can have different levels of acceptability. For instance, it's considered fairly harmless to say that someone or something is *foutu* (fucked, in the sense of broken or exhausted) or, euphemistically, *fichu*. But *je ne sais foutre rien* (I haven't a fucking clue) or *j'en ai rien à foutre/je m'en fou* (I don't give a fuck) are certainly not polite. *Se foutre*, the reflexive form, is slightly milder, as in *se foutre dedans* (put your foot in it).

The ambiguous status of *foutre* became front-page news in 1995 after a row broke out over its use in the long-running BBC radio soap opera *The Archers*. In one episode the fictitious French chef ordered someone out of his kitchen with the popular phrase: *Foutez-moi le camp*. When people complained, and in England someone always does, the BBC denied that the expression was vulgar, claiming it was no worse than saying 'get lost'. Yves Aubert, who plays the chef, said it was harmless, a phrase a French grandmother would use to her grandchildren. The French Embassy countered somewhat unhelpfully that it also means 'fuck off'. And indeed, all of these interpretations are correct: *foutez-moi le camp* means anything from 'fuck off' to 'get out my hair, children'. It just depends. The point Aubert was making was that if he really wanted to be rude he would have said something stronger, something such as *Va te faire enculer!* (Go fuck yourself!)

Like the English the French also employ *foutre* adjectivally, as in *c'est foutrement con* (it's really stupid), although *vachement* (literally 'cowishly') is more common and more polite. *Foutu* can also be used as *bien* or *mal foutu* to mean well or badly made or, if said of a person, well or badly dressed. All the above can be put together to give *il est vachement bien foutu*, which, while it translates as 'he's cowishly well fucked', means 'he's a real looker'. If you think that's weird, what about Spanish, where one woman might convey to another the fact that she fancies a man with the comment: *¡La puta que le parió!* (The whore that bore him!)? Like the Portuguese, the Spanish also use this expression to mean 'bloody hell' or 'you're kidding'.

Foutre and *foutu* share some of the English word's flexibility, where it's just thrown in to beef up a sentence such as *elle n'est même pas foutue de me le dire en face* (she hasn't the guts to say it to my face) or *il est bien foutu de le faire* (he's quite capable of doing it). And *un fouteur de merde* (a shit fucker) is what the English would call a 'piss artist'. There are numerous synonyms for *foutre*, although most of them are for the act itself and aren't metaphorical. One of the more popular is *niquer*, which can substitute for *foutre* in standard phrases such as *va te faire niquer* (Go fuck yourself). The fashionable expression *J'nique ta mère/soeur* (I fuck your mother/sister) is often translated simply as 'motherfucker'. *Niquer* appears to have entered the language from the French of the *pieds-noirs*, the descendants of French Algerian colonists, who adapted it from the Arabic *nak i nik*. This in turn corresponds to *nikah*, the Arabic word for marriage. So having saddled themselves with one word, *baiser*, that means both kissing and fucking, now they've acquired another that means fucking and marriage. Flirting in French is definitely not for beginners.

There are similar dangers in Spanish, where the widely used expression *estoy hecho polvo* (I'm worn out, literally, I'm reduced to dust) sounds perilously similar to *echar un polvo* (to have a fuck), bearing in mind that the Spanish 'h' is silent. And to the frequent embarrassment of those who learnt their Spanish in Europe, in Latin America the seemingly innocuous verb *coger* (to take) also means to fuck. Many a laugh is had at the expense of those who, believing they have asked where they can catch the train (*coger el tren*), have in fact enquired after an opportunity to go for an altogether different sort of ride. In Spain itself *joder* stands for figurative fucking and *follar* for the real thing. There are also a number of nonsense words such as *foqui-foqui* or *ñaca-ñaca* and a man who practises coitus interruptus is said to *escupir a la calle* (spit in the street).

In Latin America 'fuck', aside from *coger*, is *chingar*, derived from the Caló dialect of the Spanish Gitanos, and yet another word that apparently means to strike. In Mexico they have a curious custom on independence day of chanting *Viva Mexico! Hijos de la chingada!* (Viva Mexico! Children of the fucked woman!) This is such a peculiar thing to say it is tempting to wonder whether the chant might once have been *Hijos de la cíngara!* (Children of the Gypsy woman!). But then Spanish and Latin American people are quite capable of referring to themselves as 'children of the fucked woman' without batting an eyelid.

The use of 'fucked' to mean useless or broken is common to Greek and all the Romance languages but 'fucking' as an adjective is heard much less and scarcely at all in German and Dutch. The Dutch word is *neuken* but it's mostly only used as an exclamation and the word isn't used that often, except in the extremely rude *Ga je moeder neuken!* (Go fuck your mother!), that is to say, please go away. Stronger still, and perhaps the

worst thing you can say in Greek, is *Sou yamó tin mána!* (I fuck
your mother!), or *Sou yamó tin adelfi!* (I fuck your sister!) or
even *Sou yamó to soi!* (Fuck your entire bloodline!). In Catalan,
a language that bestrides the Pyrenees, the French influence
is clear in *Fot el camp!* and *Se me'n fot* (I don't care), while the
sense of 'You must be joking!' is rendered ¡*No me jodas!* and *No
fotis!* in Spanish and Catalan respectively. In Spanish *joder* can
also be used reflexively as *Esto me jode* (I'm tired of this). Even
better is the exasperated ¡*Hay que joderse!* which means roughly
'This is the pits', but translates directly as 'One might as well
fuck oneself'.

The Portuguese, who have never taken to swearing with the
sort of gusto shown by their neighbours, are rather shocked at
the way the Spanish throw *joder* about, as their word *foder* is
stronger. Although it's heard less, it's used in much the same
way as in Spain. But even a *Foda-se!* (Fuck it!) of shock or
surprise would be frowned upon anywhere south of Porto.
Then there's the macho expression *Fodême-los todos* (We fucked
them all), meaning 'We won'. This sense is echoed in the
Greek *Tha se yamiso*, 'I'll get my revenge', but literally 'I'll fuck
you'. Portuguese also has its version of being fucked about in
Estão-me a foder (Someone's fucking with me).

Italian has a device by which the sense of a word can be
changed radically, even to mean its opposite, simply by prefixing it with an 's'. So when *fottere* (fuck) becomes *sfottere* it
means 'to take the piss'. The main alternative for *fottere*, which
is fairly widely used, though not as commonplace as in French
or Spanish, is *scopare*. This is another one of those words that
can get you into all sorts of trouble as it also means 'to sweep
out'. Play it safe and use *spazzare*, the other word for sweeping.
Besides, it would be very vulgar to ask someone *Vuoi scopare?*
unless you really were offering to help out with the
housework.

In the course of the *Lady Chatterley's Lover* trial, one lawyer justified the attempts to ban the book on the grounds that 'it presents the forbidden acts in forbidden detail and describes them in forbidden language' – and the forbidden word 'fuck' in particular. At that time you couldn't find 'fuck' in a dictionary, now you can buy a dictionary that has no other word in it. An American called Jesse Sheidlower has even published a 232-page book called *The F-Word* which deals with nothing else but the myriad uses of the word fuck. One could go on for ever. But fuck it, let's talk about something else.

5 ★ Mary, Mary

Consider that the most lovely woman has come into being from a foul-smelling drop of semen, then consider her midpoint, how she is a container of filth; and after that consider her end, when she will be food for worms.

Petrus Cantor, Twelfth-century cleric

Sometimes it's hard to be a woman.

Tammy Wynette

The Christian likes his meek and mild, the Muslim, too, and preferably wrapped in cloth from head to toe, while first thing each morning the Jew thanks God he wasn't born one. Nitpicking and jihads aside, philosophers, mystics and men of God are all agreed on one thing – women are bad news, the origin of sin and sorrow. Why, even that nice Siddhartha had to leave his wife before he could achieve Buddhahood.

Aristotle, widely rated as one of the greatest heavyweight thinkers of all time, considered women 'a deformity', adding graciously, 'though one which occurs in the ordinary course of nature'. Nietzsche, who encouraged that little Austrian house painter to think he was superman, said that 'woman was God's second blunder', which was odd because he'd already assured us that God was dead. (And God's first blunder? Not making animals sufficiently diverting to keep men entertained, according to Nietzsche.) The fifth-century preacher St John Chryso-stom asked, 'What else is woman but a foe to friendship, an inescapable punishment, a necessary evil, a domestic danger, a delectable detriment, an evil of nature painted with fair colours?', before retiring to his desert hermitage where, one imagines, he was not much missed by the girls he left behind. And so it goes on, Schopenhauer complaining that women have no sense of justice, Hamlet whingeing that 'Frailty, thy name is woman' and Los Angeles rappers Niggaz With Attitude summing up several millennia of Western thought on the subject with the observation 'Tha bitch is a bitch'.

But men have got a case; after all women have messed up pretty badly. It's there in the Book of Common Prayer, that bon mourant's Michelin guide to life's poisoned wells: 'Man that is born of a woman hath but a short time to live, and is full of misery.' Life is misery because women are the repository of original sin which they pass on to men along with the rest of the genetic baggage – 'Behold, I was brought forth in iniquity and in sin did my mother conceive me,' (Psalms 50: 7). They also distract us men from our relentless pursuit of higher goals. Left to our own devices we boys would all be mystics and philosophers, utterly consumed by our spiritual appetites. This spirituality is the hallmark of any group of men who have been freed from the venal distractions of women; you notice it among sailors, for example, or convicts. But women continually drag us down from the heights, down into the swamp of concupiscence. It's plain that if men had not wasted so much time chasing skirt we wouldn't have made such slow progress and could well have been whizzing down the information superhighway back when Christ was still just a carpenter. St Augustine got it right when he said he was 'convinced that nothing turns the spirit of man away from the heights more than the caresses of woman'. This is the same saint who said, 'Give me chastity, but not yet', so he should know.

And not only is original sin passed on by women; they saddle us with regular, everyday sin as well. For example, across much of Europe the worst thing a man can be is the son of a whore, *figlio di puttana*, as the Italians say, a shame from which, although it's not his fault, there is no escape. A serial killer or rapist can at least plead mitigating circumstances, a war criminal can say he was only following orders, but there is nothing a poor son of a bitch can do to defend himself. Nearly as bad, he might marry a woman who cheats on him, making him a cuckold, a laughing stock. And should he behave like a woman, weak and henpecked, pussywhipped, or *under tøflen* (under the slipper) as they say in Denmark, or worst of all that he, heaven forbid, 'takes it like a woman', is a sissy or a faggot, what the Greeks call a *poústis*, well, it's probably his mother's fault for bringing him up wrong.

As for a woman, what could be worse than simply being what she is, a woman? And if it's bad enough simply to be one, then a bad woman, a whore who exchanges sex for money, is about as bad as bad gets. Or worse, a slut, a hussy who does it simply for pleasure, or because she can't control her animal desires. There seems to be complete European unanimity on this, that it's as low as a woman can fall.

And speaking of the Fall, the rot set in with Eve. Tertullian, an early Church father, says of her, 'You are the devil's gateway . . . you who softened up with your cajoling words the man against whom the devil could not prevail by force.' Poor old Adam, what a putz. He never wanted any part of it; he would have been happy to stay home and channel-surf but she kept on at him until, caramba! a quickie, *una calatina* as they say in Rome, and it's bye bye, dolce vita, *buon giorno*, sweat of your brow. Cast out of Eden, forced to become a farmer, while the kids, *che miseria*, brought forth in sorrow, start killing each other the moment they're out of his sight. Dysfunctional family or what?

Women are a calamity. And not just because they keep interrupting men's contemplation of the tinkling music of the spheres with the promise of a little *foqui-foqui* or maybe a spot of lunch down at the Lazy-Y. As though this wasn't bad enough, women have a personal hygiene problem. It's there in the Book of Leviticus, which says that if a man has sex with his wife when she has the painters in, or is among *les coquelicots* (poppies) or, as the Spanish say, *estar con el semáforo rojo* (is stuck on a red light) 'both of them shall be cut off from among their people'. Banished, sentenced to death in effect, just for having sex during menstruation. It seems pretty harsh until you hear what the Archbishop of Arles, a sixth-century pioneer of family planning, had to say. 'Whoever has relations with his wife during her period,' he said, 'will have children that are either leprous, epileptic or possessed by the devil.' Even now, despite huge advances in health education, there are still a lot of people who don't know that.

The very word 'taboo', which we borrowed from Tongan Polynesian, is synonymous with menstruation in that language. The ever-helpful Leviticus also reminds us that a woman is unclean for forty days after the birth of a son but for eighty after the even more revolting act of bringing forth a daughter. This tallies with Aristotle's calculation that the male foetus acquires a soul after forty days and the female after ninety, which is only what you would have guessed anyway. Gypsy women are traditionally considered *mahrime* (unclean) for forty days after giving birth and, in common with Orthodox Jewish women, are hemmed in by the demands of ritual purity that surround menstruation and childbirth. This does at least confer a peculiar power on Gypsy women, who can make a man unclean – a social disaster for him – merely by threatening to pull her skirt over his head.

The Church, ever adept at painting itself into an apse after a long night dancing on the head of a pin, got its tail into a terrible knot over sex, importing into Christianity the Gnostics' sexual pessimism and their characterization of the body and its desires as a 'walking grave'. Things could only get worse once the Church had embraced the cult of celibacy. It was one thing to say that sex was for reproduction, not pleasure, but St Jerome's logic drove him to declare that 'feelings of sensual pleasure such as those had in the embraces of a harlot are damnable in a wife'. For sheer stupidity this must rank with Rome's advice to women in 1916 that if a husband wore a condom they should behave exactly as if he were a rapist (lie back and take the blame, presumably), or Pope John Paul II's ruling in 1988 that it was better for a man with HIV or Aids to infect his wife than to wear a condom.

The cult of the Virgin Mary – she is scarcely mentioned in the Gospels – has been shown to be another Gnostic import, borrowed from the Greeks' obsession with virgins and virgin births. But the Church fathers made much of Mary and her virginity. St Augustine described her as a 'sealed fountain', a condition that sounds excruciatingly painful. St Ambrose chose virginity – not toolmaking or the power of reason – as 'our exclusive possession', the feature that set us apart from other beasts. In Portugal a woman's virginity is called *os três* (the three), the trinity in question being the cunt, arse and mouth, and a woman who loses her virginity *perder os três*, loses the three.

The Church celebrated celibacy as the ideal state and it was claimed that the afterlife offered greater rewards to virgins than to those who had entered the lottery of marriage. But St Jerome can't have been playing with a full deck when he tried to bluff his way out of a tight theological corner with the conclusion that the only good that comes from marriage is that 'it produces virgins. I gather the rose from the thorns, the gold from the earth, the pearl from the mussel.'

Notwithstanding St Jerome's confusion over where pearls come from, this is the earliest known record of the now widespread use of 'mussel' as a euphemism for a woman's sex. A French woman, for example, might remark that she has *la moule qui bâille* (a yawning mussel) meaning she's feeling horny, though she's not yet so far down the track as to have *la praline en délire* (a delirious sugared almond, one of many edible French euphemisms for the clitoris), at which point she would be about ready to *vider ses burettes* (empty her *burettes*, or orgasm – the wine and holy water for Mass are kept in *burettes*, a touch that would have appealed to Jerome, whose writings on sugared almonds sadly have not come down to us). On the matter of bivalves in general, in the Antipodes men sometimes speak of 'spearing the bearded clam with their pork sword', allegedly a reference to sexual pleasure, though probably not the clam's. But I digress.

Men have always had to be men, strong and brave and generally in the right, but women have had a choice of role models: Eve or Mary, the whore or the Virgin, the one whose uncontrollable sexuality has brought sorrow upon us all, the other blessed by apparently not having a sexuality at all. St Jerome – God, don't you just love this guy? – put it in a clam shell when he said, 'Death came through Eve, but life has come through Mary.' Mary was also blessed with Joseph, a husband whose breathtaking gullibility has made him the patron saint of cuckolds. As the cult of the Virgin Mary spread across Catholic Europe her antithesis came to be not so much Eve as Mary Magdalene, whose name became a byword for homes for fallen women in eighteenth-century England and who wept or slept her way into the language as the word 'maudlin'.

Irene Pivetti, the speaker of Italy's Chamber of Deputies who famously remarked that no one had done more for Italian women than Mussolini, was described in 1994 by the Italian daily *Corriere Della Sera* as: *Pura come la Madonna, abile come Maria Maddalena* (Pure as the Madonna, cunning as Mary Magdalene). Since the time of Christ women have been dancing around the same two handbags, mother and whore, saint and slut, good Mary and bad Mary. They're dancing still, as is revealed

by the pejoratives for women, which show a dispiriting con-
sistency across the European spectrum.

Once again there is a clear divide between north and south.
Northern Europeans are taken aback by the frequency with
which the word 'whore' crops up in the everyday speech of
their southern neighbours. For many of them it's as fundamental to their speech patterns as 'fuck' is to some English speakers
or *Scheiße* to some Germans. But it's only acceptable as an
abstraction; you may call a traffic jam a whore, but not a
woman, which isn't to say that no one ever does, of course.
In France, Spain, Portugal, Italy and Greece there is no doubt
that the second to worst thing to call a woman is a whore –
respectively *putain, puta, puta, puttana, putana* – and the worst is
a slut – *salope* or *connasse, zorra* (literally, a vixen), *cadela* (bitch),
troia or *mignotta*, and *tsula*. And in Euskera, *trapu*, literally, a rag,
means a slut. The rag theme is also found in the Italian *straccio
di mignotta* (rag of a slut), a withering condemnation.

But *puttana* is bad enough. The Italian film director Federico
Fellini was an uxorious man who it was thought had few
lovers in his lifetime. So when shortly after his death a woman
claiming to be his former lover put his *billets doux* up for sale,
it stirred up more interest than normal. But Fellini's sister
Maddalena – and who's going to argue with a woman named
after the 'bad' Mary – dismissed the significance of the corre-
spondence with the scathing observation, 'Federico had many
puttane, not just one.'

A 1970s study turned up 220 different English pejoratives
for a promiscuous woman but only twenty for men, and a
similar result could probably be obtained anywhere in Europe.
Ask an Italian, for example, for a word that would serve as a
put-down for a womanizer and you get one of those polite
laughs people reserve for psychotics and foreigners. But
although the underlying values and hypocrisy are much the
same, the choice of words isn't, and in northern Europe the

word whore (German *Hure*, Swedish *hora*, Dutch *hoer*) sounds old-fashioned and appears to be falling into disuse. This whore business forms one of the most clearly defined north–south slanguage barriers. In the north the exception is Finland where *huora* is quite common, and is perhaps even becoming à la mode in a rather negative way, the way 'bitch' is in America. And in Holland, *kankerhoer* (cancer whore) is an especially strong insult. Whether the relative decline of 'whore' words in the north mirrors an underlying shift in attitude seems unlikely. There's no hard evidence that northern men are any less sexist, despite the view of many of them that Latin men are all macho mama's boys. Surveys among English school-children, for example, regularly show little change in the tra-ditional view that some girls do and nice girls don't.

Attitudes may be slow to change but language doesn't stand still. A number of the more common English insults that have been hurled at women, words such as sluttish, harlot, shrew and coquette, had originally referred to men, but by the six-teenth century were applied exclusively to women. A similar transition, only in reverse, seems to be under way in Ireland where 'hoor' – the Irish rendering of the English word whore – is nowadays said more often of men than women, particu-larly in the epithet 'a cute hoor', to describe a somewhat shifty character who's not above a little sharp practice.

The various northern forms of 'whore' are ancient and have always meant an adulteress, but the southern *putain*, *puta* and so on derive from the Latin *putus* meaning a boy. This in turn is redolent of the Greek *poústis*, itself originating in the Ottoman Turkish *pust*, meaning a boy kept for sexual pleasure. So, what-ever the route, it would appear that with the *putain* family of words, women have once again been saddled with an insult that was originally directed at men. 'Punk', on the other hand, which in Elizabethan times meant a female prostitute, some-how changed sex early this century to denote a young male prostitute. More specifically it meant a boy kept for sex, a 'gunsel', from the Yiddish *gendzel* (little goose), a word that Dashiell Hammett brought back from the dead in *The Maltese Falcon*.

If *whore* itself is seldom used in northern Europe, there's no shortage of terms meaning 'slut'. Again, you hear them less in the north but they have lost none of their force. There is little that is ambivalent about words such as the German *Luder* (minx) or *Flittchen* (tart). The German *Schlampe* (slut) is profoundly insulting, the more so because it is only used in earnest, and never in a casual or figurative way. *Schlampe*, for example, wouldn't be said of an educated, middle-class woman. The Germans being more concerned about precision than the rest of us, by the time someone calls you a *Schlampe*, there's a good chance that that's what you've become. The Danish insult *spermsak* doesn't leave a lot to the imagination. The more oblique Danish word for slut, *mar*, is related to the English word 'nightmare', the latter part of which has nothing to do with horses. A female spirit, or *maere*, one of the medieval set of incubi and succubi, would settle on a person while they slept, producing a feeling of suffocation by sitting on their face. And that's the original nightmare. I don't know about you, but I've had worse dreams.

The southern European 'slut' words are all deeply offensive and more or less unspeakable. And the same rule that applies to *puta* – that there is no acceptable, jokey way of using it, not even among women friends – goes for words such as the French *connasse* or Greek *tsula*. The Greeks have some particularly fierce words of this variety, including *psolarpáhtra* (dick-grabber), the graphic *xekoliara*, which translates more or less as 'fucked almost to death', and *xeskismeni*, 'torn to pieces by fucking'.

The only context in which slut and slag words are acceptable is among gay men, who long ago appropriated female insults

for their own purposes. English women have successfully
reclaimed and taken the sting out of 'tart' and, to a lesser
extent, 'slag' and some English and American women have
been trying to do the same with the word 'bitch'. Most older
people would hesitate even to call a dog a bitch but the word
has recently become something of an issue thanks to black
American ghetto talk, in which women are often collectively
referred to – some would say dismissed – as bitches. That this
offends a majority of women was recognized at the Washing-
ton 'March of a Million Men' in 1995, held under the aegis
of the Nation of Islam and to which women were not invited.
The marchers were invited to repeat the pledge: 'I will never
again use the B-word to describe any female, but particularly
my own black sister.'

A bitch is Eve on four legs, a woman in thrall to her
insatiable sexual appetites, constantly on heat, and so is most
insulting in those (Catholic) countries where the Mary-Mary
dichotomy is at its sharpest. The Italian *cagna* (bitch) unequivocally means a woman who would go with just anyone, a
woman who the Welsh would say was *coc wyllt* (cock mad).
The Swedes see something malign in a *ragata* (vixen), while
the same word in Spanish, *zorra*, is the lowest of the low, and
suggests that the woman has lost all self-respect. This utter
worthlessness is captured in the expression ni *zorra* (not so
much as a vixen) meaning 'absolutely nothing, zilch'. Not
that *zorro*, the fox, is burdened with any such contempt, and
indeed Zorro was the name of a fictional masked hero, a sort
of Latin Lone Ranger. Spanish frequently reflects these double
standards, as indeed do other languages. *El hombre de la calle*, for
instance, is simply the man in the street, but *la mujer de la calle*
is a prostitute.

From the number of times you hear it said you might
imagine that the French *putain* is relatively harmless, but it is
still deeply offensive to use it to a stranger or to say it with

any venom. But men and women – even children – say *putain* constantly, to describe just about anything or anyone, or simply to round off a phrase with a dash of brio. It's one of the most common French epithets and, after *merde* (shit), probably the most common exclamation. It's taboo, of course, but certainly less so than in the other Romance languages or Greek. Maybe sending the royal family to the guillotine makes a nation more at ease with itself in such matters. On the other hand the English worship royalty, yet rarely have anything to say about whores, literally or figuratively, unless they're talking about journalists. But then England never really had the stomach for revolution and only embraced the Reformation because Henry VIII wanted a divorce. These things are hard to fathom and I'm no historian.

Putain is used extravagantly as an adjective in phrases such as *Quelle putain de vie!* (What a lousy life!) and even more so in exclamations such as *Putain de bordel de merde!* (Bloody hell!, though literally, whore from the shitty brothel). To give it the full nine yards: *Putain de bordel de merde mais qu'est-ce que tu fous? Tu nous emmerdes!* (Whore from the shitty brothel, what the fuck are you doing? You've put us in the shit!), which is a fairly florid way of saying 'What's happening?'. *Bordel* is also used to mean 'What a mess!' (*Quel bordel!*), a use echoed in the Italian *si è messo in un gran casino* (make a total mess of, a casino here meaning a brothel), or the Spanish ¡*Qué putada!* (What a fuck-up!), or the Italian *puttanata*. As an insult *putain* is often shortened to *pute*, which entered mainstream French via the Provençal *puto*, and is a particularly strong insult for a man as it carries connotations of male prostitution. In a hand of poker, if you're showing four queens, you have *quatre putes*, or in Italian, *quattro puttanas*.

A Portuguese man, when he's fed up and just wants to relax, might exclaim *Putas e vinho verde!*, a whore and a bottle of wine being his idea of a good time, and when he's having a particularly good time will tell you 'Da-se! Tou com una puta! (Fuck me, I'm with a whore!), that is, 'I feel good'. The Portuguese use whore as an adjective as o puta de (the bloody) and also boast one of the few affectionate variants in putefia, which more or less means junior or trainee tart, but is used fondly of pre-pubescent girls. And young boys are sometimes called putos without any pejorative overtones. But then in Portugal a bimbo is a man, not a woman.

Another French word for tart is pétasse, which made the news during President Chirac's cabinet reshuffle in 1995. Of the thirteen ministers sacked, eight were women, allegedly because Alain Juppé, the prime minister, complained that he could no longer work with these pétasses. Pétasse is just one more in what appears to be a surfeit of terms for women of moralidad laxa who se echan a la vida (cast themselves at life), as the Spanish would say. In France a highly sexed woman is sometimes known – with almost medieval paranoia – as une mangeuse de santé (one who eats your health), and an easy lay is un garage à bites (a place to park one's bite or penis). A prostitute may be a langoustine, or may be said to wear her chignon emancipé (her hair down); perhaps she walks in les talons courts (low heels, implying that she's an easy lay), or goes au persil (on the parsley, that is to say, on the game). And if she's new to the game she may be une briquette poussière (a crumbly briquette, but equivalent to 'flaky'), suggesting she's unreliable; une étoile filante (falling star), if a part-timer and une caravelle if she's high class. A brésilienne is a transsexual, une béguineuse is in danger of developing a crush (béguin) on her clients, while un boudin (blood sausage) is getting a little long in the tooth and will soon have to hang up her fishnets. French appears to have devised a word or expression to cover every nuance and specialist service in the sex industry, almost as though it was a branch of the civil service.

To some extent in Catholic countries the word whore

signifies not just any old whore but carries in its pious under-
tow allusions to Mary Magdalene, the proto-whore, especially
in Italian forms such as *puttana Eva* or *puttana Madonna*. However,
Italian menus frequently offer a piquant sauce described as
salsa puttanesca. The other Mary, the good one, pops up in Italian
slang in expressions such as *avere le madonne*, meaning to be
really angry, for emphasis in *ho una fame della madonna* (I'm
starving hungry) and, like the *ostia* (host), to mean 'nothing'.
There's also a verb, *madonnare*, meaning to beat the shit out of
someone.

In Spanish, *puta* assumes the role that 'fuck' does in English,
and is much called upon as an adjective, as in the phrase *de
una puta vez* (this fucking time). When people say, as they often
do, *me cago en la puta* (I shit on the whore) it amounts to a
dismissive 'fuck him', or 'her'. Should you find yourself *como
puta por rastrojo* (like a whore in the stubble) you are almost
certainly in a tricky situation, and if *como putas en cuaresma* (like
whores during Lent), completely skint.

Spanish (Catalan and Gallego, too) have ingeniously combined the idea of the two Marys in the widely used expression
puta madre (whore mother), which has both pejorative and
positive meanings. The Spanish are always shitting on something – your opinion, your football team, your country – but
few things are more insulting than *me cago en su puta madre* (I
shit on your whore mother) which with great economy
embodies both Marys plus the imputation that you are the
son or daughter of a whore. This can be fortified as *me cago en
la leche de su puta madre* (I shit in your whore mother's milk),
or in the form of the popular Catalan expression *em cago en la
puta mare que et va matricular* (on the whore mother that enrolled
you – in life). When the Princess of Wales visited Buenos
Aires in 1995, a woman whose husband and son were both
victims of the Falklands War shouted at her, ¡*Hija de puta! Potra,
hija de las mil putas!*' ('Daughter of a whore! Brood mare, daugh-

ter of a thousand whores!'). The British press was suitably
outraged but by the standards of Argentine invective this was
quite restrained. The protester could easily have stepped up a
gear and shouted, '¡La reputísima madre que te recontra mil parió!'
('The twice most whorish mother that bore you again and
again one thousand times!')

Then there is the multi-faceted ¡La puta madre que le parió! (The
whore mother that bore him!) which means 'what a bastard'
but, as we saw earlier, can also refer to an admirable or
handsome man. In both Spanish and Portuguese this insult is
fortified by the fact that the verb parir (to give birth) normally
only refers to animals, with the more poetic dar a luz (bring
to light) reserved for humans.

One of the functions of 'bad language' is to stand convention on its head, and one of its own most entertaining devices
is to go one step further and stand on its own head, to first
name the evil and then make it into a virtue. So in Catalan ser
un putas (being a whore) means being very clever, and in
Spanish anything that is de puta madre is excellent, first class. Un
cocinero de puta madre (a whore mother of a cook) is a very good
cook. This same man's cooking might equally be described as
de coña (cunt-like, although coña is a nonce-word which merely
resembles coño, the word itself) or cojonudo (testicle-like). In
this context both expressions mean 'terrific' or, as some English people say, 'the dog's bollocks' which, let's face it, is just
as weird. So while convention dictates what is good and bad,
slang insists on turning it inside out. The cook, in other words,
isn't merely a good cook, he's one bad motherfucker. The
Italians would say he was un ragazzo bestiale (a beast of a guy),
the Swedes that he was grym (cruel), and the Germans that he
was oberkrass (super stark). Wicked, in other words.

As so often happens, sex has led us into the kitchen, for
which I make no apology. In the kitchen we find cherries,
cupcakes and honey pies; crumpet and even tarts, contracted

from the more amicable sweethearts, have joined the pantheon
of saccharine epithets for the edible woman. She may be quite
a dish, what the English call well stacked, the French *bien garnie*
(well garnished) and the Portuguese *um cacho* (a bunch of
grapes). The French have built an extensive vernacular around
the subject of cabbages, including the popular term of endearment *mon petit chouchou* (my little cabbage-cabbage). But in this
instance it may have nothing to do with cabbages and possibly
entered the language from the Romani *sukar*, which has given
French slang *choucard*, both words meaning 'good looking'. A
woman's sex is invariably compared to food, and not just
clams or mussels, but also to a cod, apricot, humbug, tuna,
pork chop, fig, and even as the 'little fleshy bit', *la cicciolina* in
Italian, a term immortalized as the nickname of the Italian MP
and porn star Ilona Staller. But more of this later, in the chapter
on food, where it will become clear that there is no object,
action, human characteristic or point of view that cannot be
reconstituted – in French at least – as a culinary metaphor.

Aside from damning her as a vixen or the bitch with the
baleful eye, when it comes to the beastliness of women, European man has not ventured far from the metaphorical farm,
and has seen in women mainly cows, sows and chickens.
Women are sometimes compared to mares or fillies, one suspects mainly so men can imagine themselves stallions, and the
Portuguese make a rare break with the tradition that goats
symbolize cuckolded men by using *cabra* (nanny goat) to mean
much the same as bitch or slut. Hen or chicken is synonymous
with prostitute in a number of languages, an odd comparison
given that most hens only ever encounter the one cock. The
American 'chicks' for young women, favoured by that generation of rock stars who call their steady girlfriend their 'lady',
was probably picked up from the Spanish *chica*, meaning girl,
and has nothing to do with poultry. A Greek *kóta* (hen) is a
tarty, flashy woman, but a *klossa* (a nesting hen) is a fierce and

aggressive one. The Germans have a charming expression *wir treten unsere Hühner selbst* (we kick our own chickens), which is a warning to any alien cocks who might have strayed into the farmyard to the effect of 'don't mess with our women'. This alarming idiom raises as many questions about the standards of German poultry farming as it does about sexual politics.

Whatever they do in the hen house, Germans eat a lot of pork and the German idiom is stuffed with *Schwein* epithets for men and *Sau* ones for both men and women. An *alte Sau* (old sow) is an ageing prostitute, while *du Drecksau* (you filthy sow) is a strong insult. Furthermore, an unpleasant person is described as a *linke Sau* (treacherous or mean) and a gay man as a *schwule Sau* (gay sow). The Euskera word *urdaska* (pig sty) is synonymous with slut, but in English sow mainly conveys the idea of a sexually unattractive woman. The Italian *porca* implies that a woman has unusual sexual preferences or appetites, and *porcellona* that she is obsessed with sex. Jane Mills, in her book *Womanwords*, notes that 'a further link between the sow and the female human is the hymen which is possessed by no other animal'.

Cow, symbol of motherhood and docility and therefore shorthand for sexually undesirable, has become increasingly pejorative in English. While it once conveyed lumbering, passive and fat, now it suggests much the same as bitch. A woman who is described as 'a right bloody cow' is malevolent, not docile. When something turns out badly or amounts to nothing, Italians say *l'affare è andato a vacca* (it went like a cow), and in this sense *vacca* is interchangeable with *puttana* (whore). It's not always so clear what Italians mean when they say something is *vaccata* because, depending on context, it could mean disgusting, badly done or simply idiotic. The Finnish *lehmä* (cow) means fat when said of a woman, although corpulence can also be considered a virtue, witness the Galician saying *a muller e a vaca e mala sendo fraca* (women and cows shouldn't be skinny). In Portugal *vaca* is a particularly strong insult of the 'bitch' variety – one of the worst – although *vaca leiteira* (milk cow) is less so. A *vaca tourina* is also strong, suggesting promiscuity, as it implies the cow goes to the *corrida* in pursuit of bulls. Even worse is *vaca do caralho* (prick cow), which speaks for itself. Although in French *vachement* is just an emphatic 'really', *vache* by itself means 'nasty' and *une vacherie* is a dirty trick. But let's get off the farm, let's shut the *lade port* (barn doors), which is how the Danes describe a woman with a big arse, leave these milk cows alone and find us some real ballbreakers.

There's a gulf of meaning between old master and old mistress, or between bachelor and spinster. And there is no positive, complimentary word that is the female equivalent of 'virile'. Such a woman is butch, a dominatrix. Where a manly man is 'a real mensch' in Yiddish, his female counterpart is a *yenta*, once a Jewish girl's name, now a byword for a nag. Conventional language, never mind slang, unequivocally condemns assertive women as counterfeit men, dangerous upstarts. The word virago, for example, is rooted in the Latin *vir* (man), Amazon comes from the Greek *a mazos* (breastless) and the modern Greek for a big, bossy woman is *androyinéka* (an androgyne, literally a man-woman). In Portuguese, Spanish or Euskera a mannish woman is transmuted into yet another Mary, this time a masculine one – *mandona*, *marimacho*, *marigizon* – all of which also mean or imply that she's a lesbian. A real Italian nag is a *cagacazzo*, that is, she shits on your dick, while in Danish she is more explicitly a *slavepisker* (slave driver) or a *ja-mor* (yes, Mum, i.e. bossyboots) when she isn't just being a *sur kalling* (sour bitch). The German *Schreckschraube* (literally, a scary screw, although screw doesn't have sexual connotations in German) manages to combine the ideas of old, wealthy and ugly into the one woman. The Irish *an seán stripeach* means 'the old whore', but conveys the sense of 'old battle-axe'. Be aware, however, that the French *casse-couilles* (ballbreaker) is usually applied to men, generally to mean a bore or a pain in the arse. French women are too busy plucking their eyebrows and waxing their legs to bust anyone's balls.

At each turn, a double-bind. 'Behold the handmaid of the Lord. Be it unto me according to thy word,' says the mother of God in her New Testament walk-on part. But apart from St Jerome and his ilk, no one really has any time for a virginal goody-two-shoes. Such women are decried as *cursí* (prim) or *pénible* (painful) and, far from their chastity being admired, a lack of interest in men will only arouse suspicions of either frigidity or lesbianism. Or else she's a pricktease, a *calientabraguetas*, or heater of men's flies as they say in Spain, or in France *une allumeuse* (a lighter). Or simply a bimbo, a dumb blonde, what the Greeks call a *glastra* (flower pot).

Virgin or whore, ballbreaking bitch or docile doormat – it's a raw deal, and however she's cast, a woman faces a different battery of insults. For many women it's not the words so much as how they're said and who's saying them; like being called 'love' or 'darling' by men in the street, or *guapa* (gorgeous) or *muñeca* (doll) in Spain, *ragazza* (girl) in Italy, or *febra* (bit of pork) in Portugal. But the ultimate put-down and the one in which men in the English-speaking world seem to take particular pleasure, is to reduce women to the one thing, to skirt or pussy or cunt or gash or beaver or snatch or any number of other unlovely and unloving words. Harsh, unspeakable words in English, and in German too, but not everywhere; in France, Italy and Spain the words are taboo, of course, but not insulting. Like mother said, men only want the one thing. But what do you call it, this unnameable object of desire and fear that Italians sometimes call simply *la cosa*, the thing?

6 ★ Concerto in C

> Fuck's only what you do. Animals fuck. But cunt's a lot
> more than that. It's thee, dost see: an' tha'rt a lot besides
> an animal, aren't ter? – even ter fuck?
>   Cunt! Eh, that's the beauty o' thee, lass.
>
> D. H. Lawrence, *Lady Chatterley's Lover*

The language of love is impoverished, starved of nuance: I
like you, like you a lot, love you, am in love with you. And
it's been said that when it comes to talking about sex we're
forced to choose between the vocabulary of the nursery, the
gutter or the anatomy class: nookie, fucking, intercourse;
willy, prick, penis. As for *la cosa*, the thing that brought about
the Fall, you'd think that after more than a thousand years of
the English language we might have come up with something
better than the triptych of 'front-bottom', 'cunt' and 'vulva'.
Well, you would, wouldn't you?

Women generally find themselves at a loss to find a word
with which to describe their sex. Can there be many women
who really think of it as their vulva? I doubt it. As for cunt,
attempts to reclaim what remains the most fearsome word in
the English language have so far met with failure. But if there
isn't a satisfactory English word – and this isn't just an English
problem – it's not for lack of trying. In *Slang Down the Ages*,
Jonathon Green lists over 900 English euphemisms for a
woman's sex, second in number only to slang terms for drinking and copulation. By contrast *Harrap's French–English Slang Dictionary* can muster only 63, Neves Pinto's *Dicionário do Palavrão e
Afins* scores 74 for Portuguese and Victor León's *Diccionario de*

Argot Español a mere 38. Only the Italians come close. Gianfranco Lotti's *Le Parole Della Gente* lays claim to 825, with an impressive 29 terms for clitoris as opposed to 14 in French and a negligent 3 in both Spanish and English.

'Cunt' remains the most taboo and insulting word in the English language; even those films, plays or books that fuck themselves from the opening fucking scene to the fucking denouement recoil from 'cunt'. When Robert De Niro says cunt in *Taxi Driver* it has the ring of untruth about it, as if it had been thrown in simply to shock. Its German sister, *Fotze*, is if anything even more taboo but otherwise its status varies enormously across the European vernacular. Just as the Swedish for 'fuck' has no figurative meaning, neither does the Danish *kusse* (cunt); it is what it is. In Greece *mouni* is as insulting to men as it is in English. And while men might say *oreo mouni* (nice cunt) about an attractive woman, you can't call a Greek woman a *mouni*, not because it's not the done thing but because it wouldn't 'mean' anything. We've seen that across the water in Italy, however, *figa* is never an insult and is in general complimentary. It's sexist sometimes, when women are objectified as *figa* the way in English men say 'skirt' or 'pussy'. Of course it's still considered 'bad language', but it's not the ugly word it is in English and German. And, like the Spanish, Italians don't understand that this word can be used to insult someone. The Spanish use of *coño*, it's true, is often negative but it's neither an insult nor a compliment; Spaniards are never cunts. But more of this later; firstly, a look at this troublesome word's background.

The C-word has struck such terror into the hearts, and perhaps other organs, of lexicographers that it didn't manage to force itself upon the mighty *Oxford English Dictionary* until 1972, although the latter had not balked at an entry for 'prick'. The *Oxford* entry reads: cunt. 1. The female genitals, the vulva. 2. A very unpleasant or stupid person, and gives the year 1230 as the first reference to it in English, citing Gropecuntlane, a now-defunct street in the St Pancras area of London. An interesting address by any standards and, if streets were twinned the way towns are, matched by the still-extant Via Fregatette (Tit Massage Street) in Bologna.

Defining a cunt as a 'vulva' posts an early warning of the etymologists' confusion and discomfort. *Vulva* is Latin for womb which, let's face it, is hardly the same thing at all. Other dictionaries unselfconsciously define it as 'the female pudendem', derived from the Latin *pudere*, 'to be ashamed'. Ashamed of what though? As for vagina, this is another straight Latin import meaning a sheath, and by implication a handy place to park one's sword, a word that epitomizes the male perspective governing sexual vocabulary. In German, a language that likes to strap as much ideology on to a word as it can bear, the two have been brought together in *Schamscheide*, the 'sheath of shame' or 'shame slit'. It lives shamelessly in the company of *Scham* (genitalia), *Schamhaar* (pubic hair) and *Schamlippen* (labia).

Although the word 'cunt' has long been taboo it was only at the turn of the century that it became a term of abuse, although why is not clear. It appears that, accompanied by 'fuck', it tramped back from the First World War, from whose trenches the British working class emerged – the lucky ones – even more foul-mouthed than before. Certainly the word was once considered harmless, if perhaps a little coarse. Chaucer's Wife of Bath is quite matter of fact when she declares: 'For, certeyn, olde dotard, by youre leve, / Ye shul have queynte [cunt] right ynogh at eve.' And Hamlet's 'Do you think I meant country matters?' remark to Ophelia is vulgar and teasing but it's playful and there's no sense that the word had acquired the edge it has today. However, by the eighteenth century, although not yet a personal insult, it had become so taboo as to be unspeakable. The aptly named

Francis Grose, whose *Dictionary of the Vulgar Tongue* (1785) was an early attempt at a comprehensive lexicon of slang, could not bring himself to print it in full. The entry reads: 'c**t: the χοννος of the Greek and *cunnus* of the Latin dictionaries; a nasty name for a nasty thing'.

Mr Grose was not alone in his fear and revulsion. It wasn't until the late 1980s that any British newspaper dared to print cunt in full, without asterisks, an event prompted by that most English of pursuits – cricket. The occasion was the 1987–8 tour of Pakistan when England were captained by Mike Gatting. In a report on an altercation between Gatting and umpire Shakoor Rana during the Faisalabad Test, the *Independent* published 'cunt' in full. This prompted Kelvin McKenzie, doyen of the yellow press and then editor of the nation's moral guardian the *Sun*, to report the *Independent* to the Press Council for printing the 'nasty' word in a family newspaper, thus lowering the tone of British journalism. It is one of the curiosities of the British tabloid press that, while it will lie without compunction, destroy often defenceless people's lives and exploit to the full every nuance of human prejudice, it doesn't approve of bad language, at least not in print.

No doubt the resistance to speaking or writing the word has contributed to the ongoing dispute about its origins. It doesn't appear in any Old English texts. Those who claim that it's of Germanic ancestry point to the Old Norse *kunta* and Middle Dutch *kunte* but fail to explain why in modern German, Finnish, Swedish, Danish and Dutch it is, respectively: *Fotze* (from *Vut*, meaning mouth), *vittu*, *fitta*, *kusse* and *kut*. It has also been linked to the Old English *cwithe*, meaning womb. The classicists, on the other hand, say it derives from the Latin *cunnus* (another word for womb) or *cuneus*, meaning a wedge. A what? This appears to confirm suspicions that the wordsmiths of ancient Rome were gay men whose intimate knowledge of women didn't extend beyond a glimpse of a pubic triangle.

If anyone was going to follow in Rome's footsteps you'd expect it to be the Italians but in modern Italian the word is *figa* (this is the usual spoken form; it's more often written as *fica*). *Figa* is also used in Catalan, but it's more frequently rendered *cony* there. In its more common 'c' or 'k' forms, however, the word may well have started its journey further east. In both Arabic and Hebrew the word is *kus*, which is related to the words for cup and pocket – still a receptacle, but surely an improvement on a wedge. In Hittite, a dead Indo-European language deciphered from cuneiform, the word for a bride was *kusa*. European historians tend to overlook the influence of Islam on southern Europe. Much of Spain and Portugal were Islamic for centuries and the Moors made their mark as far north as the Loire basin until they were defeated at Poitiers by Charles Martel in 732. Perhaps they brought the word *kus* with them, bequeathed it to the Spanish in the form of *coño*, the Portuguese as *cona* and the French as *con*, which the latter brought to England with the Norman conquest. Well, it's not impossible. Etymologists object that a route beginning at *kus* and ending at cunt doesn't explain how the word acquired an 'n', and they're absolutely right; I have no idea where that 'n' came from.

Whatever its origins, the word marks one of Europe's great divides. Northern Europeans fancy themselves as sexually liberated and often disdain their southern neighbours as repressed and sexually inept, as strangers to pleasure and prisoners of guilt. And yet in much of the north the various 'cunt' words are more or less unspeakable and are invested with loathing and disgust, particularly in Britain and Germany. By contrast, many southerners are often baffled that such a word could be a term of invective. They are also amused by the idea that people as stiff as the English, Swedes or Germans regard themselves as sexually liberated. Just look at the way they dance.

Grose's sentiments about 'a nasty word for a nasty thing' seem to hold good for Germany where the words *Fotze* and *Möse* attract the same loathing as 'cunt' does in English and are regarded by women as especially *frauenfeindlich* (misogynous). Middle-class Germans will assure you that no one ever uses these words, but this is not true. What they really mean is they don't mix with working-class people. Down south in Bavaria, which is 60–70 per cent Catholic, the word is not so strong, at least in that it appears in expressions such as *Halt dei' Fotze!* (Shut your trap!) or *Der hat dir eine Fotze* (There speaks a true bullshitter). *Fotzig* is used to describe someone malicious or spiteful but when Chancellor Kohl publicly condemns a political opponent as *hinterfotzig*, it's not what it seems. The *Fotze* in this case reverts to its earlier meaning of 'mouth', and translates roughly as 'two-faced'. *Fotze* follows the German pattern of combining two words to make a third but the results, such as *Fotzenfummeln* (cunt fumbling) for heavy petting, are often a triumph of precision over passion.

In Welsh *cont* is an expression of contempt although in Caernarfon it can apparently be used between men to mean 'mate', as is *a chuint* (oh, you cunt) between men in Connemara, although elsewhere in Ireland *chuint* is an insult. In Swedish *fitta*, when said of a man, means inept rather than unpleasant. It is also used to refer to women generically. Stieg Malm, general secretary of the Swedish trade union federation until his resignation in 1993, will be remembered not for his skilful handling of industrial relations but for referring to the Social Democratic Party's women's organization as *fitt-stimmet* (a shoal of cunts).

The exclamation *Voi vittu!* (Oh cunt!) is quite common in Finnish but is still considered strong language. In English 'cunt' is more often directed as an insult towards men than women but the Finnish vittupää (cunthead) is a strong insult for a woman. The Finns also use it in the form of vittumainen (cunt-like) as an adjective, the way 'bloody' or 'fucking' are used in English. The word is becoming much more widely used and the resourceful Finns have recently devised a past participle vituttaa, meaning 'to be annoyed'. The Danish kusse has almost no metaphorical life and is mostly confined to describing the thing itself. You can't call a woman a kusse; a man, yes, but it wouldn't cut any more ice than if you called him a squirrel or an omelette. If you want to pick a fight in Denmark, don't call a man a kusse, call him shorty or spotty or big nose. Better still, say his girlfriend's got a fat bum – then you'll know what trouble is.

The Danes tend to break the rule that insults shouldn't be literally true. The worst way to insult a Danish woman, for example, isn't something metaphorical, such as calling her a slut, but some direct and personal remark about her appearance, that she's fat or ugly or looks like she's had her hair styled by the Copenhagen parks department. The Danes aren't much given to abstractions. As for the Dutch, kut is widely used as an interjection the way in English one might say 'Shit!' or 'Damn!' and is little used as an insulting epithet although they do boast some nasty expressions such as kutwyf (cunt-wife), meaning 'bitch'. As you can imagine, the arrival of Silk Cut cigarettes on the Dutch market was the source of much merriment.

Let's lie back for a moment and think of England. It's clear that thirty years after 'swinging', anything-goes London cocked a Biba hat at sexual convention, 'cunt' remains the most taboo and insulting word in English, holding its own against successive waves of iconoclastic teds, mods, rockers, hippies, punks, ravers and new age crusties. The various euphemisms – growler, quim, gash, minge (from the Romani), twat and the cat with its throat cut – offer little in mitigation. One of the most hated is 'snatch', which has been around longer than you might think. Robert Burton wrote in *The Anatomy of Melancholy* in 1621, 'I could not abide marriage, but as a rambler, I took a snatch when I could get it,' which is not quite the language we've been led to expect from an English clergyman.

The word cunt, in its pejorative role, is more or less universally loathed by women in the English-speaking world. Nothing is more venomous on an Englishman's lips – and the same goes for the Welsh, Scots and Irish – most of whom feel it necessary to affect a particularly nasty grimace when they say it, as though they'd just eaten something disgusting. This is the word that is most likely to raise the ante in a dispute between men in Britain and Ireland, the one most likely to provoke the response, 'What did you call me?' It's surprisingly little heard in American English, even on the lips of those whose every other word is motherfucker. There the word 'pussy' is preferred for the thing itself, while for insults Americans seem content with a repertoire that extends from 'asshole' through 'cocksucker' to 'motherfucker'. They don't appear to miss 'cunt' at all.

The French word con occupies some middle ground between northern and southern Europe. It's certainly not a term of admiration or endearment, but as an epithet it has come to mean little more than twit or fool and is a mild and commonplace insult. *Fais-pas le con* (don't play the fool) is something every French child hears most days. It may have been stronger once, which could explain why it was felt necessary to supplant the old word for rabbit (connil) with lapin a couple of hundred years ago. This might also account for the disappearance of coney, formerly the English for rabbit, which lives on as Brooklyn's Coney Island. But today con is probably less taboo and more widely used than in any other European tongue. Even in expressions such as *espèce de con!* (species of cunt!) it only amounts to 'Bloody fool!' and *le roi des cons* (king of cunts) is merely a 'total idiot'. The word is innocuous and its connotations, if we may use that word, are of foolishness rather than unpleasantness. *Quelle connerie!* for example, means What rubbish!, and a *déconneur* is a bullshitter. And if you imagine I'd take your *boulot à la con* (lousy job) then you're wrong; *je ne suis pas la moitié d'un con* (I'm not stupid, literally, not just half a cunt).

There are myriad euphemisms. Among the most popular are *chatte* and *chagatte*, leading inevitably to such phrases as *bouffer la chatte* (eat the cat) for cunnilingus. But for real invective the French resort to the word *connasse*. Probably the worst thing you can call a French woman is a *connasse* or a *salope*, both of which suggest she is something between a bitch and a whore, the sort of words that, as we have seen, are key weapons in the southern European misogynous arsenal.

Where French really scores is in its many charming if predictably gourmandizing words for clitoris such as *bonbon*, *framboise* (raspberry), *grain de café* (coffee bean), *berlingot* (humbug) and *praline*. If the vernacular's any guide, the clitoris has yet to come to the Englishman's attention which, given his antipathy to cunts in general, is only to be expected. 'Love button' and 'little man in a boat' pretty well exhaust the vocabulary. Probably a minority of those who helped make Anita Ward's record of the 1970s, *Ring My Bell*, such a hit were aware that 'bell' is African–American slang for clitoris.

All around the Mediterranean the various cunt words, while not exactly positive, enjoy what is at least a playful metaphorical life. It comes as a surprise to a northern European that the words are relatively benign in most of Catholic Europe. And then there are the Greeks; not Catholics but Mediterranean none the less and, one would have thought, washed by similar cultural and ideological waters to their neighbours, but whose use of *mouni* is overwhelmingly negative. Whether this is attributable to Eastern Orthodoxy is open to question, though it's noteworthy that the word is used with similar abrasiveness by their fellow Orthodox in Russia. *Mouni* has no positive figurative uses; calling a man a *mouni* is a strong insult, as it implies he's not all the man he should be. Otherwise it's used in negative metaphors such as *Tákana mouni* (I messed up) or *Sto mouni mou!* (I couldn't care less, literally, to my cunt!).

In common with Spain and Italy, the Portuguese don't use *cona* as a personal insult, but it's more taboo and heard much less often than elsewhere in Catholic Europe. In the north people might say *Na cona!* (No kidding, literally, no cunt), but otherwise it's not much used. In Italian, however, *figa* is always positive. After *cazzo* (prick) Italians probably get more mileage out of *figa* than any of their other *parolacce* (dirty words). *Che figa!* is lighthearted and widely used of people, things and situations, and as well as meaning 'What a looker!' can mean 'What good luck!' It can also be used in combinations to produce phrases such as *Che macchina figa!* — What a nice car!; *Che festa figa!* — What a great party!

The association with figs may be a reference to the succulence of the fruit or perhaps to Adam and Eve's choice of undergarments. D. H. Lawrence favoured figs among his sexual metaphors, and the Italian 'Get lost!' gesture, in which the thumb is placed between the first two fingers in an unmistakeably sexual symbol, is known as the 'fig'. In Biblical times the fig was also the symbol of the Temple and the Talmud advises Jews to ward off evil by making sexual gestures, either the fig (sex act) or by placing the thumb in a closed fist (a symbol of pregnancy). Italian shares the expression 'I don't give a fig' with English, and in French a man with *les figues molles* (limp figs) can't get it up. Greece again breaks with convention: *síka*, a fig, is a gay man.

Young Italian women have 'reclaimed' *figa* in the form of *figo*, simply changing it to a masculine noun, so that *Che figo!*

means 'What a looker!'. It can also be used adjectivally as
fighetta/fighetto. If something is *figata* it is excellent, terrific, a
usage mirrored in the Spanish *de coña* or *cojonudo*. Or it can be
said of a person, for example: *Charlie Parker era un figo del jazz*
(Charlie Parker was a great jazz musician). Prefixing *figa* with
an 's' radically alters its meaning. Thus *una sfiga* is a misfortune
or a cock-up, while *sfigato* means unlucky and also describes
someone who is uncool. To some extent *sfiga* is also used as a
euphemism, the way some people say 'sugar' or 'fiddlesticks'.

The greater the taboo, the greater the impact, which is why
taboo subjects are invoked to express disbelief, almost as if
one is saying 'if this is true, then anything is possible'. We
see this in ¡*El coño de tu hermana!*, a common Spanish expression
to the effect of 'You're kidding!', although its literal meaning
is 'Your sister's cunt!'. The Portuguese mean the same thing
when they say *A cona da tua mãe!* (Your mother's cunt!). These
expressions may reflect Arab influence, as *Kus ommak!* (Your
mother's cunt!) is a fairly common Arabic interjection. However common, such phrases should be used with care and only
among close friends. As any mention of his female relatives and
in particular any reference to their sexuality is likely to provoke
an extreme reaction in the Mediterranean male, ¡*El coño de
tu hermana!* is not the recommended way of conveying one's
astonishment to a stranger in Spain. Such expressions will be
reviewed in greater detail in the next chapter, in which we
will examine just what it takes to enrage the European male.

People are often shocked at the sheer quantity of *coños* in
Spanish discourse. It is of course taboo, but the words *coño*
and the euphemistic *coña*, while they are not polite, pervade
popular speech. They're not used harshly and are employed
to convey a wide range of sentiments. Sometimes it might
mean nothing at all; *coño* can be an emphatic way of rounding
off a sentence, the way we might say, 'But he's married, for
fuck's sake'. In Spanish *coño* will often assume the 'for fuck's

sake' role, in the same way that the French will finish sentences
with *con* or *putain*.

In the Basque country the Euskera *alu*, which stands, as
expected, outside the Indo-European frame, is more taboo and
more pejorative and in the form *alubita* means 'son of a whore'.
Likewise in Galicia in the north-west, *conacho* (of a cunt) means
a stupid man in Gallego. But in Castilian Spanish you cannot
call a person a *coño*, neither as an insult nor in the complimentary *Che figa!* mode exhibited by Italian. This isn't a question
of taboo, such a usage simply doesn't exist; *coño*, while it might
be negative, is not pejorative. Spanish students of English are
nonplussed when they are told that they would be well advised
never, ever to use its English equivalent.

¡Coño! as an exclamation means 'Really!' or 'Oh, my God!'
or 'You're kidding!', or it might be used for emphasis as in
Coño, no, to mean 'Of course not', or 'Don't be silly'. ¡*Ay qué
coño!* however, is a sympathetic interjection to the effect of
'What a shame!' or 'How awful!' One doesn't expect to hear
a woman exclaim ¡*Otra pena pa mi coño!* (Another pain in my
cunt!), which amounts to 'One more thing I have to contend
with!' but in Spain it's fairly commonplace. ¿*Qué coño?* can convey anger, doubt or indifference in the manner of, 'And what
of it?' In the same way that the English earned the monicker
les fuckoffs, *coño* is such a feature of European Spanish that in
Chile and Mexico Spaniards are popularly known as *los coños*.

In common with the French practice of making words for
the female genitals masculine nouns and the male parts feminine, *coño* is masculine but has a feminine form *coña*. However,
defying all logic *coña* can only be used metaphorically, as in
de coña (great, brilliant) and not to describe the female anatomy,
which remains resolutely masculine. *Coña* can mean a joke in
bad taste but a *coña marinera* (of the sea) is a source of irritation,
as is anyone or thing earning the epithet *coñazo*. In many
common expressions *coño* is interchangeable with *polla* (penis

which, naturally, is a feminine noun). So it makes no difference whether you say *es el coño/la polla* (it's the absolute limit) or *estoy hasta el coño/la polla* (I'm up to here with, i.e. fed up). In Spanish, when you're fed up, you can be up to your cunt, prick, arsehole, balls or nostrils; it's entirely up to you and the company you keep.

Tocarse el coño (playing with or touching it) has nothing to do with masturbation but is said of someone who is idle or frittering their time away in the sense of someone who stands around scratching themselves. The Spanish are not averse to *comer el coño* (cunnilingus), but this shouldn't be confused with the contentment conveyed by *como comerle el coño a bocaos* (like eating cunt by the mouthful) which merely suggests that an experience – and not a sexual one – is, as British prime minister John Major is fond of saying, most agreeable. Earthiness is quite acceptable in Spain, where food is often described in sexual terms, such as the comment on a succulent steak that it is *más dulce que la teta de una novicia* (sweeter than a novice nun's tit).

The Catalans' use of *cony* doesn't differ much from the Spanish *coño*, although they probably say it less often. In common with most seafaring peoples, Catalans traditionally believe that it's bad luck to allow a woman on a boat, but they also ascribe unusual powers to a woman's sex, embodied in the saying, *La mar es posa bona si veu el cony d'una dona* (The sea calms down if it sees a woman's cunt). So for luck, fishermen's wives would expose themselves to the sea before the boats put out. It was also believed that a woman could cause storms if she urinated in the waves.

But the most bizarre use of *coño* is the expression *en el quinto coño*, common throughout Spain, meaning the back of beyond or the boondocks or, for an Antipodean, beyond the black stump. Why an out-of-the-way place should be described as 'the fifth cunt' is something of a mystery. Evidently it's a parody of the rustic custom of naming remote areas or very small villages after their most prominent feature, such as the two streams or the three pines. But why a cunt, and why the fifth? Ask a Spaniard to explain and all you'll get is one of those fatalistic shrugs that means either they don't know or, if they do, they aren't going to tell you. In Gallego, the back of beyond is rendered as either *no quinto carallo* (the fifth prick) or *no quinto demo* (the fifth devil). Bingo is also known as *quinto* in Spain and, while we're on this theme, the expression 'fifth columnist' for a spy is a legacy of the Spanish Civil War. The Francoist General Mola claimed that he had four columns surrounding Madrid and *una quinta columna* (of sympathizers) inside the city. Not that the Civil War is germane to the subject of cunts in a federal Europe, but what is pertinent is that probably few people in Brussels knew when they voted to let Spain join the Community that they were admitting a nation whose citizens thought of an out-of-the-way place as 'the fifth cunt'. This is just one of the many imponderables that lie in the path of a united Europe. In fact, the Spanish have an even better expression for the back of beyond, but I'm saving it for later.

It would be satisfying to conclude this essay with the neat paradigm that 'cunt' is a nasty, bitter word in the cold and Protestant north and a nice-ish one in the languorous Catholic south, but sadly this just isn't so. In Denmark, Holland and Belgium it's either little used or innocuous, while its role in Finnish is closer to Mediterranean than to Nordic culture. Then there's Portugal, Catholic and laid back, but a country where the word is best not said at all. And Ireland, Catholic enough, but where English slang has been superimposed on the indigenous culture along with so much else. Or the Greeks, a people who always appear comfortable in their own skins, but for whom the word is as vituperative as it is in Germany or Britain.

To an Italian, a Spaniard, a Dane or a Belgian it's never a personal insult. In those countries where it is, it's mainly directed at men, and it's considered absurd to say it to a woman. Even in Britain it's used much less by and of women. But any attempt to measure the relative misogyny of nations using the status of the word 'cunt' as a yardstick are, in my opinion, futile. I don't know what it says about Italy or Spain that *figa* and *coño* aren't nasty words, but what it definitely doesn't say is that the men there aren't sexist, or that these societies aren't patriarchal. After all, in both countries, and many others besides, the worst a man can be is the son of a whore. The worst insults for men nearly all come back to women: to being a cunt, what a woman is; a bastard, which is a woman's fault; or a queer, like a woman. As men are so fond of saying, 'Life's a bitch'.

7 ★ Take It Like a Man

> ... son of a whore!
> There is not such another murdering-piece
> In all the stock of calumny; it kills
> At one report two reputations –
> A mother's and a son's.
>
> Thomas Middleton, 1580–1627

When the Japanese car company Datsun launched the Cherry, they had been warned that this could make them and the car a laughing stock, that since the nineteenth century 'cherry' had been slang for virginity. Imagine the smirks when someone announced that they'd acquired a brand-new Cherry; the barely stifled giggles when they reported to the police that their Cherry had been stolen. But the Japanese followed their noses, no one laughed, the car sold well and life for Datsun was one big bowl of cherries.

So maybe no one said anything when Mitsubishi brought out the four-wheel-drive Pajero, a name they had apparently concocted out of the Spanish words *pasajero* (passenger) and *pájaro* (bird). From Sitges to Santiago de Chile, however, a *pajero* is a wanker, literally someone who makes a straw (*paja*) of themselves. In 1994, the United Nations human rights mission to Haiti was forced to jump into its Pajeros and high-tail it across the border into the Spanish-speaking Dominican Republic. As if being driven out of Haiti by a handful of rechauféed Tontons Macoute wasn't humiliating enough, they then had to endure the jibes of Santo Domingo's children as they danced around their white-painted Mitsubishi 'wankers'. Sega, the

video games company, may also have raised the odd smile in
Italy, where a *sega* is a wanker. Advertisers are always falling
down these vernacular pits. Braniff Airlines, for example, had
to pull a Spanish ad that offered passengers the opportunity
to fly *en cuero*, that is, in leather seats. But most Spaniards are
far too modest to consider travelling *en cueros* (stark naked) and
too proud, for that matter, to drive around in a wanker, even
a four-wheel-drive one.

Considering the low esteem in which women are held,
you might imagine that a wanker would be admired for his
independence and integrity. After all, as Woody Allen pointed
out, masturbation is sex with someone you love. But no,
masturbation is shameful and sinful. St Thomas Aquinas – I'm
not making this up – said it was worse than having sex with
your mother. And D. H. Lawrence, a puritan at heart, was of
the opinion that 'masturbation is certainly the most dangerous
sexual vice that a society can be afflicted with, in the long
run'. Masturbation is viewed as the resort of failed and feeble
men. Women are seldom called wankers, presumably because
they still aren't thought capable of it. Except in Japan. The
Japanese word for male masturbation is *senzuri*, which means
a thousand slippings and slidings. The female variety is *manzuri*,
ten thousand slippings and slidings, suggesting that Japanese
women have either poor technique or a surfeit of leisure time.

The old-fashioned word for masturbation is Onanism, after
Onan, one of Judah's sons. In fact Onan's sin was to practise
coitus interruptus, which he did because he felt guilty about
screwing his sister-in-law, even though his father had ordered
him to screw her. But God struck him dead, not for shtupping
his brother's wife, but for spilling his seed on the ground.
The Bible is quite clear about this: spermatozoa is a precious
resource that is not to be wasted, not spilt some place where
it hasn't a cat's chance of fertilizing an egg. Considering that
it would be theoretically possible for any half-way healthy

man to father about five billion children, more or less the current world population, from a single ejaculation, this seems like needless anxiety on the part of the divine authorities. What with the pressure on living space, you'd think the more that ended up on the duvet the better. But we mustn't ignore the health risks. As recently as 1985 a conference of German bishops confirmed what we had long suspected, that masturbation makes you impotent, blind and brain damaged. It is not known by what method they carried out the research that led them to this withering conclusion.

Every nation has its favourite dirty word and, as we've seen, for Greeks the hands-down winner is *malakas* (wanker). Greek men say it all the time, as an exclamation of surprise or disbelief, for emphasis, or simply to pad out their sentences. As an insult it's not particularly strong, mostly because it's so commonplace, and it has a friendly side of the 'you old bastard' variety. No one knows where wanker comes from, but *malakas* derives from winnowing, the separation of the wheat from the chaff. The word *malakós* on a packet of flour signifies that it's been well winnowed until it is soft and smooth. So *malakas* manages to pack the literal sense of physical rubbing while carrying the word's metaphorical baggage of a soft, ineffectual man.

There are worse things in life than being called a wanker. Just about anywhere it's considered more insulting to be called a poof, for example, and in southern Europe it isn't a patch on calling a man a cuckold, or the son of a whore, or any other slurs on the honour of his mother or sister. On the other hand, you can walk right up to a German and say what you please about his sister, you may even suggest his *Frau*'s been putting the boat out lately, but *bitte schön*, don't call him a wanker. He won't like that at all. A *Wichser* is nearly as insulting as *Fotze* (cunt); worse still is a *Trockenwichser* (a dry wanker). As for the French, they're not really that bothered; *branleur* really just means incompetent. But, whatever Mitsubishi might think, calling a Spaniard a *pajero* or *pajillero* isn't too clever, nor is anything else that suggests he might not be up to par as a man. For many Spanish men, being a man is more than an accident of nature; it's a calling and a full-time occupation.

The whole point of being a man is that no one, but no one, fucks with you. No one fucks with your business, no one fucks with your car, and sure as God made little green apples, no one ever, ever fucks with your woman. Everything else is secondary. Being a man is a serious business and so sometimes things inevitably get out of hand. People get hurt, killed even; OK, so sometimes a lot, millions even, get killed. But that's the way it is. A man's got to be tough. Better to be harder than Chinese algebra than to be *menos fuerte que el pedo de un marica*, weaker than a faggot's fart, as the Spanish say. No one wants to be a wimp, what the Welsh would call *hen frechdan*, an old sandwich, a *mou* (spineless) French *pantouflard* (stay-at-home) who, like a Spanish *mierda de tio* (worthless shit), *cuelga los cojones detrás de la puerta* (hangs his balls behind the door).

A man has got to act like a man. Take Hitler. The man was born with three strikes against him: he was short, ugly and Austrian. No one would buy his watercolours so he was forced to become a house painter. His real name, Schicklgrüber, had second fiddle written all over it and, to put the tin lid on his resentment, the story goes that he caught the pox from a Jewish whore in Vienna. (See the trouble women cause?) Like they say in Yiddish, Hitler was *tsu kleyn tsu zayn a mentsh un tsu grys tsu zayn a shmok*, too small to be a man and too big to be a prick. But he saw to it that no one ever called him a *Pantoffelheld* (slipper hero) or a *Waschlappen* (sissy, literally a flannel) to his face. No one ever went up to him and said, 'Leck mich am Arsch, Hosenscheißer' (Lick my arse, pants shitter), which is the kind of thing Germans come out with when they're pissed off. It's said that he often referred to himself as a *Scheißkerl* (shithead) but that was his prerogative; you can bet Eva Braun never called him that.

And you can be sure that Mussolini was never accused of being a *mozzarella* (wimp) and that no one in Franco's Galician hometown of Ferrol called him *miñaxoia* (the Gallego for gutless, literally 'my jewel'). These men had their faults, and some liberal *vat nisse* (cottonwool gnome) from Copenhagen or a Helsinki *mamanpoika* (mama's boy) would probably say that they were monsters, fascists even. But they showed they were men, and they saw to it that nobody fucked with them.

Rather confusingly the Swedes say of a gutless man that *det är ingen kuk i honom* (he's got no cock in him). Now this is odd, because in general that's just how a real, red-blooded man prefers things to be. Perhaps it's the Swedish equivalent of having no balls. But then in Swedish a man who is *långkukig* (long-cocked) is not, as you would assume, blessed with that most prized of human attributes, a seriously long shlong, but is extremely tedious and boring. The Swedes are full of surprises. To recap: in Sweden, a man who does not have a male member inserted in him is regarded as being in a position of weakness, and a man sporting an abnormally large member is dreadfully dull. Is that clear?

To be both dull and a complete wimp is not that remarkable, but to have an expression that encapsulates both is impressive and is to be applauded. The Italians, or at least people from Perugia, do. They say of such a man that *il latte scende fino ai coglioni* (his tits droop right down to his balls), a figure of speech that is bent double under the weight of its ideological baggage and which surely requires no further explanation. More commonly Italians say of bores that *mi rompi i coglioni* (he's busting my balls), or *che scassacazzi* (what a dick-breaker), also rendered *Che rompicazzi!* Italians take a close interest in *coglioni* (balls) which, in common with many other languages, they associate with three things: manliness, tedium and nonsense. The expression 'he's busting my balls' has been revised by Italian-Americans to mean 'he's getting on my back', but in all other respects a real bore seems to hit an Italian right between the legs.

A Dane, on the other hand, experiences tedium between the ears. A bore is said to *at halde vand ud af øreme*, pour water out of their ears, an odd expression but scarcely more peculiar than the Dutch judgement on a dull man that he's a *zeiksnor* (a pissing moustache). If you really bore the pants off a Portuguese they'll say *aquele gajo é um cola* (this guy's like glue), or *é chato como potassa*, he's as flat as a plain of potassium, which you have to admit does sound pretty dull. The French bore easily, which is why French intellectuals constantly make up new words. They insist it's because their ideas are so new the existing vocabulary cannot express them, although everyone knows they do it just to stay awake. But however many new words they come up with, when their book is published, the critics just shrug and say *ça pisse pas loin*, it doesn't piss very far, by which they mean it's pretty boring.

The French like to argue, too; about anything at all. Jean-Paul Sartre wrote a book called *Being and Nothingness* in which he argues for over six hundred pages about whether anything actually exists. Now, you couldn't accuse someone who isn't even sure they exist of being *un je-sais-tout* (a know-all), but Sartre leaves you with a clear-cut choice: either his attempts to clarify whether existence is all it's cracked up to be make him the greatest philosopher of the twentieth century or he's what the more down-to-earth French call an *enculeur de mouches*, a fly-fucker, a rather picturesque alternative to what we call a nit-picker. They might also say *il cherche midi à quatorze heures*, he's looking for noon at 2 p.m., that is, for problems when there aren't any. This same idea is conveyed in the Spanish *buscar los tres pies al gato* (searching for the three-legged cat), which is not to be confused with *chercher le mouton à cinq pattes* (looking for the sheep with five hoofs), which is what you do when you try to find a needle in a haystack. Anyway, enough about bores, it's boring. As the Basques say, *Hori ez da gero ahuntzaren gauerdiko eztula*, it's only the cough of a goat at midnight, which, as you can imagine, is of no importance whatsoever.

When the Irish say *Ghabhfadh sé suas ar bhruach na maidine* (He'd screw the crack of dawn) the man in question is a ladykiller, a squirrel hound, a Don Juan or Casanova (new house) or any one of a number of flattering epithets for a man who puts it about. Outside of gay circles, there's no way of calling a man a slut any more than a woman can be called a 'manizer'. Nor is a 'dog' merely a male bitch, although one of President Clinton's associates from his Arkansas days, when asked to comment on his alleged infidelities, remarked: 'Bill's a good man, but he's a hard dog to keep on the porch.'

We saw earlier that Italians haven't been able to think up a pejorative for a womanizer. The nearest they get is a *farfallone* (butterfly), *galletto* (young cock) – neither of which is exactly a dire insult – or *paraculo*, one of those untranslatable words that means all at once a skirt-chaser, wide boy and low-life but has a literal sense of 'bum-dodger'. The literal-minded Danes are more explicit with *trusse tyr* (knicker thief) and the French don't mince their words with *enjambeur* (literally one who gets his leg over). As for Spanish, which can muster thirty or forty words for whores and tarts, for a womanizer there is only one, *mujeriego*, which combines *mujer*, the word for woman, with *riego*, meaning irrigation. This implies that philandering serves some useful function as a branch of Spanish agriculture. There's an echo of this in the French expression *arroser le bouton* (water the button), meaning to ejaculate inside someone.

The purpose of this double standard, by which a woman is vilified for her 'easy virtue', while a man enhances his reputation by playing the field, is all part of a forlorn effort to curb women's infinite capacity to be a man's undoing. No one has the power to harm a man and his reputation quite the way a woman can. It could be his mother, it could be his sister. Or it could be his wife, the woman in his life, his main squeeze or whatever you choose to call her. Then again, his daughter might disgrace him. Any one of a man's female relations may cause irreparable damage to his standing in the community. At first glance this might seem unfair. After all, no one can choose their parents and a man can't help it if he's the son of a whore. But someone should have prevented this disgrace, some man in his family – his father, his uncle, someone – because that's what men are supposed to do. And if they've failed to protect or control their women and, by extension, safeguard the family line and the inheritance, he must bear some of the blame.

We are talking, of course, about southern Europe. Northern European men just don't seem to care what their women do any more. Call a Swede or a German a son of a whore and he'll think you're nuts. Call an Englishman a cuckold and the chances are he won't even know what you mean. A survey of men born north of Paris since, say, 1960, would almost certainly reveal that a majority simply don't know what a cuckold is and probably a large number don't know that a bastard is someone born out of wedlock. But head south, and from Porto to Piraeus the two worst things you can say to a man are either that he's a cuckold, someone who 'wears the horns', or is the son of a whore.

This business of the horns, which has the same meaning all over Europe, requires some explanation. Across southern Europe the word for a cuckold means 'the horned one'. And just so you remember never to say such a thing to any man from south of Chantilly, here they are: cornudo or cabrão in Portuguese, cornudo Gallego and Spanish, in which it's also cabrón, cornut (Catalan), cocu (French), cornuto (Italian) and keratas (Greek). Even the Euskera adarduna, although it doesn't appear to fit the pattern, derives from adar, meaning horn. Why the horns? Why should a Spaniard who is being deceived llevar los cuernos (wear horns)? Why should a cuckolded Frenchman be mocked with the observation that tes cornes sont si grandes que tu ne passes pas la porte (your horns are so big you can't get through the door)?

The explanations, which involve stags, bulls, goats, cockerels and devils, are generally unsatisfactory but entertaining none the less. The origin is often traced back to the story of Actaeon in Greek mythology. Actaeon was a hunter who, as a punishment for seeing Diana bathing, was turned into a stag and torn to pieces by his own hounds. Now I don't have any sympathy with peeping Toms, but this seems a pretty harsh punishment. More to the point, what has it got to do with being cuckolded? All it shows is that things turned out badly for Actaeon once he started sporting horns. Besides, among real-life stags it's the one with the best set of antlers that gets to monopolize the females.

Horns have long been associated with male sexual prowess; that's why licentious men are called goats in so many cultures. It's also why the rhinoceros is facing extinction, because some men believe its horn is an aphrodisiac, and surely goats lie behind the origin of the expression 'feeling horny'. So how, when horns are otherwise so strongly associated with virility, did 'wearing the horns' come to mean a cuckolded man in cultures as remote from each other as Germany and Portugal?

Perhaps its origins lie in the tale of Zeus and Europa, in which horns figure prominently. Zeus fancied Europa from the moment he saw her on the beach at Tyre. So he transformed himself into a dazzling white bull with crescent-shaped horns and appeared beside her. As soon as Europa climbed on to his back he walked into the sea and swam away with her to Crete where they had a whirlwind holiday romance that produced three sons: Minos, Sarpedon and Rhadamanthys. Zeus then sent his white bull persona to the heavens to become the constellation of Taurus and 'gave' Europa to Asterius, the king of Crete who, unable to father children with Europa, adopted Zeus's three sons. So that's one set of horns, in the sense that Asterius got lumbered with the white bull's offspring, but there's more.

When Asterius died, Minos proclaimed himself king of Crete and to prove to his jealous brothers that he was the rightful king he asked Poseidon to make a bull emerge from the sea, promising to sacrifice the bull to the god in return. Poseidon did as he was asked but Minos refused to sacrifice the bull. In revenge the sea god sent the bull mad and, for good measure, afflicted Minos's wife Pasiphae with a compelling desire to have sex with the beast. The artist and architect Daedalus built her a wooden cow which she could get inside so that the bull could mount her. The product of these couplings was the Minotaur, half man, half bull. So there's two more sets of horns, Pasiphae's bullish paramour and the Minotaur. Despite having a bit of bull on the side herself, Pasiphae was jealous of Minos's affairs and put a curse on him whereby any woman he slept with was devoured by serpents and scorpions that emerged from all over his body. One can imagine the effect this had on Minos's pulling power once word got out. Minos, incidentally, is often credited with being the first homosexual, possibly because he ran out of women who enjoyed being eaten alive by scorpions. This was Crete, after all, not Los Angeles.

The horn explanation preferred by etymologists has nothing to do with stags or devils but comes from the world of cock-fighting. Apparently aficionados in the Middle Ages would graft the spurs of a castrated cock on to the bird's head, where they grew as horns several inches long. This explanation, combining as it does horns with emasculation, at least has the virtue of making sense and gets some semantic support from the fact that *Hahnrei*, meaning a capon or castrated cock, is the German for a cuckold, likewise *hanrej* in Swedish, not that anyone in Germany or Sweden ever uses these words. But I don't buy it. The idea that a specialized practice from the cockfighting arena could become a metaphor for adultery I can accept. But that the same metaphor should be taken up by men as far apart – in all senses of the word – as Stockholm and Palermo is frankly hard to swallow.

My own feeling is that it derives from the devil, one of whose names is Old Horny. Once the concept of God's evil alter ego had been established – the devil is very much a creature of the New, Christian, Testament – it was inevitable that Satan would get lumbered with Christianity's sexual paranoia. Women who displayed an 'excessive' sexual appetite – i.e. any appetite whatsoever – were regarded as being in the grip of possession. In the Middle Ages there was even a widespread belief that the devil might join a couple engaged in sex, an uninvited guest at the concupiscent feast. If asexual Mary is the Lord's handmaiden, it follows that the venal Mary Magdalene must be Lucifer's moll, and once Old Nick's got to a girl, it's only a matter of time before she starts fitting her old man with a set of replica horns. This is made clear in Spanish, where the unfaithful woman by her actions *pone* (places) the horns while her husband is said to *lleva* (wear) them. However, we're unlikely ever to get to the bottom of this and, whatever its true origin, one senses in this image of a man putting on horns something quintessentially pagan.

There are signs that the horned insult is beginning to lose its impact in parts of southern Europe. Among young Greeks *keratas*, once a deadly insult, is these days more likely to be used as a meaningless exclamation. And sometimes a person is called a *keratas* when they've been really lucky or have in some way excelled themselves. In Italy the strength of the insult varies depending where you are, north or south, city or country, but calling a man a *cornuto*, especially accompanied by the index and pinky finger horn gesture, is still best avoided. The alternative and much more common Spanish word for *cornudo* is *cabrón*, meaning goat-like. This is one of those words whose acceptability is entirely governed by context. Among male friends it's used all the time, like *hombre* or 'mate' or 'you old bastard'. It even has an affectionate diminutive, *cabronito*.

But said in anger, or even casually to a stranger, *cabrón* is fighting talk, as is *cabrão*, its Portuguese equivalent, which has no 'matey' usage. Portuguese is unusual in that it has a feminine version, *cabrona*, for a woman who is being cheated on, and that a crazy person is said to have *passon-se dos cornos* (parted company with their horns). One of the strongest Portuguese insults is to call someone a *cabrão filho de puta* (a cuckolded son of a whore). Curiously, in the north of Portugal, where they swear a lot, *cabrão* is considered a bad insult, while they're prepared to let the odd *filho de puta* pass. The reverse applies in Lisbon and the south, where they swear much less. The only softer use in Portuguese is *Os cornos do teu pai!* (Your father's horns!) which, while it can be insulting, as often as not merely amounts to 'You're pulling my leg!' The worst thing you can call a man in Portugal is a *paneleiro*, once an innocuous word for a cook – because he stood over his cooking pot or *panela* – but somehow transmuted to mean 'faggot'. Portuguese men don't like being called faggots. Asked for their opinion on a party or club or concert that they didn't much enjoy a Portuguese might comment that *só putas e paneleiros* (there were only whores and faggots).

The word *cornute* was introduced into English by the Norman conquest and was in use until the sixteenth century when it was overtaken by cuckold, a word derived from the cuckoo's habit of laying its eggs in other birds' nests. In *Love's Labours*

Lost Shakespeare teases: 'Cuckoo, cuckoo! Oh, word of fear, / Unpleasing to the married ear!' Why the word, and therefore the insult, should have become redundant in northern Europe I couldn't say, but the fact is that this matter of wearing the horns delineates another of the fundamental European slanguage barriers. Southern Europeans must find it exasperating trying to pick a fight with a northern European man. How do you provoke a man who shrugs when you call him a bastard, laughs at son of a whore, goes blank at cuckold and doesn't even flinch when you say 'Your mother!'? Does this man hold nothing sacred? Doesn't he care about his wife and his mother? His family's honour? Is he a man at all?

Another north–south divide is drawn on the issue of parentage. Across northern Europe you can call a man a 'son of a whore' more or less with impunity and it doesn't appear ever to have had the impact it has in the south. In England, 'whoreson' came into fashion during the early sixteenth century and can be found in the works of almost every Elizabethan dramatist. Shakespeare employs it in *King Lear* when the Duke of Kent belittles Goneril as 'Thou whoreson zed! Thou unnecessary letter!', and also put into *Troilus and Cressida* the line 'Dog . . . thou bitch-wolf's son', a forerunner of sonofabitch. Sonofabitch, an all-American favourite, is whoreson's only living heir in spoken English, although it almost certainly entered the American vernacular in translation from the Italian *figlio di puttana* (son of a whore) and not via English. 'Whoreson' and its northern counterparts such as the German *Hurensohn* are now found only in dictionaries, the entries marked *arch.* for archaic. A Belgian or a Dutchman, for example, would consider *vulle klootzak* (dirty scrotum), more insulting than *hoere jong* (son of a whore).

Unlike among its northern neighbours, however, 'bastard' hasn't fallen out of favour in English. And while it's lost its literal impact, it can still be used with venom to signify a deeply unpleasant person. John Major gave it new life in a 1993 TV interview when, thinking the camera had been switched off, he referred to a particular set of rivals in his Cabinet as 'bastards'. This was a gift that was gratefully received by headline writers and political columnists. In future, instead of some clumsy definition of this right-wing coterie, they could now refer to them simply as 'the bastards'. This illustrates the capricious fate of 'dirty words'. In normal circumstances convention curbs the sub-editor's natural inclination to include the word 'bastard' in headlines, especially on political stories. But once the prime minister has sanctioned it, just try stopping them.

No one has taken 'bastard' to their hearts quite the way Australians have. They have a flair for picturesque sayings. They'll complain that a footballer 'couldn't get a kick in a stampede', or say someone is 'as busy as a one-armed taxi driver with crabs'. With greater irony, a miserable person is said to be 'as happy as a bastard on Father's Day'.

Some Irish people have bastard built into their names. After they invaded Ireland, the Norman aristocracy found it a useful place to dump all their unwanted, illegitimate progeny, of which they had rather a lot. The routine was to give the bastards a few acres of Co. Dublin or Wicklow and allow them to allude to their noble origins by adopting names such as Fitzgerald or Fitzmaurice. The 'fitz' prefix means fils (son), by which everyone understood that this was Maurice or Gerald's 'bastard', one of the clan, therefore, but clearly not in line to inherit the family Calvados business back in Normandy. In Welsh they rather quaintly call a bastard a plentyn siawns, a child of chance.

But in much of southern Europe bastard isn't taken lightly. Were you to say of a Frenchman c'est une vieille salope ce type (he's a real bastard) it's metaphorical. But if you say he's un bâtard, it means just that: born out of wedlock. This isn't to say that *bâtard* is never used metaphorically, just that it has retained a strong literal sense of illegitimacy, which of course has undertones of son of a whore. The same goes for all the Mediterranean countries. As we've seen, *bastardo* is the worst thing you can call an Italian. No greater calamity could befall an Italian than to be without family. It is everything, the fundamental social and economic unit. You can't get along in Italy unless someone owes you something and without family you can't get on the first rung of the grace and favour ladder. The family gets you your job and your housing and without these connections you never know who to bribe or how much. The strength of this unit and the extent of its influence is bound to be undermined by Italy's unusually low birth rate but for the time being, an Italian without family, a *bastardo*, is *fottuto*, well and truly stuffed. In English women are almost never called bastards but in southern Europe, where it still means what it means, there is no such discrimination. A *bastarda* is as ill-starred as her male counterpart.

The French expression *fils de sa mère* (his mother's son) seems innocuous enough, but although it sounds like it might mean 'chip off the old block' it is in fact another way of saying *fils de putain* (son of a whore). The same applies to the Galician *fillo de cura* (son of a priest). Bastard and son of a whore go hand in hand and there is little to choose between them. In Greece *yios tis putanas* (son of a whore) is probably worse than bastard and the same applies to Spain, where bastard is not much used. There is really no restriction on what is acceptable among friends, and son of a whore is commonplace as jocular men's talk – especially in southern Spain – and is becoming increasingly common among women. But its power and taboo shouldn't be underestimated. A son of a whore is an outcast, without family or bloodline, however humble. And in a culture that has made a shibboleth of the Virgin, a son of a whore is de facto thrown into the camp of her antithesis, the other, fallen Mary. As if that's not enough, he's also a bastard in the English sense of the word.

It has been argued that we once belonged to matriarchal societies, where women ran the show guided by a pantheon of goddesses. This is not the place to conjecture over how, when and if matriarchy succumbed to patriarchy in one part of Europe or another, but for whatever historical or religious reasons, the issue of female relatives is very fraught for the Mediterranean male. The Spanish may say jokingly that *su madre sera una santa, pero él es un hijo de puta* (his mother may be a saint but he's a son of a whore), and they may try to diffuse the mother issue by making a positive concept out of *de puta madre*, but really this is no laughing matter. To say to a Portuguese man *Vai mamar na cona da tua mãi* (Go suck your mother's cunt), or to a Greek *Sou yamó ti mána* (I fuck your mother), or *Sou yamiété i mána* (Your mother fucks around) is really to book yourself into an early grave. And it's enough just to say to a Greek *Tis mánas sou!* (Your mother's!) as it is in Spanish ¡*Su madre!* or Italian *Sua mamma!* to land yourself in very hot water. The same effect can be achieved by saying 'your sister' or indeed anything that implies a sexual familiarity with a man's sister. In Arabic and Urdu it's possible to insult a man by calling him 'brother-in-law', which implies that you 'know' his sister.

A more unusual version of this can be heard in the Pied-Noir French *La figa ta ouela!* (Your grandmother's cunt!), an expression that illustrates Pied-Noir's multilingual components, taking *figa* from Italian and *ouela* from the Spanish *abuela*. Alone among English speakers, African–Americans and Afro-Caribbeans say 'Your mama!' in this way, of which more later. In a piece on so-called 'Britspeak' in the *Independent on Sunday* in 1995 a London teacher reported that an eight-year-old boy at her school had been reduced to tears by another child taunting him with the cry, 'Your mum, your mum!'.

To summarize: if you're looking for trouble you can find it easily in Germany, Sweden and among English-speaking European men by calling them cunts. This will generally do the trick. But it won't faze the Dutch or Belgians, for whom scrotum is a safer bet, while in Denmark you'll have to use your imagination. It's strange to think that when the Danes invaded England all those years ago our languages were so similar they could communicate with the native English without recourse to an interpreter. Frankly, when you look at the Danes today, it's hard to picture them invading anywhere, let alone sweeping down from Gateshead on a tide of blood. Something in the lager, perhaps. Now if you want to provoke a Finn you can start with *paskapää* (shithead) and if that doesn't do it try *kyrvänimijä* (cocksucker), which suggests that he's a homosexual, something Finns are rather touchy about. You could also call him a Swede, a double-edged insult because the Swedes not only ruled Finland for centuries but are synonymous with homosexuality. Well, they are in Finland anyway. As for France, there's every chance that a Frenchman who doesn't bite on *salope* won't be able to let *fils de pute* pass. And in Greece, Italy and the entire Iberian peninsula from Cadaqués to Cabo San Vicente, if a man doesn't get his knife out for 'cuckold', 'son of a whore', 'bastard' or 'your mother', you've probably picked on a German tourist by mistake.

Astute readers will have noticed the conspicuous absence of idioms and insults connected with what has long been recognized as the driving force behind art, literature, philosophy and, let's face it, civilization, the one attribute that has propelled us to the higher consciousness that divides humanity from the beasts of the fields. I refer, of course, to the mighty love muscle, a thing of such wonder and magnificence it deserves a book all to itself. But size isn't everything and, due to pressure of space, we shall have to try to confine this awesome beast within a single chapter.

8 ★ How's It Hanging?

> When the prick stands up
> The brain goes to sleep.
>
> Yiddish proverb

You could find no better paradigm of the European dream than the Eurofighter. Here you have Britain, Germany and Italy – sworn enemies so often in the past – pooling their wits and emptying their wallets to produce a state-of-the-art killing machine. Each country has the task of producing certain key components, the sum of whose parts will be a federal fighter plane capable of defending the Union against its enemies. It's not clear right now who our enemies are but some are bound to show up, they always do. Before they do, we've got to get the Eurofighter off the ground. The project is, predictably, years behind schedule and millions over cost, zillions if we're working in lire. But then that, too, epitomizes the European ideal. There is every possibility that at the end of fifteen years' effort and after scraping the bottom of a very large pot of gold, these three great nations will unveil a flying machine that, having been discussed, amended and compromised by so many sub-committees and working parties, is of no danger to anyone except its pilot. Many would salute such a feat and welcome it as progress.

Brussels, were it to play to the vernacular strengths of the member states, would need to initiate a similar transnational project in order to produce a sexually active European male. We have established that 'fuck' is the English speciality while 'wanker' is the province of the Greeks. However, neither activity can be pursued without the necessary equipment and for this we must turn to Italy for the *cazzo* (prick) and to Spain for the *cojones* (balls) or, as they are also commonly known, *huevos* (eggs). We need look no further than Belgium and Holland for the *klootzak* (scrotum) in which to cosset these precious eggs but to achieve orgasm we might need help from the Portuguese, who are inclined to splutter *Porra!* (Come!) when taken by surprise.

Even though we've been able to exclude the French and the Germans, it's asking a lot to achieve such a high level of co-operation on such a delicate and fundamental issue. One suspects that the fully federal, integrated Euromale is still some way off. But, like the Eurofighter, these things can't be rushed, and France will no doubt continue to veto the project on the grounds that, without French components, it could never be said to be *bien outillé* (tooled up), that is to say, well hung.

The Italians would disagree. There is nothing an Italian can't do, linguistically speaking, with a *cazzo*. It turns up in every part of speech. Consider, for example, this assessment of the then prime minister Bettino Craxi, made in 1984 by fellow left-wing deputy Fabio Mussi: '*Ah, sei incazzato? Vedrai che poi scendi dal cazzo e vai a piedi.*' The gist of Signor Mussi's comment is: 'If you're fed up now, just wait till later when you have to stand up for yourself.' But his exact words to the prime minister were: 'So you've got a cock up you. Well, wait till you have to get down off that cock and go on foot.' This must set some sort of benchmark for political debate, a challenge even to Australia's former prime minister Paul Keating, famous for his colourful language. As for Silvio Berlusconi, the millionaire premier who was going to save Italy from its own corruption, he soon acquired the contemptuous nickname 'Berluscaz', courtesy of Umberto Bossi, the leader of Italy's Northern League.

Italian men measure out their conversation in *cazzi*. A *cazzo* is thrown into a phrase to augment the rhythm or to add emphasis, or just to be saying something while they're thinking about what to say next. There are many, many synonyms for *cazzo* in Italian, so many that in 1832 an anonymous Roman published a poem, entitled *Er padre de li Santi* (The Father of the Saints), which consisted of nothing else. It begins:

> Er cazzo se pò ddi rradica, uscello,
> Ciscio, nerbo, tortore, pennarolo,
> Pezzo de carne, manico, scetrolo,
> Asperge, cucuzzola e stennarello.

(The cock may be called a root, a bird, a whip, a dove, a feather, a piece of meat, a handle, etc.) There are five more verses and suffice to say that every word, bar the odd conjunction, means the same thing in the Roman dialect. But *cazzo* is the word everyone uses and mostly it's just friendly banter. But you never know when some *ragazzo* who's *incazzoso* (easily angered) might fly into an *incazzatura* (huge rage) just because someone's accused him of being *cazzuto* (tedious) or a *cazzaturo* (a nobody) who *non vale un cazzo* (isn't worth a damn). And if he doesn't like it? Well, that's just his tough luck, *cazzi amari*, literally 'bitter cocks'.

However, for all their enthusiasm for the *cazzo*, even Italians recognize that one of the few places it doesn't belong is in the space designed to house the brain. No one wants to be called a dickhead, *testa di cazzo*, a fool in just about any tongue. The Swedish *kukskalle* is a little stronger, however, suggesting the dickhead in question is not merely stupid but despicable. In French he's just a stupid *tête de noeud* unless he's exceptionally dumb, in which case he's *con à bouffer de la bite* (a dick-eating cunt), meaning 'thick as two short planks'. In Portugal, one way of saying 'a likely story' is to recite the little rhyme *Bonito, bonito, são os colhônes a bater no pito* (Beautiful, beautiful, the balls banging against a cunt). These expressions manifest an awareness, arrived at with some reluctance, that although the most important thing in the whole world is what a man has between his legs, it helps if he has something else between his ears. Even if it's just a little one.

Let's relax for a moment. You're on holiday, the sun's going down and you're pouring out the early evening in a quiet bar on Spain's Costa de la Luz. Across the purpling Mediterranean you can make out the coast of Morocco, just as 1200 years earlier Tariq ibn-Ziyad had looked across at Visigothic Spain from the opposite shore and thought, I'll have that. Unlike Tariq, however, you're not planning to conquer anything in the name of Islam, but you do quite fancy another drink. Unfortunately you can't catch the waiter's eye, so you call out to him. Now you'd think it was a pretty safe bet that the worst way to go about getting the *camarero* to come to your table would be to call out: ¡*Oiga, pichi!* (Hey there, little dick!). But, hey, it works a treat and there he is, all smiles, taking your order. In Andalusia, Spain's southernmost province, *pichi* is a common greeting between men and is no more offensive than 'mate'. Not so long ago this was also the case with *shmuck* (prick), now only used as an insult, but which was once a friendly monicker among Jewish men in eastern Europe. And in parts of England men call each other 'cock' or 'my cocker', and in Bristol and Nottingham men unselfconsciously address each other as 'my lover'.

Pichi is a nursery word for the male sexual organ; the female equivalent is *chichi*. So, given that Spaniards don't regard the subject of their manhood as a laughing matter, it comes as a surprise when, at the end of the Spanish football season, the top goal scorer is dubbed *el pichichi* and is awarded a special trophy of the same name. For this we have to thank Rafael Moreno Aranzadi, Athletic Bilbao's prolific goal scorer at the turn of the century, whose nickname was *el pichichi*. Not that this explains how he came by the nickname, but no one in

Spain thinks anything of honouring a footballer with such an unlikely title. Somehow it taxes the imagination to picture an English or Dutch footballer warming to the monicker of 'the wee dick-cunt'.

Pichi at least has the virtue of being a masculine noun. A grown-up pichi, una polla, is not only feminine but is perilously similar to pollo, a chicken, which is masculine. One of the things that helps a Spanish waiter get through the day is the procession of hungry tourists who solemnly ask to have their dicks fried, diced or cooked on a spit. The word for the male of the hen species is gallo but polla is firmly in the tradition of analogies between farmyard cocks, servicing and serviced by their harem of hens, and the mighty male member. Polla isn't used as an insult the way 'prick' is in English, and on the whole Spanish vernacular is more enthusiastic about balls than pricks. La polla seems to be more a source of irritation than delight, witness such expressions as ¡Pollas en vinagre! (Pricks in vinegar!) or Esto es la polla encima del pan, this is the prick on top of the bread, that is to say, the last straw. A common exclamation is ¡Y una polla! (And a prick!), which means 'No way!'. The key thing is to have una polla lisa, a smooth dick. This will put you on a par with an Italian who has molto culo (a lot of arse). In either case, it's understood that you're enjoying good fortune.

Given the reverence in which the purple-headed love god is held, the European mind displays an uncharacteristic lack of imagination when it comes to naming it. Not that there's a shortage of euphemisms but the analogies, predictably, are almost entirely between things of vaguely phallic dimensions – carrots, cucumbers, sausages, poles – or weapons such as chopper, mutton dagger, dard (French for a bee sting) or kamaki (Greek for harpoon). The Euskera zakilpistola (pistol prick) at first sight appears to belong in this category but actually denotes a Basque who suffers from premature ejaculation.

You'd think that the many militaristic euphemisms – rapier, ramrod, torpedo, Patriot missile – would be matched by equally daunting metaphors for a woman's sex, but this isn't the case. The target of these mighty weapons usually appears to be unfortified and poorly defended. You never hear a vagina described as a fortress, for example, or a minefield, the Maginot line or a tank trap. Not much of an adversary for the all-conquering Dick, Dr Feelgood, Johnson or Charles-le-Chauve (Charles the Bald).

'Cock' has meant the same thing in English slang for at least five hundred years. Only 'tool' has survived longer (first recorded in 1252) whereas 'prick' first appeared in the sixteenth century. 'Cock' didn't become taboo until Victorian times but the prudish Americans replaced it long ago with 'rooster', just as their 'ass' gave way to a 'donkey'. One suspects these euphemisms have survived for so long not so much because no one has had the wit to think of any better ones but because 'cock', 'dick' and 'prick' all incorporate the harsh, plosive sounds that are the meat and drink of bad language.

However, some languages are so onomatopoeic they scarcely need to resort to metaphor. What else could the German *Schlappschwanz* mean except 'limp dick', and the Dutch *slappe zak* (slack scrotum) clearly refers to an ineffectual man, a drip or a wimp. Although it sounds like one of those Old English words, wimp appeared from no one knows where early in the twentieth century. The French call a wimp *une couille molle* (a limp ball) and when they say *il y a une couille* (there's a ball) they mean that there's a problem, the singular ball indicating that something is amiss. Indeed this is one area on which there seems to be pan-European unanimity, that it's good to have balls, to be assertive, *poner los huevos encima de la mesa* (to put your balls on the table). In the Yiddish rendering of this, of getting down to brass tacks, you put your *toches afn tish*, your arse on the table, not your balls.

The balls, los cojones, are what really count; they're the very stuff of life. But although the Spanish think very highly of their nuts, they don't go as far as the Venetians, reputedly the most blasphemous people in Italy, who honour theirs with the handle i santissimi, the most holy sacraments. We've established that to a Spaniard something that is cojonudo (testicle-like) is terrific, absolutely brilliant, but it gets better still and at best achieves that superlative state of having tres pares de cojones (three pairs of balls). It's axiomatic that, whatever the culture, a real man has balls, both a literal pair and a pair of idiomatic ones. But somehow cojones carry more weight than just any old balls, more even than Italian coglioni which, quite frankly, sound smaller, though not to an Italian. Both as a word and a concept cojones found a ready home in the works of Ernest Hemingway, iron man's amanuensis. Immersed in the corrida and the Civil War, drunk on the manly scent of blood and leather, or just plain drunk, Hemingway liked to give the impression while he was in Spain that he had más cojones que nadie (more balls than anyone) or even más cojones que Dios (more balls than God).

But sometimes a situation gets so out of hand that no one, not even a man's man like Hemingway, can save it. At this stage you might as well give it up as a bad job because it's clear that no tener más cojones, there are no more balls, it's beyond redemption. If you're lucky, it won't matter much anyway, in which case no importa tres cojones (it doesn't matter three balls). And as often as not it becomes clear that no hay cojones que valgan, there aren't any balls that are worth it, the game's not worth the candle. Catalans, on the other hand, when they're really fed up, say they've got els collons plens (full balls), presumably irritated by the lack of an opportunity to void them. But Catalans are a bit jumpy; give them a fright they end up with els collons per corbata (balls for a necktie).

When huevos (eggs) are substituted for cojones things can get very confusing, as in the case of the Spanish restaurant that put up a sign which read: *Aqui igual se plancha un huevo que se frie una corbata* (Here we are as happy to iron a testicle as to fry a necktie), a rather abstruse way of saying 'at your service'. But as sure as eggs is eggs, wherever you go, you know that sooner or later someone is going to demand their pound of flesh. The thing is, you never know where they're going to take it from. In London, for example, you pay through the nose but it costs you an arm and a leg; in Paris, they take *la peau des fesses* (the skin off your buttocks). In Madrid, however, when you pay a heavy price it costs you *un huevo y la yema del otro* (one egg and the yoke of the other i.e. your balls).

From bad eggs to sucking eggs, few items of food are such a rich source of metaphor. A French *oeuf* is a fool, and a fool doesn't get the point even when it's *l'uovo di Colombo*, Columbus's egg, which in Italy means as plain as the nose on your face. The Germans say *Ach, du dickes Ei!* (Oh, you fat egg!) as a way of saying 'Bloody hell!'. But by far the commonest egg metaphor, ranging through the Romance languages to German and Romani, is for the testicles. Those Freudians still stuck on penis envy should take note of what must surely be an epidemic of ovary envy.

However, balls are also regarded as worthless, as when we say something is bollocks or the Greeks say *arhithia*, and when a Corsican's really down on his luck he says that *sta à coglie in manu*, he's got his balls in his hand. What a Corsican does with his hands is one thing, what he puts in his mouth is another. This is a matter on which there is consensus – cocksucking. The insult is identical across Europe, straightforward and without nuance, as is 'arselicker', and there seems to be complete agreement that such abject activities are not worthy of a man. For all that, 'cocksucker' is not much used, at least not to the extent it is in the United States, where both 'cocksucker' and the aggressive exhortation 'Suck my dick!' never seem to be far from some men's lips. Compared to the vast menu of

edible metaphors for a woman's sex there are very few for a
man's. Heterosexual men evidently regard performing fellatio
as the absolute nadir, the sort of thing, in fact, that's only fit
for a woman to do. In Portuguese they say *mama aqui a ver si e
deixo* (try to suck here and see if I let you) as a way of saying
'I'm not as stupid as you think'. It's surprising to discover
that Gypsy men may sometimes say *Hav te kar* (I eat your cock)
as a placatory gesture if an argument is threatening to get out
of hand. It's a metaphorical offer, of course, but even so it's
a very unusual, and very direct, way of offering reconciliation.
It's not to be confused with the confrontational *Ha miro kar*
(Suck my dick).

But the metaphor is everything. Most things in life are pretty
average and dicks are no exception. It all comes down to
talking it up as best you can. Europe is punctuated by statues
of little men perched atop some mighty erection: Nelson in
London's Trafalgar Square, Columbus at the foot of the
Ramblas in Barcelona, Napoleon in the Place Vendôme. Or
there's the childish jumble of competing Renaissance towers
in San Gimignano, each built by some wretched Tuscan duke
to prove to another inbred fop that his was bigger.

Few of us can expect our manhood to be immortalized in
statues and architecture, but we have a common language to
help us along, a lingua franca not just of words but, perhaps
more importantly, of symbols. Listen to the money men gath-
ered round the flickering screens, shirtsleeves rolled, ready to
face a bear or a bull market. They talk the same language;
they understand each other perfectly when they speak of performance, stripping, rollovers and penetration. They buy short
and sell long. When a French woman loses her virginity it's
said that she *entame son capital*, breaks into her capital, but a
businessman raises his. Or there's sport. No one laughs when
a football commentator reports that after a limp first half Spurs
stiffened their resolve and showed what they were made of.

They went in hard and penetrated the Arsenal defence to go one up, then after mounting a final surge, came again at the death.

Men have to talk a good game because, even if he wanted to, a man can't display his magnificence in public. The trick is to somehow signify the enormity of his sexual assets through the careful choice and confident display of that most vital of male accoutrements – the proxy phallus. The phallic accessory *sans pareil* is a gun; nothing speaks louder or clearer about a man's potential. What could be more awe-inspiring than a man who displays on his hip an instrument of death while the seeds of life swing insouciantly between his legs? Surely this is as close as a man can get to dwelling in God's image. Regrettably, unless you join the police or armed forces, there is no country in the EU where you can legally walk around with a Magnum or an Uzi on your hip – except during the hunting season, of course.

Still, there's an old saying, 'If you can't get ahead, get a hat', and if you can't carry a gun, improvise. The next best thing to a gun is an electric guitar, but it's hardly street attire, and besides there's something forlorn about an unplugged guitar. Furthermore, *chitarra* (guitar) is Italian slang for the female genitals, which is definitely not the message you're trying to convey. A mobile phone clipped on to the waistband can serve as a symbolic gun, plus it suggests that you're someone important, someone whose expertise or opinion might be sought at a moment's notice. Alternatively, hang an ostentatiously large bunch of keys from your belt loop. Only those with single-figure IQs will fail to make the connection that you're a man who opens doors. At the very least, wearing a wide leather belt with a mammoth buckle speaks volumes about the wild beast you're having to restrain.

But the most eloquent and accessible surrogate penis is without doubt the car. Everybody speaks car, it transcends all language barriers; it's Esperanto with bells on. Up to a point one is confronted by a simple matter of economics: more money, more motor, more manly. Few of us can afford a Ferrari but thankfully it doesn't really matter. In a social democracy you don't need money to be a dickhead. Just make sure the car is the right colour; black or red is ideal. And as soon as you have the cash, fit wide wheels with big shiny wheelnuts. And jack up the rear suspension so that the driver behind gets a full, in-your-face view of your fat, chromed differential. That'll show him who's boss. And install tinted windows; then nobody need know you're a nobody. Oh, and don't forget the sexy bumper sticker. Something like 'Windsurfers do it standing up'. Now you're talking the talk, man's talk. Pure bollocks.

9 ★ Wearing the Feather

Like a bad farmer, the homosexual lets the fertile land lie
fallow and toils night and day with the sort of land from
which no fruit can be expected.

Philo of Alexandria

The foregoing chapters should have made it fairly plain to
both men and women what is expected of them by the divine
and pastoral authorities. The essential thing to remember is
that sex is a vile and hideous activity that is best avoided.
However, for the species to survive, a certain amount of sexual
activity is unavoidable and the authorities are prepared to turn
a blind eye to this so long as it takes place in the context of
marriage and doesn't entail any pleasure. Engaging in acts
simply in order to gratify sexual desire puts a soul on the
autoroute to damnation, and such acts between members of
the same sex puts those souls in the fast lane of that autoroute.
But what the hell, the sinners say, let's face the music and
dance.

Homosexuality is uniquely linked to place names. Although
fellatio, lamentably, is not an Italian resort, Sodom did once
stand on the shores of the Dead Sea, along with its twin city
Gomorrah. And not only do sodomites hail from Sodom, but
buggers come from Bulgaria and lesbians from Lesbos,
although it's also claimed the latter derives from a Greek verb
lesbiázein, meaning 'to lick the sexual organs'. You'd think that
English, which is such a magpie tongue, might have picked
that one up, plugging an obvious gap in the language. Sadly

not, and indeed there is very little reference in any language
to lesbians – almost as if they had never existed.

Sodom was Sin City, and the name has a ring of doom
about it beloved by hellfire preachers. During the Gulf War
President Bush was at pains to pronounce Saddam Hussein's
name with an equal emphasis on each syllable, conscious of
its echoes of Sodom. And Gulf War T-shirts were produced
bearing the slogan 'America will not be Saddam-ized'. But
rereading the Biblical story of Sodom you wonder whether
God got the right guys when he launched his own version of
Desert Storm.

What happened was this. Two angels arrived at Lot's house
needing a place to stay and Lot did what anyone else would
do in the circumstances, he offered to put them up for the
night. But word got out and the men of Sodom surrounded
Lot's house demanding that he let them get to 'know' his
guests. Lot was so appalled at the proposal and the bad impression it might make on his visitors that he tried to placate the
mob with the offer of his two virgin daughters, to do 'to
them as is good in your eyes'. But the Sodomites weren't
interested in his daughters and tried to break down the door,
whereupon the angels, evidently of the avenging variety,
smote the intruders blind. They then told Lot to take his wife
and daughters and leave the wicked town because God was
going to wipe it off the map. And so they left Sodom, but
Lot's wife couldn't resist one last backward look at the destruc-
tion and was turned into a pillar of salt for her pains.

So now Lot is a single parent living in temporary accommo-
dation, a cave near Zoar, with his virgin daughters. With their
mother dead, the daughters are naturally concerned that their
father no longer has anywhere to spend his seed. So the first-
born daughter gets him so drunk on wine that he passes out,
and while he's in this condition she has her way with him.
(It's well known that a woman who wants a child will stop

at nothing.) The next night the other daughter does likewise. Sure she did, Lot. But no one remembers this part of the story. No one remembers that Lot offered his virgin daughters to a bunch of strangers to do with as they pleased, nor do they remember this preposterous story that in a drunken stupor he unknowingly deflowered both of them. And why should they remember? After all, God didn't seem to mind, Lot wasn't punished. But God didn't like those faggots hanging around Lot's house one bit and so he trashed the whole town. And that's what we remember, that's the message: God hates queers.

Sodomites, queers and buggers. Buggers started out as *bougres*, an eleventh-century sect of Gnostics based in France and what is now Bulgaria. As was the custom with heretics, they were accused of just about every conceivable crime against God and nature, including the sexual practice to which they've given their name. In 1239 the authorities burnt 180 of these *bougres* at the stake on Mt Wimer in Champagne and there were many more burnings to come. The Italian equivalent of 'poof', *finocchio* (fennel), is said to originate from the practice of throwing fennel on to such a fire to cover up the smell of burning flesh. However, there is no evidence to connect the common epithet 'faggot' with the faggots of wood used to light *autos-da-fé*. As for bugger, the word has not only stayed with us – and in Britain 'buggery' remains the legal definition of anal sex – but for some curious reason has always been considered an acceptable swear word among Britain's upper and middle classes. A loud 'bugger orf' doesn't raise an eyebrow in the sort of posh company that would blanch at a whispered 'fuck'.

But whatever might be acceptable in the drawing rooms of England, homosexuality has been unequivocally condemned by Western religions; first by Judaism, then by Christianity and Islam. Despite claims to the contrary, all these religions hold women in low esteem, so it's only to be expected that

any man who wantonly renounces all the advantages intrinsic
to being male in order to behave 'like a woman', would also
be despised. Philo, who is quoted above, was a Greek Jew and
a contemporary of Christ who believed that the homosexual
male 'should not be allowed to live a day, indeed not for an
hour, since he shames himself, his house, his fatherland, and
the whole human race'. But Philo's fellow Greeks thought
otherwise, which is why 'Greek' continues to be synonymous
with anal sex in the majority of European languages.

According to the ancient Greeks, there had originally been
three sexes. In Plato's *Symposium*, Aristophanes explains that
each sex was its own companion, so a man was a double man,
with two sets of limbs and organs, and a woman likewise.
The third, hermaphrodite sex had one set each of male and
female sexual organs. But the hermaphrodites, who sprang
from the moon, unlike men and women who sprang from
the sun and earth respectively, were so successful that, when
they weren't busy taking advantage of themselves, they began
to threaten the gods.

Zeus removed the threat by cutting them all – men, women
and hermaphrodites – in half and making them stand upright
on two legs. The result, Aristophanes laments, is that,

'Each of us then is the mere broken tally of a man, the
result of a bisection that has reduced us to a condition
like that of flat fish, and each of us is perpetually in
search of his corresponding tally. Those men who are
halves of a . . . hermaphrodite are lovers of women, and
most adulterers come from this class, as also do women
who are mad about men and sexually promiscuous.
Women who are halves of a female whole direct their
attention to women and pay little attention to men; Lesbians belong to this category.

'But those who are half of a male whole pursue males,

and being slices, so to speak, of the male, love men throughout their boyhood, and take pleasure in physical contact with men. Such boys and lads are the best of their generation, because they are the most manly . . . When they grow to be men, they become lovers of boys, and it requires the compulsion of convention to overcome their natural disinclination to marriage and procreation . . . It is clear that the soul of each has some other longing which it cannot express, but can only surmise and obscurely hint at . . . The reason is that this was our primitive condition when we were wholes, and love is simply the name for the desire and pursuit of the whole.'

With a manifesto like that under their belts it's not surprising that the 'Greek' tag stuck to the Greeks long after the Orthodox Church had driven Plato and his queer friends into the Aegean. You can also see why the Catholic Church appointed Aristotle and not Plato as its philosopher-in-residence. The word *poústis* (faggot) entered the Greek language during the era when Turkish men were wont to keep harems of boys, and a boy so kept was called a *pust*, which derives from the Persian for 'arse'. This admirable clarity shouldn't have left any room for doubt in the minds of naive boys who imagined they were being employed as wine waiters. Greeks are fond of a little intensification, and so *poústis* can be cranked up to *poustára*, meaning mega-faggot, more or less, or to *paliopoústis*, which is like saying 'a faggot from way back'. It's not unknown for heterosexual male friends to call each other *paliopoústis*, and *poústis*, when it isn't being used literally, can mean someone clever or lucky. In modern Greek *síka* (figs) is a gay man, a reflection perhaps of the fig's association with female sexuality. But the more fluid concept of sexuality prevailing in ancient Greece is expressed in Aristophanes' poem *The Peace*, written in 422 BC:

Now live splendidly together,
Free from adversity,
Pick your figs.
May his be large and hard.
May hers be sweet.

Today in Greece, as in many other countries, the non-pejorative word is 'gay', of which more later.

After Greece came Rome, and among the other facets of Roman life so perfectly preserved when Vesuvius buried Pompeii was the graffiti. Comments such as 'Phoebus the perfume-maker fucks excellently', and *Cosmus Equitiaes magnus cinaedus et fellator est suris apertis* (Equitias's slave Cosmus is a big queer and a cocksucker with his legs wide open) uncovered in the vicinity of the Pompeii baths suggest that the gay bath house scene didn't begin in San Francisco in the 1960s. But the manly Romans disdained passivity and didn't like to be thought of as effete, a strange word for an effeminate man as it derives from foetus and, in so far as it suggests feebleness, means 'worn out from childbearing'. As no red-blooded Roman wanted to be cast in the passive role, they employed legions of male prostitutes, the *puti* who we noted earlier are the antecedents of today's *putains* and *putas* (whores). Evidently this wasn't an underground or illegal profession as the *puti* paid special taxes and also had their own national holiday when they could get some well-earned rest.

Aside from *finocchio*, which is of Florentine origin, the most common pejoratives for gay men in modern Italy are *frocio*, more or less equivalent to 'faggot', and *recchione* (sometimes rendered *ricchione*). The latter originated in Naples and may derive from *orecchio* (ear), touching their earlobes being one way that men would signal to others that they were gay. In Mafia slang a gay man is a *seicento* (six hundred), a reference to the rear-engined Fiat 600.

This is fairly typical of the slang for gay men, which is dominated by anal sex analogies, whether it's the German *Arschficker* (arse fucker), the Irish *cigire tónach* (arse inspector), the Danish *røv cuer* (arse cuer, a snooker analogy), the French *être de la pastille* (of the anus, i.e. gay) or *pédé comme un phoque* (queer as a seal). The Swedes show a little more originality in their description of gay sex as *ollonkrock* meaning 'a crash of cock heads'. More affectionately, German gays are known as *warme* Brüder (warm brothers) or *Schwestern* (sisters).

In Portugal a gay man is often called a *bicha*, which is the feminine form of both 'beast' and 'queue'. But more typically they follow the Iberian tradition of associating homosexuals with that most definitive of women, Mary, giving *maricas* in Portuguese, *maricón* in Spanish and similar words in Gallego, Euskera and Catalan. In Cuba the word is simply *pájaro* (bird) and in Spanish there are numerous bird references, such as the expression *más maricón que un palomo cojo* (queerer than a lame pigeon), an observation on the waddling, mincing gait of pigeons. Spanish gays and lesbians who are 'out' are said to *llevar la pluma*, wear the feather.

In keeping with calling sex 'it' and sexual organs 'things' homosexuals have often been referred to simply as 'one of them'. This is echoed in the French *en être* (being) and the Spanish *entender* (understanding), both of which are generally accompanied by an 'explanatory' swivelling action of the hand. In the Middle Ages homosexuals were often called 'Ganymedes' after the Trojan shepherd boy whom Zeus abducted for his pleasure and from which we have tortuously derived the word catamite, meaning a boy kept for pleasure. Compared to 'shirt-lifter', or the Swedish *stjärtgosse* (tail boy), Ganymede was relatively neutral but since it died out homosexuals have lacked a non-pejorative or positive word with which to describe themselves. That is, until the late 1940s, when 'gay' emerged.

Aside from meaning 'pretty' or 'cheerful', in the nineteenth century gay's sexual connotations were entirely heterosexual. A gay house was a brothel and a gay woman one who was 'loose'. There's some evidence that the French *gaie* was a homosexual sobriquet as early as the sixteenth century and some even fancy that it derives from Gaia, the Greek goddess of the Earth and mother of the Cyclopes and Titans. The word wasn't widely used by gays until the 1930s but it quickly spread through the American gay scene after Pearl Harbor, when America entered the war. By the early 1970s, in the wake of 'gay liberation', it had worked its passage out of the gay underground and into the English mainstream. It has since been adopted by languages as diverse as Finnish, Italian and Japanese, fulfilling a need for a neutral, non-judgemental word. In most of Europe it's become the acceptable, neutral term for a male homosexual.

But the word in its modern sense has met fierce resistance from those whose idea of a gay scene was one depicting pastoral contentment, posies and buxom milkmaids. In 1980 Roger Scruton, the right-wing British historian, whinged about 'the kidnapping and debauching of the innocent word "gay" . . .', conjuring an image of some green country boy being dragged into a hedge by cosmopolitan perverts and schooled in their unnatural pursuits.

Inevitably, as the word has gained widespread acceptance, many gays have spurned it in favour of 'queer', an insult that has been reclaimed by the more assertive gays much as 'nigger' has by the most disaffected blacks. In a similar fashion gay men like to flaunt 'women's words' such as 'tart' and 'slag' and 'queen'. The latter, which had long been applied to women to mean 'whore', acquired its gay meaning in Australia in the 1920s. Up until the late 1960s, before gay liberation, the need to be clandestine often drove English gays to resort to an argot known as Parlyaree or Polari, when having a conversation in public. Polari, from the Italian *parlare*, meaning to speak, was a lingua franca, consisting mainly of Italian, originally used as a patois among sailors around the Mediterranean. It was later adopted by circus people and other travelling performers and probably found its way into gay speech via the theatre. Typical Polari words such as *donah* (woman), *omee* (man) or *mungaree* (food) are recognizably Italian (*donna*, *uomo*, *mangiare*). Some remain in the language, notably *khazi* (toilet), from *casa* (house). Greek gays also had a private language called *kaliardá*, some of which survives among older gays and transvestites.

But Polari has gone the way of much of the compromise and duplicity that for so long was a condition of homosexual life. By the early 1990s the rejection of such dissimulation had triggered a campaign of 'outing' prominent public figures, whether churchmen, politicians or entertainers, who were known but 'closet' homosexuals. Posters would appear in the street showing the person in question above the legend 'Queer as fuck'. This is pure vernacular; instantly understood by the native speaker, utterly impossible to translate. As a slogan, 'Queer as fuck' is so replete with semantics you could hang an entire treatise from it.

While Church and State have hounded gay men – Henry VIII made sodomy a capital crime and it remained so until 1861 – lesbianism has rarely been recognized in statute, not even in those countries where male homosexuality is or has been punishable by death. Islam and Christianity have tended to condemn lesbians to a relatively light sentence in purgatory, while men were damned to hell without appeal. Perhaps because the ideas and language of sex are so male-defined, sexual acts between women have been considered unthinkable, impossible or simply ridiculous. Perhaps men feel less threatened by a woman behaving 'like a man' than by a man behaving like a woman. From a heterosexual male point of view, the worst thing about a lesbian is that she doesn't want to have sex with him; the worst thing about a gay man is that he might.

This ignorance or indifference is reflected in the poverty of the language. For a start, lesbian is the universal and in some countries more or less the only word for a lesbian, a sure indicator that something is either unmentionable or unthinkable. Even English, with its insatiable appetite for synonyms, has little to offer beyond 'lezzie' or 'dyke'. Imagine, for example, that 'penis' was the only word for penis, not just in English but in a dozen or more languages. In seventeenth-century England lesbians were often called *tribades* or *fricatrices*, both from Latin words meaning 'to rub against', and *tribade* remains one of the few Italian synonyms. This rather dreary picture of sex between women is also expressed in the Swedish *slå flat*, beat flat, or *flatknulla*, flat fuck, both of which mean lesbian sex. It's also possibly what lies behind *tortillera*, pancake seller, the widely used Spanish word for a lesbian. It's conceivable but unlikely that there is a connection here with *tortilla* (omelette) which, as everyone knows, you can't make without breaking a few *huevos* (eggs), the favourite Spanish euphemism for balls. In Portugal, though no one can explain why, a lesbian is a *fufa*.

But the anal sex terminology associated with gay men isn't matched to any degree by 'muff-diving' epithets for lesbians. The French come close to having a verb meaning 'to lick the sexual organs' with *brouter*, which in other contexts means to graze or browse and from which French derives *une brouteuse* for a lesbian, who are also known as *bottines* (little boots) and *gouines*. In French, male homosexuality is sometimes called *la brioche infernale* (the brioche from hell), but this is a men-only *boulangerie*. French lesbians hang their hats – and their little boots – at *la maison tire-bouton*, push-button house, the button in question being the clitoris.

The American Judy Grahn, having already derived 'gay'

from the goddess Gaia in her book *Another Mother Tongue*, pro-
ceeds to claim that the origin of 'dyke' lies in Gaia's grand-
daughter Dike. She also asserts that 'fag' as a word for a
cigarette derives from 'faggot', in the sense of a firestick, 'the
agency by which the magic of fire passed from the old female
domain into the newer, more male-oriented Greek tradition'.
Yup. Apart from Ms Grahn, however, no one seems to have
a clue where dyke comes from, nor why the more butch
'bulldyke' should also be rendered 'bulldagger'. In recent years
this has been overtaken by 'diesel dyke', which is represented
in Greek by *dalikieris*, truck driver, and *betadzís*, a builder's
labourer. As we saw earlier, the Greeks also express the idea
of butch with *androyinéka* (literally 'man-woman') and the
Portuguese do much the same with *Maria-rapaz* (Maria-boy).
The Spanish also enlist the ever-willing Mary in forms such
as *marimacho*. On the whole lesbians haven't embraced the word
gay, which is used almost exclusively to refer to men, and
mostly settle for the relative neutrality of the word lesbian.

At present there is arguably less stigma attached to being a
European homosexual than at any time since the fall of the
Roman empire. Furthermore the ethos of gay pride has
allowed gays and lesbians to be more visible, vocal and assertive of their rights. Attempts to discriminate against them are
met with a militancy and self-confidence epitomized by the
slogan: 'We're here. We're queer. Get used to it.' But the
arrival of Aids, which in the West is still tagged the 'gay
plague' even though worldwide the overwhelming majority
of HIV-infected people are heterosexuals, has given moralists
and homophobes new heart. The very word plague plunges
us back into the Bible and those virtuous souls who can still
tell a Pharisee from a Philistine at a hundred paces have not
been slow to see in Aids a repeat of God's judgement on
Sodom and Gomorrah. Even Donna Summer, whose disco
music provided the soundtrack to gay liberation, turned her

back on the bulk of her fans when she declared in 1984, 'Aids has been sent by God to punish homosexuals.' But not lesbians, Donna, who occupy the same low-risk group as nuns. Now what does that say about divine judgement?

10 ★ You and Whose Army?

'Okey, Marlowe,' I said between my teeth. 'You're a tough guy. Six feet of iron man. One hundred and ninety pounds stripped and with your face washed. Hard muscles and no glass jaw. You can take it. You've been sapped down twice, had your throat choked and been beaten half silly on the jaw with a gun barrel. You've been shot full of hop and kept under it until you're as crazy as two waltzing mice. And what does it all amount to? Routine. Now let's see you do something really tough, like putting your pants on.'

Raymond Chandler, *Farewell My Lovely*

Tough guys, they're everywhere. Hard cases looking for trouble, bent on causing grief; muscle men, black belts and kung fu crazies itching to show off a few moves. Wide boys and dudes, gangstas and ragamuffins, strutting their stuff and flexing their attitude. So just a word about tough guys, because you can't avoid them, not even in Denmark.

In Denmark they call them Johnny Brians and really they're not that tough. Johnny Brians all wear the same outfit – blue trainers, blue jeans and blue and white check shirts and one earring. They wear their hair cut short on top with long wispy bits over the collar, like 1970s throwbacks. They drive Opel Mantas, try to look mean and talk shit about cars and girls. Their girlfriends are called Leilla Konnies. Until the biker wars broke out in the mid-1990s, this was about as tough as it got in Denmark.

In Italy, on the other hand, it can get very tough indeed. Everyone laughs at the Italians, writes them off as a bunch of flakes and posers who couldn't organize tutti-frutti in a gelateria. But, hey, no one laughs at Cosa Nostra, do they? And you don't hear a lot about Italian comedians doing stand-up routines about the Neapolitan Camorra or Calabria's 'Ndrangheta. Nothing flaky about them. More in keeping with the stereotype of the Italian male as a show pony, all mouth and well-cut trousers, are the paninari (the bread rollers), so-called after the Bar Panino in Milan where they first appeared in the 1980s. These are young, rich Milanese who have made an art form of hanging out and looking cool. They follow a strict dress code, wearing only the most expensive designer clothes, in which they then strike tough poses against a backdrop of their favourite cars, especially BMWs. In fact the toughest thing about a paninaro is probably his Moschino belt buckle. Nevertheless they attracted enough attention to become the subject of a Pet Shop Boys' record in 1986. The song, called Paninaro, summed up the Weltanschauung of these young Italians with the words:

> Passion, love, sex, money
> Violence, religion, justice, death
> Girls, boys, arts, pleasure
> Food, cars, travel.

But what really put the paninari on the social map were two cases of parricide that shocked Italy in the early 1990s. In the first a 21-year-old Milanese, Corrado Ferioli, strangled both his parents, while over in Verona, Pietro Maso, nineteen, bludgeoned his parents to death in order to get his hands on a £750,000 inheritance. Neither showed a trace of remorse and offered as a defence their need for more money in order to maintain their lifestyles. Both of them received piles of fan mail from sympathetic peers who evidently felt that doing away with mama and papa was nothing compared to the dismal prospect of a life without Armani and Versace.

But a *paninaro* is little more than a yuppie with attitude, a spoilt kid whose motto is *Non me ne fotte niente* (I don't give a fuck). Only money separates him from the *paraculo*, who does just what he pleases, without a care for anyone else. He certainly isn't a *uomo d'onore* (a man of honour) that is, a mafioso, although the code of *omertà* (silence) ensures that such a man would *fare il finto tonto* (play dumb) if you enquired too deeply into his affairs. Italians are fascinated by power and in a society that runs on influence, where connections are everything, everyone dreams of being a *pezzo grosso*, a fat piece, a big fish. And any *capo* or Mafia boss would hope one day to be a *pezzo da novanta*, a 'ninety-piece', or top dog.

In Mario Puzo's *The Godfather*, just before he dies Vito Corleone confesses to his son Michael that he'd hoped by now they would have become respectable. 'I thought that when it was your time that you would be the one to hold the strings,' the old man says. 'Senator Corleone, Governor Corleone, something . . .' 'Another *pezzo da novanta*?' his son interrupts, with heavy irony. 'We'll get there, pop.' And why would a 'ninety-piece' be top of the heap? No one is really sure, though some claim it's because ninety is the highest number in tombola and in the lottery. Another sobriquet for a top mafioso is *mammasantissima*, most holy mother, mother of all the saints. This sanctification of the mother of all tough guys neatly binds together the two most enduring and best organized institutions in Italian society – the men of the cloth and the wise guys.

When it comes to being tough, the Mafia are the genuine article, but your regular tough guy is all talk. This is the whole point of talking tough; you don't talk tough to make trouble but to avoid it, to make sure no one messes with you. Well, that's the theory anyway. In France you get your everyday *mec*, who's just a guy, or you get *un bon mec*, who's a good guy. But *le mec des mecs* is another pair of shoes altogether, a real tough nut, *un dur à cuire*, a hard-to-cook. Yes, another food metaphor. In France, as we shall see, even gangsters live and die by the culinary sword. But if he's a real *sacré lapin* (streetwise guy, though literally a sacred rabbit) people might look up to him as a *manitou*, a big shot. *Manitou* must have been picked up by French colonists in the new world as it's a Native American word that in the Narragasett tongue means a supernatural being or an object of religious awe. Somehow this mystic being has found its way into the vocabulary of *tatoné* (tough guy) talk.

A handy ice breaker if you're trying to make an impression in the Greek tough-guy scene would be: *Yamó tin panayia su* (Hey, fuck your Virgin Mary). This amounts to going up to some hard case and saying 'suck my dick'. Try it some time, they'll just love it. A real Greek hard case, faced with a demand for money or any other claim, will respond: *Páris ton poutso mou* (You'll get my dick), or *Na sou skiso to kolo sou* (I'll tear your arse apart). In Portugal and Spain the pose-striking tough guy is such a common phenomenon they have coined a special word for him: *gajo* in Portuguese and *chulo* in Spanish. *Gajo* seems to have entered Portuguese from Gitano speech. Unlike most Gypsies, Gitanos don't speak Romani but a variant of Spanish called Caló, meaning black. *Gadjo* is the Romani word for any non-Gypsy but the Portuguese *gajos* probably owe their name to the Caló *gachó*, which means a guy, a bloke.

A real *gajo* will assure you that *me der na real gana*, I do just as I please, which is very much in the spirit of the Spanish *chulo* who, when challenged about his behaviour, will retort *hago lo que me sale de los huevos* (I do whatever issues from my balls), which sums up the *chulo* mentality rather nicely. Although *chulos* were originally associated with Madrid and the word is still used to describe a particular type of strutting, working-class Madrileño, the term is used throughout Spain. An editorial on Catalan leader Jordi Pujol recently appeared in Spain's *La Vanguardia* newspaper under the headline *Más chulo*

que un ocho (more *chulo* than a figure of eight), an expression
applied to anyone who is very astute or a smooth operator.
A *chulo putas* is a pimp – which is what *mec* meant at the outset,
as did *hoon*, the Antipodean for a wide boy – but your average
chulo is a pretty harmless creature, all attitude and little action.
He likes to strut, the more so if he's a little on the short side.
He'll sneer a good deal and no woman will get past without
him calling out or hissing ¡*Oye guapa!* (Hey, gorgeous!).

A *chulo*'s definitive characteristic – aside from a total lack of
anything that could be construed as class – isn't the clothes
or the swagger or the strut but a manner of speaking that is
tough, dismissive and unyieldingly masculine. A *chulo* is never
impressed, he is far too *chulito* (cool) to be impressed by
anything. For example, when presented with some truly aston-
ishing information the true Catalan *chulo* will shrug and offer
a dismissive *Me la porta fluxa i pendulant*, my dick is drooping,
that is to say, big deal. Or a Spanish *chulo* might respond with
his own version of 'big deal', ¡*Tócame los huevos!* (Touch my
balls!). A *chulo* must never appear threatened or show fear.
Threats will be dismissed with ¡*Me lo paso por el forro de los
cojones!* (That's wearing out the lining of my balls!), or the
super-contemptuous ¡*Me suda la polla!* (Oh yeah, my dick's really
sweating!). As you can see, there's much more to being a *chulo*
than wearing tight jeans and a black leather jacket; it's a whole
modus vivendi.

A final word on hard cases. Even if it is all talk, you have
to be prepared to put your money where your big mouth is.
So, sticking with the hardboiled idiom, you don't want to be
writing cheques with your mouth that your body can't cash.
Tough guys like to pick fights, often with the gambit 'What
are you looking at?' Of course, there is no good answer to
this because the question's rhetorical, a tough nut's idea of
foreplay before he gets down to the serious business of doing
you over. In Dublin, a town with its fair share of gobshites,

the equivalent of a chulo is a gurier (from the French guerrier, a warrior). And the word is that if a gurier gives you any of that 'What are you looking at?' bollix, the smart reply is 'Search me, they don't put labels on shite'. Go on, I dare you. Say it next time.

11 ★ *An Irish Wedding*

> Prejudice, not being founded on reason, cannot be
> removed by argument.
>
> Samuel Johnson

The French have had a bad press. As individuals French people
are much like anyone else, some good, some bad. But everyone
has the same gripe about the French as a nation: that they're
arrogant. Even the English and the Germans think so, and they
should know. They complain that the French act as if they
had invented culture, as if no one else could cook with élan,
write poetry with panache, or behead aristocrats with finesse.
For proof of French arrogance, people say, one need look no
further than their generous contribution to the lexicon of
snobbery, to which they have donated nouveau riche, parvenu,
arriviste, petit bourgeois, faux pas and chauvinist, among
others. The English, always grateful for new ways of emphasiz-
ing class distinction, returned the favour with 'snob', a word
that appeared in the 1850s and which has been adopted
unchanged by the majority of European languages. How on
earth did social hierarchies get along without it for so long?

In America the socio-linguist Irving Lewis Allen unearthed
more than a thousand epithets to describe fifty ethnic groups,
a quarter of them pertaining to blacks, over one hundred to
whites, with the Jews, Irish and Italians leading the rest of the
field. But we can do better than that here in Europe. Here
there's no room for petty prejudice; that is, we don't see
anything petty about it. Here we have terms of abuse not just

for other races and nations, but for people from the next province or town, the next valley or the other end of the village. And probably no nation has attracted as many as the French.

The French get the blame for everything and they certainly copped it for the pox. Girolamo Fracastoro, the sixteenth-century physician-poet, entitled his medico-historical poem 'Syphilis: or a Poetical History of the French Disease', even though he accepted the received wisdom that it was the Spanish who introduced it to Europe. Columbus's sailors are said to have picked it up in Santo Domingo, now Haiti, which has also been blamed as the source of Aids. (Aids is gathering its own grim epithets. In most of Africa it's known bleakly as 'slim', but in parts of Tanzania they call it 'Juliana', after a popular dress fabric worn by women in neighbouring Uganda.) The theory is that the French picked up syphilis when they besieged Naples in 1495, although this isn't thought to be the origin of the saying 'see Naples and die'. Naples was at that time part of the Catalo-Aragonese empire which explains why it was occupied by Catalans and Spaniards. However, the French had hired some mercenaries in Barcelona, several of whom had accompanied Columbus to America and, well, you know what they say, what goes around comes around.

The impact of syphilis on the European psyche – not to say health – was immense. It can hardly be a coincidence that as this new plague, which unlike leprosy was sexually transmitted, spread across the continent, so, too, did Puritanism, nor that the abstemious merchant class saw its fortunes rise as the suppurating aristocracy vanished in ever greater numbers behind the doors of Europe's lunatic asylums and sanatoria. Syphilis has in its time been known as Spanish, Turkish and even Polish pox; in Japan they call it *mankabassam*, the Portuguese sickness. France fought a rearguard action, calling it the

Italian disease, but French pox stuck. The French have also given us 'the clap', from clappoir, a large boil.

But not all the associations between France and sex are unpleasant. If Britain's contribution to pan-European understanding is 'fuck', then we must thank France for 'French', a byword for oral sex throughout the Union. Europeans are also united by that other French number, soixante-neuf. For the less ambitious, there's French kissing, which the Portuguese call beijo à francesa and the Spanish beso francés. Italian, which couldn't possibly import French words into the language of love, plays on lingua, meaning both tongue and language, to produce a lip-smacking slinguata. The French themselves open wide and lécher les amygdales (lick the tonsils).

Then there are the indispensable French ticklers and French letters, which the French sometimes call capotes anglaises (English raincoats) and the Germans, playing it safe, call variously ein Engländer, ein Londoner or ein Pariser. And then, pardon my French, there is the matter of Greek, another component of the sexual Esperanto. Except in France where – how could they resist? – the verb to sodomize is anglaiser. This is further evidence of the French belief, famously put forward by former prime minister Edith Cresson, that a large number of rosbifs are closet homosexuals. The Greek connotation is retained in Va te faire foutre par les Grecs, one of the many versions of 'Go fuck yourself!'. In Greece frang (French) is synonymous with anything that is either foreign or Catholic; a frangópappas, for example, is a Catholic priest.

We get an insight into the Spanish view of English sexuality through the fact that those inclined towards sexual masochism are said to have a taste for inglés (English). However, people with el humor inglés have a predilection for nothing more exotic than irony. The Italian montar a la inglesa (riding English-style) doesn't have anything to do with sex either, unless riding side-saddle is your thing. As for the Portuguese, they seem to regard 'wife-swapping' as a peculiarly English pursuit, in any case they call it *casamento à inglesa* (marriage English-style).

Portugal is so isolated people often forget about it altogether, as though it was merely Spain's Atlantic sea wall. It's a long time since the heyday of Vasco da Gama and the riches that came from the colonization of Brazil. In 1974 the Portuguese woke up for ten minutes, overthrew the dictatorship, and then went back to sleep. No one notices them, least of all the Spanish.

The Portuguese, for their part, have some pretty strange things to say about their neighbours across the mountains. For example, a roundabout way of saying 'don't touch' is *és como os espanhóis, vês com as mãos*, which means 'you're like the Spanish, you see with your hands'. The expression *de Espanha nem bom vento nem bom casamento* (no good wind or marriage comes from Spain) harks back to the ill-starred marriage of Alfonso V of Portugal and Juana of Castile. It's used to depict the unequal relationship between the two countries and is reminiscent of the Irish assessment of their economic relationship with Britain that 'when England catches a cold, Ireland gets pneumonia'. Among the stranger Portuguese expressions about the Spanish is *casamento à espanhola* (marriage Spanish-style), a form of matrimony in which the bride sleeps with the best man on her wedding night. Spaniards are at a loss to explain how the Portuguese came by this idea. But then neither are they particularly chuffed that the French call breast-fucking (I'm sorry, but is there another word for it?) *une branlette espagnole* (a Spanish wank). The Italians agree and call it *una spanola*, but the Portuguese call this kind of rub-a-dub doing it *à florentina* (Florence-style).

Where we get these ideas about each other's sexual habits is anyone's guess. Why, for instance, do the English call the aphrodisiac made from the blister beetle 'Spanish fly'? At least it's clear why there's no need to dress up for an 'Irish wedding'.

(masturbation, in gay slang) and also why, as the pioneering sex-change operation on Christine Jorgensen was carried out in Denmark, a transsexual was for a long time called a 'Danish pastry' in gay circles.

At the dawn of what has become known as the permissive society, Sweden and sex were one and the same in the popular imagination. At that time you needed only give a movie a title such as Swedish Au Pairs and everyone would know it was about young blondes who burst out of their dresses like the Incredible Hulk every time any man wearing an orange body shirt and brown flares entered the room. When tourism first hit Spain and hotels shot up along the Costa Brava, among Spanish men una sueca (a Swedish woman) became synonymous with any foreign and therefore sexually available woman. Not so in Finland, however, where we've seen that they call gay men Swedes or sometimes some common Swedish name such as Björje.

Can there be any greater comfort than to spend an evening at home, toasting one's stale prejudices at the fireside of national chauvinism? Heaven knows, we've had plenty of opportunity to burnish our stereotypes, especially as at some time or another just about everyone in Europe has been at war with just about everyone else, or been colonized by them. We could choose to forget that Normandy is so called after the Norsemen who conquered it, that Spain once ruled Holland, that Corfu and Minorca were British or that Naples was once at the centre of a great kingdom and not the dump it is today. But like war memorials, the vernacular keeps the memories alive long after the battles have been fought. It's 1,500 years since the Vandals devastated Gaul but they still get the blame for graffiti and broken public toilets.

Without even considering the Balkans, there's no shortage of unfinished business. England has yet to conclude its eight-hundred-year war with the Paddies, nor has it resolved its dispute with the Jocks and Taffs. Corsica continues to resist Paris, while in Spain the Basques, Catalans, Galicians and Andalusians – about four-fifths of the nation – reject to varying degrees the authority of Madrid. In Belgium the Flemings despise the Walloons. As for Italy, a nation which its own citizens will cheerfully assure you doesn't exist, the drive against corruption threatens to wash away the very dirt that's held the place together. And at the heart of nearly all these disputes there is a conflict not just over sovereignty, but language.

It's a maxim that war is politics by other means, but football is both war and politics by other means. This is one of Britain's great contributions to Europe and, even if the English themselves can barely play it any more, the fact that to this day football managers in Spain are called *el Mister* or that AC Milan hasn't changed its name to AC Milano is testimony to Britain's role in spreading the gospel of 'the beautiful game'. The longest-running war to be played out on the football field is that between England and Ireland – and between the Catholic and Protestant Irish – which has been fought twice a season for over a century when Glasgow Celtic meet Glasgow Rangers for what is known as the 'Old Firm' game. Celtic, founded in the 1880s by and for the expatriate Irish, is almost entirely Catholic, while the Protestant and royalist Rangers didn't field a Catholic player until the 1980s. All the old insults – Fenians, Billy boys, Orange bastards, Papists – apply as Glasgow plays out the Irish conflict by proxy.

The causes of Basque and Catalan nationalism were kicked around in a similar fashion during the Franco era. Franco saw a populist opportunity in football and allied himself with the capital's great team Real Madrid. Real's matches against both the Basque team Athletic Bilbao and the Catalan FC Barcelona became the focus of nationalist sentiment. Supporters sang and chanted in their banned languages and for Catalans the claret and blue colours of *el Barça* became the surrogate national flag. Twenty years after Franco's death these games remain highly charged encounters at which many of the Madrid fans deck themselves out provocatively in fascist regalia. Football matches, where there is safety in numbers, often provide an outlet for nationalism. Simon Kuper, in his book *Football Against the Enemy*, cites an Armenian fan who, sensing the possibility of Armenian national independence after Gorbachev came to power, was emboldened to shout at a match: 'Referee, go fuck your wife in front of the Lenin mausoleum.' More often, however, football is a vehicle for more everyday prejudices. For example, the Amsterdam club Ajax and London's Tottenham Hotspur, both of which traditionally have a large Jewish following, are nicknamed the Yids.

But if war – or winning the World Cup – was the mother of sobriquets the Germans would have acquired more names than anyone, yet they haven't. In English there's the phrase 'be a good German', meaning 'play by the rules', and authoritarian types are called 'little Hitlers', but that's about it. The French might call them *boches*, more or less the same as 'krauts', and the Dutch call them *mofs*, after the cuffs of their uniforms, but the Nazi occupation made little impression on the language. In Yiddish someone totally inept is sometimes called a *kranker daytsh* (a sick German) and southern Italians refer to their northern compatriots as *tedeschi* (Germans), when they're not calling them *polentone* (polenta eaters). Italians also call Germans *crucchi* and their admiration for the English is summed up in the description of them as *lumaconi scivolosi* (slippery snails).

In Greek if someone says *mi kaneis to Germano* (don't pretend you're German), they mean 'don't deny that you did it'. As for Portugal, if a man drops his trousers just enough to expose his buttocks for sex with another man, they say he's doing it *assim que a Alemanha perdeu a guerra* (as though Germany had lost the war). Spanish sentiments are encapsulated in the term *alemanita*, little German, meaning masturbation. Considering the havoc Germany wreaked during the first half of the century, doing penance as Spanish slang for a wank has to be regarded as pretty lenient.

Relations between France and England have always been a little strained, what with William the Conqueror, Agincourt, the Hundred Years War, Waterloo and Eric Cantona. But when a French woman shakes her *anglaises* (ringlets) in irritation and announces that *les anglais ont débarqués* (the English have landed), don't panic, she's only signalling the start of her period, not an international incident. The French, notoriously, take French leave. The Spanish agree, although for them *despedirse a la francesa* means leaving without saying goodbye rather than without permission. But in Italy and France it's the English who *filare all'inglese* or *filer à l'anglaise*, unless you're on the run from the law, when naturally you *filer en Belgique*. Germans will have none of this, and take Dutch leave. Give them a shot of Dutch courage and the English will do the same, whatever the dire warnings from their Dutch uncle about landing themselves in Dutch.

Ultimately, of course, the French *s'en fout* what the *bifteks* (English), *flahutes* (Flemings), *espingouins* (Spanish) or *macaronis* (Italians) think of them; their opinion isn't worth *une carte de France* (a map of France, i.e. a wet dream). They'd rather *boire en suisse* (drink in Switzerland, i.e. alone), or with *un cousin à la mode de Bretagne* (distant cousin), or *travailler pour le roi de Prusse* (work for the king of Prussia, i.e. for nothing) than admit someone else's point of view. And anyone who disagrees or *fait une réponse de Normand* (gives an evasive answer) can expect *un coup de tête de Breton* (head butt, or Liverpool kiss) at the very least. *Les homards* (English, but literally lobsters), in particular, are nothing but *un bonbon anglais* (an English sweet, that is, a tiny pimple) on the face of Europe. And there's no point arguing with them because *ils ont les portugaises ensablées* (they're deaf, literally their oysters are stuffed with sand).

Sobriquets are based on a simple trick; pick on a physical characteristic (slanting eyes, dark skin) or a common name (Mick for an Irishman, or Janke, from whence Yankee) and Bob's your uncle. Speech patterns are another source. In nineteenth-century China the English were known as the 'I says' and, for the same reason, during the Napoleonic campaign, the Spanish called the French *didones* from *dis-donc* (I say). This process lies behind the origin of *wop*, the (mostly American) monicker for an Italian. This, too, dates back to the Catalo-Aragonese empire when southern Italian men – who later emigrated to America in huge numbers – acquired the Spanish habit of addressing each other as *guappo*, meaning handsome, which is pronounced hwoppo. *Guappo* is still used in southern Italy, although in the argot of the Camorra, the Neapolitan mafia, it has acquired the specific meaning of a thug.

Occasionally epithets derive from people's eating habits, such as the *rosbifs* for the English or spuds for the Irish. Calling French people frogs presumably relates in part to their penchant for frogs' legs and this nickname has been adapted in America to describe a French-Canadian as a *crapaud* (toad). Liverpudlians are called scousers after lobscouse, a sailor's dish made of corned beef, potatoes and onions (lob is dialect for 'boil' and scouse for 'sauce'). In the same way Swedes and Norwegians are called 'herring chokers' in America while US Jews call Italians *loksh* (Yiddish for noodles, which is all anyone can think of calling Italians). The Jews are paid back with the nickname 'bagel benders', and Mexicans are 'taco benders'. Not that you'll be served any tacos with a Mexican breakfast, which consists of a cigarette and a glass of water. This is at least a little more substantial than what the Australians call a drover's breakfast, which is no more than a cough and a look around.

While we're on the other side of the world, this must be

why an Italian says they're *al kiwi* when they've hit rock
bottom; because it's 'down under'. Some epithets are harder
to understand. Why, for example, do Basques call Spanish
immigrant workers 'Koreans'? But then Basques from Vizcaya
dismiss their neighbours from the province of Guipuzkoa as
giputxis robasetas (mushroom thieves) and those who can't speak
Euskera as *bellarimotzak* (short ears). Elsewhere in the Spanish
peninsula Catalans are called *polacos* (Poles) because no one can
understand them. *Pareces de Madrid* (you must be from Madrid)
is said everywhere – except Madrid – of someone who never
closes the door behind them. In the northern province of
Aragon they call immigrants from other parts of Spain *matracos*
(yokels), while elsewhere an obscure comment is sometimes
called a *galleguismo*, suggesting it was made by someone from
Galicia in the north-west. A citizen of Málaga is known simply
as *un boquerón*, a type of anchovy. Catalans, the wealthiest and
– they think – the most 'European' people in Spain, frequently
dismiss other Spaniards as *murcianos* (after Murcia, a poor area
of the south-east) and people from the southern province of
Andalusia as *africanos*. In most of Spain foreigners are referred to
as *guiris*, a term originally applied to soldiers of the reactionary
nineteenth-century Carlist movement who supported the
Bourbon pretender to the Spanish throne.

Gringo, the Spanish-American for an Anglo-American, probably derives from *griego* (Greek), which in Spanish is also used
in the 'it's all Greek to me' sense or, as they put it in France,
pour moi, c'est de l'hébreu (it might as well be Hebrew). The
Chinese, who have managed to survive a long time in Europe
without suffering serious persecution, are mainly denigrated
as a byword for the incomprehensible. The French *c'est du
chinois* (it's incomprehensible) reflects the European view of
them as an impenetrable sub culture, as does France's term
for red tape: *chinoiseries administratives*. Inability to speak or understand a language has inspired many epithets. The Russians

call the Germans *niemets*, meaning someone whose speech is unintelligible. The Finns' appreciation of the Russian tongue, meanwhile, is expressed in *puhua venäjää*, which means both to speak Russian and to fart. The French are notoriously touchy about how their language is spoken; they say of someone who speaks it really badly that they *parle français comme une vache espagnole* (speak French like a Spanish cow).

Everyone needs their whipping boys, someone to be their fall guy, the butt of their jokes. For the French and the Dutch it's the Belgians, about whom they tell the same jokes that the Germans tell about the Poles or the English about the Irish. *Tu es du belge ou quoi?* (Are you Belgian, or what?) means 'Are you thick?' One of the strangest French expressions is *Fume! C'est du belge!* (Smoke it – it's Belgian!), which, taking the cigar as a penis metaphor, means 'Suck my dick', but is used in the sense of 'Get lost'.

The English believe that the Irish are congenitally stupid, a conviction that an eight-hundred-year barrage of Irish confetti (bricks) and blows on the head from an Irish screwdriver (hammer) has done nothing to shake. Such is Irish contempt for the British, they haven't even bothered to think up any insulting names for them. They used to call them sassenachs but for the most part are content to call them Brits. The Irish reserve their worst barbs for those who have thrown in their lot with the Brits, whom they deride as West Brits and castle Catholics. Nearly as bad are *soupers*, who proselytized to the Protestant Church in exchange for soup during the famine of 1845–9, or *gombeen* men (literally usurers) who bleed the Irish on behalf of the ruling class, the Anglo-Irish, the type whom Brendan Behan dismissed as 'a Protestant with a horse'.

The English may think the Irish thick, but in Ireland it's people from the south-west corner, from Kerry, who are the butt of jokes. They're *culchies* (bumpkins), par excellence, although they're so called after the remote Co. Mayo town of

Coillte Mághach. In Germany the jokes are about the southern Swabians, in Italy about Neapolitans or anyone from the *mezzo-giorno*, the midday, as they call the south, in Greece about the Vlachs. To the southern Portuguese it's the northerners who are *salois* (bumpkins); to northerners it's the Alentejanos from the province above the Algarve, and for coastal dwellers it's the *transmontanos* who are the real hicks. Lisboans, who call people from Porto *tripeiros* (tripe eaters), say *Lisboa é Portugal o resto é paisagem* (Lisbon is Portugal, the rest is just scenery). And so it goes on: in Finland it's anyone not from Helsinki, in Denmark it's people from Århus or the *halv-svensker* (half-Swedes) from Bornholm.

City people have always looked down on their uncouth brethren from the boondocks, a term imported by American GIs from the Philippines; in the local Tagalog *bundok* means mountain. In Scotland the highlanders are dismissed as *teuchters*, in Italy the *zappaterra* or farm labourer is named after his hoe (*zappa*), while his Irish counterpart, the wretched *spailpín*, owes his name to his *spail* or scythe. Despite or perhaps as a result of this contempt, the idea of 'the back of beyond' has been a great source of inspiration to Europe's phrasemongers. The everyday French expression for this metaphorical wilderness is *en plein bled* (open desert), a North African import via Pied-Noir French, but there is also the picturesque *Tripatouille-les-Oies* which, in so far as it can be translated, means 'the place where they tamper with geese'. Italians, who love cowboy movies, talk about the *terrone* (peasants) who come from *nel far ovest* (the far west), regardless of geography. Most languages have hit on the concept of *am Arsch der Welt* (the arsehole of the world) but few have an expression as touching and as fanciful as the German *wo sich Fuchs und Hase gute Nacht sagen* (where the fox and hare bid one another goodnight).

But the prize has to go to the Spanish. Not only do they write off the remote parts of their country as *en el quinto coño* (at the fifth cunt), they also describe the back of beyond as *donde a Cristo se le cayó el mechero* (where Christ dropped his lighter). This is the very essence of Spain, the country that gave us on the one hand Ignatius de Loyola, founder of the Jesuits, and Torquemada the Grand Inquisitor, and on the other Salvador Dalí, doyen of surrealism, and Don Quixote, the heroic failure. Forget all this sun, sand and sangría; the Spanish tourist board should adopt this as their slogan. You can just see the posters: Spain – where Christ dropped his lighter. Spain could become the market leader in existential holidays. And the Portuguese could run a similar campaign under their equally bizarre expression for the sticks: *onde Judas perdeu as botas* (where Judas lost his boots). And for good measure, so could the Cubans, with the delightfully surreal *donde dios pintó a Perico y no alcanzó bicicleta* (where God painted St Peter and didn't get round to the bicycle).

Frogs and eyeties, *rosbifs* and *espingouins*. Sticks and stones, but names can always hurt you. Sometimes they stick, sometimes people become what you call them. Look at the Welsh, who were the original Britons, whose language King Arthur almost certainly spoke. And yet Wales is from *welisc*, the Saxon for foreigner; no wonder the Welsh prefer to call their country Cymru, the land of their *cymry*, or compatriots. Or the Gypsies, so called because they said they had come from Egypt. Gypsies and Jews need no other sobriquets; their very names are insults, but that's another chapter.

Most of the name-calling in this chapter has been relatively harmless, but it isn't always so. In Romance languages the word for 'stranger' also means foreigner, outsider. It has a clear 'them and us' dimension. So does the German *Ausländer*. Since the 1950s many new strangers have come to Europe – Turks, Indians, Africans and Arabs – 'guest' workers and former colonial subjects, some of whom are now second-generation Europeans. But there is a widespread reluctance, to put it mildly, to accept them as fellow Europeans. The Italian press has found a new name for them, a novel way of calling people black without saying so. They call them *extracomunitarios*, meaning from outside the European Community, which disregards the large number who are European citizens. The expression has caught on, but in shortened form. Now Italians, who were never shrinking violets when it came to racism anyway, have a dismissive if outwardly innocuous little word for the dark and unwelcome strangers in their midst. They call them *extras*.

12 ★ Skin-Deep

Our brotherhood is based on the fact that we are all black, brown, red or yellow. We don't call this racism, any more than you could refer to the European Common Market, which consists of Europeans, which means that it consists of white-skinned people . . . as a racist coalition.

Malcolm X. 1964

When the 1990 World Cup kicked off in Milan something strange happened. During the opening game between Argentina, the reigning champions, and rank outsiders Cameroon, the Italians all cheered on the African side and booed Argentina, saving their biggest jeers for the champions' star player Diego Maradona. After the match which, against the odds, the Africans won, the handful of Cameroon supporters who had made it to Milan weren't treated with the disdain usually reserved for *extras* and *culi neri* (black arseholes) but hailed as friends and heroes by the Italian *tifosi* (fans), a social group not renowned for racial tolerance.

Why? Because the fans were nearly all northern Italians and Maradona, when he wasn't playing for his country, played for the Italian club side Napoli, from the despised *mezzogiorno*, southern Italy. Thus, as the enemy of my enemy is my friend, the Africans had, by humiliating Maradona, jumped a few rungs on the ladder of prejudice and won a temporary home in the hearts of northern Italian *tifosi*. It's one of the curiosities of Italian football – and another indication of how little allegiance Italians feel towards the state – that in later games Napoli

fans supported Argentina and their beloved Maradona in preference to the Italian national side.

But football fans, and white people in general, are perfectly
capable of holding black individuals in reverence without it
affecting their fear and contempt of black people as a whole.
Whatever their local ethnic squabbles and national disputes,
Europeans are united in their antipathy towards dark-skinned
people and in their desire to exclude them from what's become
known as 'fortress Europe'. To its former colonies Europe says
au revoir and thanks for the memory. Oh, and thanks a million
for the raw materials and the cheap labour, but please forget
all that rash nonsense about being welcome in the mother
country, we simply haven't room. And yet, despite the fortress
mentality and Malcolm X's uncharacteristically parochial view
of Europe as an all-white continent, there are millions of black
people in Europe.

Europe's 'blacks' include Africans from all over the continent, Arabs, Afro-Caribbeans, Indians, Pakistanis, Moluccans
and Turks. In Britain, France, Belgium, Holland and Portugal
they represent an imperial legacy; in Germany and Scandinavia
they are largely 'guest workers' or refugees, likewise to some
extent in Italy and Greece. In Portugal, Spain and southern
Italy they are part of a continuum of relations with the Arab
world that stretches back centuries. In Portugal they also comprise the *retornados* from the former colonies of Angola and
Mozambique. But in every European country, any one of these
people will as likely as not be called, and forced to define
themself as, black.

Europe's blacks have no linguistic flag of convenience, no
equivalent of 'African-American', that they can fly. Black
Americans have defined themselves at various times since the
turn of the century as negro, coloured, black, African-
American or 'people of colour'. In a debate on racial terminology the Reverend Jesse Jackson said: 'Black tells you about

skin colour and what side of town you live on. African-American evokes discussion of the world.' Maybe, but at the same time many young urban blacks in the US have contributed to the debate by reviving 'nigger', which they use with a sort of bitter pride. Their attitude to the term African-American was voiced by the New York rapper KRS-1 who dismissed it as meaning 'not fully American but getting there very slowly'.

But no good is ever going to come of a vernacular based solely on skin colour. Even the word 'Creole', which leaves a better taste in the mouth than most, turns out to have a previous conviction as the Portuguese verb criar, meaning 'to bring up', and refers to a mixed-race African raised in the house of a white 'master'. 'Piccaninny', the once common generic for a black child, still heard as pickney among some Afro-Caribbeans, is also from the Portuguese pequenino (little child). Naughty Portuguese children are often scolded with the words preta, feia, má (black, ugly, evil) or pretinho de Guiné (little person from Guinea). As for kaffir, the standard white South African pejorative for black Africans, it comes from the Arabic kafir, meaning an infidel, in this case, a Christian.

The language of racism exhibits a depressing uniformity across the Union, and Europe's wits and word players haven't overheated their imaginations devising insults for blacks. In Sweden all blacks are svartskaller (black heads), in Denmark they're Afro-abe (Afro apes), in Germany eine Rolle Dachpappe (a roll of roofing paper). It doesn't get any better, believe me, whether the party in question is an African, Turk, Arab or – in the case of Britain – someone from the Indian sub-continent. Despite this lack of imagination, whites still invent far more epithets for blacks than vice versa. In Britain it's telling that black terms for whites in general and the police in particular are often one and the same, as with the now passé 'Babylon' and the current 'blue boys'.

In much of Europe the 'blacks' are Turks. Even before the Ottoman empire, Turks were maligned by everyone west of the Bosporus and they remain outsiders throughout the EU. In Greece they have an insult *Tourkóyiftos* (Turk-Gypsy) – handy for anyone who can't tell the difference. The Greeks also say of someone who's lost their temper that *eyine Toúrkos*, he became a Turk. Greece does at least have a historic quarrel with Turkey, but the Italians have little cause, given their own propensity to curse, to say *bestemmiare como un turco* (swear like a Turk). Even in Portugal they say *parece um turco* (like a Turk) of an ill-mannered or uncouth person, while in Spain *turca* is a byword for drunkenness.

In Sweden Turks have become the target of racist attacks and mounting right-wing violence, while in Denmark, where Turks are the largest foreign group, they call them *tyrkersvin* (Turkish swine). But it's in Germany where the hostility is most acute. Germany is now into its third generation of *Gast-arbeiter*, so-called 'guest workers', mostly Turks and Kurds, who comprise a significant but disfranchised part of the German working class. Since German unification there has been an upsurge of arson attacks on Turkish homes and businesses in which a number of people, often women and children, have been murdered. The German political right seems to have recruited the Turks to fill the role of scapegoat left vacant by the Jews. *Kruzi Türken!* (Crucify the Turks!) is an everyday exclamation, especially in Austria, roughly equivalent to 'Bloody hell!', and is just one example of how the old poison is recycled to nourish the new lies. *Negersau* (black pig) is another, redolent of the medieval *Judensau* (Jew pig).

In Spain the 'blacks' are the Moors, and to some extent the Gypsies. Fifteen hundred years ago the Visigoths, always on the look-out for more *Lebensraum* (living space), rolled down from Germany and elbowed the Romans out of Spain. Three hundred years later the Arabs looked across the Straits of Gibraltar and saw the northern Goths gone soft in the Andalusian sun and a country ripe for the picking. It took the Arabs, high on the newly minted faith of Islam, a mere two years to conquer all but the most inaccessible parts of Spain. As it took the Spaniards eight hundred years to complete the Christian *reconquista* of their country, they are understandably reticent on the subject of their Islamic and African background, even though it's apparent that what makes the Spanish such a handsome people is not the legacy of the blue-eyed Visigoths. Gazing into the dark pools of a pair of Spanish eyes – and there are worse ways of spending your time – it's not unusual to glimpse a ray of African sun. Nor is it difficult to discern among the Gypsy and Jewish elements of flamenco a singing style that ululates with Islam.

Castilian Spanish is full of Arabic; virtually the entire vocabulary of agriculture derives from it. And the common cry ¡Ojalá! (I wish!) is a corruption of *Inshallah* (If Allah wills it). But the expression *hay moros en la costa* (the Moors have landed i.e. the coast's not clear) betrays Spain's unease with its Islamic past. Nor does it have a high opinion of present-day Arabs. A jealous, possessive man is called *un moro*, but *el moro* is Moroccan hashish, which can be obtained by *bajarse al moro* (going down to the Moors). Throughout northern Spain, Portugal and Italy people from the south of the country are derided as 'Moroccans', although a large percentage of the citizens of Madrid, Lisbon and Turin are from the south or are the children of southerners. In northern Portugal they say *abaixo de Valongo são todos mouros* (everyone from south of Valongo is a Moor). The Marroquís themselves call each other *jai*, meaning brother.

As for the French, the fact that in the wake of the bombs planted in Paris by Algerian extremists in 1995 it was possible to deport over 10,000 Arabs without provoking an outcry speaks volumes about the hostility of the white French towards French Arabs. Not that *les nègres* from Côte d'Ivoire and France's

other former African colonies aren't subject to the same
racism, but Algeria and Morocco lie at the heart of France's
unfinished colonial business. Known pejoratively as *bicots* (kid
goats), *figuiers* (fig trees), *ratons* (young rats) and *sidi* (presumably from the name Said), French Arabs are subject to continual
racist attacks as well as official harassment from an openly
racist police force. For example, all branches of the French
police are bound by law to use the formal *vous* form when
addressing members of the public, but as a matter of routine
they address Arabs as *tu*, tantamount to calling them 'boy'. In
Mathieu Kassovitz's film *La Haine* (The Hatred) the young Arab
Seyid remarks after an uncharacteristically civil encounter with
a Parisian *flic*, 'Il m'appelle "vous" et tout!' (He called me *vous* and
everything!). In the slang known as *la tchatche* spoken by young
French Arabs, white people are dismissed variously as *fromagers*,
fromages blanc or *pots de yaourt*.

The colour *noir* has all the negative connotations in French
that it has in other languages but it is often distinct from *nègre*
(racially black). For instance, someone who is *complètement noir*
is blind drunk, while the patronizing *parler petit nègre* (speaking
little black) means pidgin French. But although it's possible
to see the thought processes behind calling a ghost writer un
nègre — because they do all the work — or a good red wine *une
négresse*, why a flea should also be *une négresse* is hard to fathom.
When in doubt the French retreat to the kitchen, which is
why a mixed marriage between Arab and non-Arab French is
called *couscous-pommes frites*.

Oppressed people, outsiders, the colonized, all feel a need
from time to time to speak in a code the 'enemy' can't understand. Sometimes, as with Romani and Yiddish or for many
European Turks and Arabs, they have recourse to another language. In other circumstances, as with Catalonia or the Basque
country under Franco, the Irish under British rule or the early
years of the black diaspora, speaking in one's mother tongue

posed a danger in itself, so any form of dissent had to be codified. In Ireland, because the British forbade the speaking of Irish, there emerged a tradition of poetry and song known as *aisling* in which political messages were delivered in the guise of love songs addressed to a woman. The woman, as all but the colonizers understood, was Ireland itself. As we've seen, before gay liberation gay men in Britain spoke Polari and even cockney rhyming slang may have arisen from a need to speak privately in front of the bosses.

The development of a private language by diaspora blacks in America and the Caribbean has led to a rich and fast-changing slang tradition which has been invigorating main-stream English since the early 1900s. Black street talk dates faster than any other argot and as a general rule by the time it's been picked up by the white world it's facing extinction in the black one. So when honkies (from the Wolof *honq*, meaning pink man) were diggin' hot music, the brothers were probably already rapping about cool, and when the ballheads got hip (also Wolof, *hipi*, to open one's eyes) to cool cats, the bloods were chillin' to some bad muthafucka. And so it goes on, as blacks, driven constantly to reinvent themselves and to stay one step ahead in a white world, scatter new words and nuances in their wake. Cool, for example, is cool in many languages, as are many other musical terms: jazz, gig, riff, and so forth. Every youth culture, from the beatniks onwards, has borrowed its slang from black American speech. Clarence Major, an authority on black American slang, remarks: 'African-American speech and slang form is, in a sense, one of the primary cutting edges against which American speech – formal and informal – generally keeps itself alive.'

An early form of secret language was pig Latin in which words were constructed by moving the first letter of the word to the end then adding 'ay'. So girl becomes *irlgay* and boy *oybay*. This is the origin of the now dated word for white people, *ofays*, which derives from 'foe'. Forms of patois serve the same purpose. The majority of black Britons of Afro-Caribbean descent, even those who have never set foot in the Caribbean, can speak patois. This form of English, based on an extremely broad Kingston ghetto dialect, is virtually unintelligible to the uninitiated. It allows black people to have private conversations in the presence of whites but among black men can also be fighting talk. In any stand-off or argument a sudden switch into patois, especially the use of the derogatory *bwoy*, signals that the stakes have been raised. Jamaican patois doesn't employ a specialized vocabulary. But what makes it impenetrable to outsiders is the broad accent, unorthodox sentence structure and some grammatical quirks such as sometimes saying 'I' for 'me' after a verb ('he cheat I') and 'me' for 'I' before one ('me cheat him'), 'we' for 'us' and 'ouno' for 'you lot'. Take, for example, this sample of dialogue from Victor Headley's *Yardie*:

'You ha fe believe we, D. The hit don't come from here, it's the truth.'

'So wha'? You soon tell me seh Blue nah work fe ouno again!'

Patois appears to have become broader and more enigmatic over the past twenty years, possibly as a reflection of the growing alienation of young blacks, and TV interviews with dance hall and ragga stars now carry subtitles as a matter of course. But some things endure and among the most common insults to emerge from the Caribbean are *raas clat* and *bumber clat*, both of which mean 'arse wipe'. Just as enduring but more unusual is *blood clat* (sanitary towel), a unique insult in English. The nearest thing to it is the American 'douche bag'. Afro-Caribbeans who talk dirty are often rebuked for their 'slackness', sometimes with a condemnatory *cho* or a dismissive 'tssk' sound produced by 'teeth kissing'. Both of these are probably of African origin and teeth kissing can be heard throughout the black diaspora.

The primary function of secret languages such as patois is to act as a code. But they also serve as an assertion of cultural identity and as a forlorn defence against cultural plundering. The rapid evolution of both black slang and black music reflects this need to keep something of their own. Black people are understandably resentful at the way in which what is probably their most distinctive contribution to Western culture, music, has from the very beginning been imitated and exploited to the benefit of white people. Thus early this century the (white) Original Dixieland Jazz Band made more money out of 'hot' jazz than King Oliver, whose music they merely copied; thus the white Benny Goodman became the key of swing and Elvis Presley the king of rock 'n' roll. And sax-playing President Bill Clinton appointed as his 'secretary of state for jazz' Kenny G, a white musician whose contribution to the development of jazz music is so small we must await the invention of instruments sensitive enough to measure it.

This isn't to say that there aren't white jazz musicians who are respected, even revered, by black players. But in the general run of things it's as though the world had decided that James Last's rendering of Mozart was better than the real thing. In *Black Nationalism and the Revolution in Music*, Frank Kofsky quotes an unnamed black be-bop musician who says, 'What can we do? We must go on inventing something new all the time. When we have it, the whites will take it from us, and we have to start all over again. It's as though we were being hunted.'

The supreme irony is that the principal consumers of rap music, the bleakest and blackest expression yet of the ghetto experience, are young middle-class white American males. This audience, which cruises the suburbs and small towns of middle America talking about 'bitches', slapping high fives and calling out 'Yo muthafucka', has identified itself so closely with black ghetto music that the term 'wigga' (white nigga) has been coined for them. The irony isn't lost on the rappers of Compton and Flatbush, but then nor are the royalty cheques. Thanks to rap music and the emergence of young African-American film-makers, 'motherfucker' has entered the American mainstream.

A word about motherfuckers, as we are bound to hear more of them in years to come. We've seen that insults concerning mothers are more or less unknown in northern Europe. However, typically 'Mediterranean' insults of the 'Your mama!' variety are common among African-Americans and Afro-Caribbeans. It seems likely that this is something that was brought over from Africa with slavery rather than something picked up by African slaves from Europeans. But older still is the form of ritualized insult, still practised by young black men, known as the 'dirty dozens' since 1620 and more recently as 'snaps', in which the participants trade insults about their mothers and sometimes other female relatives. The ritual originated among the Bantu and Yoruba but boys can be heard playing variations of it in the playgrounds of Britain and America. Similar games are played by boys in the Middle East, Turkey and in Mexico, where it's known as *albures* (puns).

In these games it's essential that, however strong the insults, they're not factually true, so that the process remains in the ritual domain. The exchanges, examples of which are featured in the film *White Men Can't Jump*, typically go something like this:

'Your mama like a police station, dicks going in and out all the time.'

'At least my mama ain't no cake, everybody get a piece.'

'At least my mama ain't no doorknob, everybody get a turn.'

'Your mama like a railroad track, laid all over the country.'

Less frequently the insults will focus on poverty, though again not if it is known for a fact that the opponent's family is going through especially hard times. These will run along the lines of, 'Your family so poor the rats and roaches eat lunch out', or 'Your mama so poor I saw her kicking a can down the street and I said, "What you doing?", and she said "Movin".' And so on in what, until the 1920s, was a pattern of twelve insults and retorts, hence the 'dozens', although this structure has fallen into disuse. The point is to show off your verbal skills while at the same time keeping your cool in the face of provocation.

Among Turkish boys the subject matter is the same but the insults must also rhyme. The boys have to show that they have mastered the traditional, set patterns while demonstrating an equal ability to extemporize, rather like a gymnast being marked for both technical excellence and artistry. Each boy portrays his opponent and his opponent's female relatives as wanton sexual receptacles. Failure at the game, even a failure to rhyme, casts the loser in the dreaded female role, that is, a passive homosexual. His opponent will seize this opportunity to say something particularly disgusting about his female relatives or to suggest that his opponent has been 'taking it up the arse' again. The purpose of these widespread rituals appears to be to enable boys to repudiate the female world of their mothers and so become 'men'. In any case, the 'dozens' have helped hone a particular fast-talking, sharp-shooting style of black talk that first came to the attention of the wider world on the lips of the then Cassius Clay, whose style of pre-fight bragging was straight out of the 'dozens' tradition. So, too, is the high-speed rhyming of rap and Jamaican 'toasting' and DJ styles.

Europeans like to think that the traffic across the Mediterranean was all southbound. It was Europeans, after all, who 'discovered' Africa, even if some Arabs had earlier made the northward journey and ruled large swaths of southern Europe for a few centuries. They left behind some pointed arches, a few words and some clever ideas about irrigation. But they also seem to have bequeathed this taboo on insulting a man's mother. If, as appears likely, this taboo travelled to America with slavery in the sixteenth century then plainly not only has it been around a long time, but it's as African as it is Arabic, and as Islamic as it's Catholic. But unfortunately this maternal link to Africa hasn't made southern Europeans any less racist than those in the north.

On this issue, at least, there is little to choose between Stockholm and Salerno. James Baldwin, who said that 'you can't tell a black man by the colour of his skin', argued that American identity was forged partly through 'white' immigrants – Poles, Italians, Irish, Jews et al – agreeing that, whatever their differences, they had this one important thing in common, something most of them hadn't even thought of before: they were 'white'. Of course they were no such thing; how can people as dissimilar as, say, a Latvian, a Sicilian, an Armenian and a Portuguese Jew all be lumped together as white? But it was another way of saying that they weren't black which, when it came to the crunch, was all that seemed to matter. It would be nice to think that in Europe we could find some other grounds for unity.

13 ★ Two For the Road

> If I am to be like him, who will be like me? And if I am
> only for myself, what am I? And if not now, when?
>
> Hillel the Elder, First-century rabbi

Gypsies and Jews have always occupied a special place in
people's hearts and have a niche of their very own in the
European vernacular. Both have the privilege of being bywords
for sharp practice and hard bargaining. The Welsh might object
that they, too, have been saddled with the same libel. However, you can welsh on a deal only in English, but you can
be gypped by a Jew, or words to that effect, in almost any
European tongue. Other pejoratives need not apply; vagabond,
bohemian, sheenie and kike – none have quite the sting of
the names themselves, Gypsy and Jew. Whatever their views
on the single currency or a common defence policy, there is
one thing on which everyone in Europe can agree: they don't
like Jews and they don't like Gypsies. They never have.

According to stereotype, the Gypsy who once would have
sold you a handsome and apparently healthy horse that
dropped dead the following morning will now sell you a
low-mileage, only-one-owner car that blows its big end a
hundred miles down the road. But compared to Jews, Gypsies
are strictly small time. A Gypsy might steal your car, give it
a quick respray, then sell it to someone in the next street. But
a Jew will lend you money to buy a sofa and then buy your
house from under you with the interest he's made on the
loan. The Gypsy in his oil-stained overalls might have

£20,000 in cash under the mattress but the Jew next door, who says he's an accountant, is part of a global conspiracy to take over the international banking system. And if a Gypsy steals your child it's only so they can put it out to beg; but if a Jew abducts one it's because they need the blood of a Christian child to bake matzos for Passover. But then everyone knows that.

Although their paths have often crossed, Gypsies and Jews have had little to do with each other. As wanderers, whether by choice or compulsion, they've plied many of the same, portable trades: horse trading, metal working, music. They have been persecuted and scapegoated almost since their arrival in Europe; blamed for the crucifixion, accused of causing plagues and poisoning wells. And of all the peoples in Europe, these two alone were singled out by the Nazis as *Fremdrassen* (alien races), whose sombre genes cast a shadow over the purity of the legions of blue-eyed *Übermenschen*.

'Anti-Semitism,' said Heinrich Himmler, head of the SS, 'is exactly the same as delousing. Getting rid of lice is not a question of ideology, it is a matter of cleanliness.' Before Germany assumed the role of Europe's ethnic housekeeper, there were ten million Jews in Europe. By 1945 there were only four million and today there are less than half that many. Jews formed Europe's largest minority, a role that has now fallen to the continent's eight million Gypsies. With character-istic thoroughness the Nazis conducted thousands of tests to establish a correlation between the proportion of Gypsy blood and a propensity to crime. It's touching how the Nazis always felt it necessary to establish the scientific basis of prejudice, lest anyone should think their genocidal frenzy was rooted in something more visceral, like hatred, for instance. The algebra of the Gypsy 'problem' worked out to the same solution as it had for the Jews and as many as 400,000 perished in the gas chambers. But it wasn't until 1982 that Chancellor Helmut

Schmidt acknowledged, on behalf of the German state, that Gypsies had been murdered under the racist Nuremberg laws.

The Nuremberg laws were designed to ensure racial purity but in this respect the Third Reich had least to fear from Jews and Gypsies. For centuries both peoples – in the face of overwhelming pressures to conform, convert and integrate – have been keeping their genes to themselves, doggedly resisting the temptation to intermarry with non-Gypsies (known as *gadje*) or *goyim*, non-Jews, from the Hebrew for 'nation'. But this separateness has only served to arouse suspicion and hostility, fuelled almost entirely, it seems, by these peoples' stubborn insistence on being themselves.

Gypsy is synonymous with untrustworthy and unreliable; a person without ties, a fly-by-night. In America a Gypsy cab is unlicensed; in Spanish *gitano* means dirty, oily or crooked, and someone who *estar hecho un gitano* (is like a Gypsy) is crafty and not to be trusted. In Portuguese to say someone is being a *cigano* means they're trying to con you. The entry for Gypsies in Diderot's famous *Encyclopédie* reads, 'Vagabonds who profess to tell fortunes by examining hands. Their talent is to sing, dance and steal.'

Gypsies have always been finding themselves on the wrong side of the law. This is reflected in the significant number of Romani and Caló words (Caló, the language of Spain's Gitanos, is a Romani-Castilian hybrid) borrowed by French and Spanish criminal slang. *Chouraver*, for example, common French slang meaning 'to steal', comes from the Romani *tchourover* while the Spanish *nicabar* (steal) is a direct lift from Caló. Whether the latter bears any relation to the English 'to nick' is doubtful. The Spanish slang for jail, *trena*, is also a direct borrowing, as is the French *chtib* or *schtar*, from *star mauri* (four walls). This is also the origin of 'stir', the British and American slang for prison. French slang *enchrister* (incarcerate) has nothing to do with Christ; it comes from *klistarja*, Romani for police. The Gypsies' perpetual battle with the police is further reflected in the French *bédi* (cops, from *beda*), and the direct French borrowing *adja* and Spanish *najarse*, both meaning to make yourself scarce.

In the 1970s and 1980s English TV scriptwriters sought to 'authenticate' the south London slang of programmes such as *The Sweeney* and *Minder* by injecting words of Romani origin such as *mui* (mouth) and *chor* (steal) which were in fashion at the time. They helped to popularize *div*, meaning stupid, which derives from the Romani *dinilo*, while dekko as in 'take a dekko' is probably from *dik* (look). However, the most common item of Romani-based English is that man's-best-friend word 'pal', from *phral* (brother). Other borrowings include lollipop, from the Romani for a red apple, and cosh, from *krash*, a stick. Another Romani word that enjoyed a long spell of popularity in English slang is *minge* (cunt), but it seems to have fallen into disuse. It mainly survives in the form of 'ginger minge', still a common epithet for a redhead.

But for as long as Gypsies have been run out of town as tricksters and thieves, they have also always exerted a romantic fascination on poets and artists and adolescents. Until the turn of the century many Europeans even persisted with the fantasy that the Spanish Gitanos were the Guanches, the original inhabitants of the Canary Isles, supposedly the last survivors of Atlantis. Gypsies have never been shy about cashing in on these fantasies and it may be that they perpetuated the myth that they had come from Egypt because they found that this was what the *gadje* wanted to believe. In fact, the Gypsies spread out from northern India about a thousand years ago. Romani, their language, is related to Hindi and some Romani speakers can to this day converse with Punjabis, although along the road the language has freely acquired bits of Farsi, Greek, Armenian and Germanic tongues. An analysis of Welsh Romani found it consisted of 60 per cent words of pre-European origin; 16 per cent English; 9 per cent Greek; 6 per cent Slavic; 4 per cent Welsh, with the remaining 5 per cent made up of Romanian, German and French.

The absence of Arabic in Romani suggests that not even the Gitanos, who call themselves Pharaoh's children, had spent any time in Egypt, but that's how they got the name Gypsy and it's stuck. The people themselves don't have a word meaning Gypsy. In England and America they used to call themselves Romanichal, from *rom* meaning 'man', but these days are more likely to refer to themselves as either Gypsies or travellers. Elsewhere they simply call themselves 'black' – *calé* in Spain, *kaale* in Finland – whence Shakespeare's Caliban, from *kaliben* (darkness). In France they are *manouches* (related to the Sanskrit *manusha*, people) *gitans* or *tziganes*, from the Greek *athingani* (heathen). Unlike Jews, for whom religion is the historic wellspring of identity, Gypsies have always adopted the religion of the host nation, not that it helped them escape religious persecution. For centuries in Germany and Holland *Heiden* (heathen) was synonymous with Gypsy.

When Israeli prime minister Yitzhak Rabin was assassinated in 1995 President Clinton greeted the news with the words 'Shalom chaver, goodbye friend'. *Chaver*, a friend in both Yiddish and Hebrew, is very close to the Romani *chavo*, a boy, which has been borrowed by Spanish as *chaval*. It's possible this entered the Romani of the German (Sinti) Gypsies via Yiddish but, in the absence of written records, whatever evidence there was of such cross-fertilizations perished at Auschwitz. One place they wouldn't have picked it up, however, was Palestine, despite the popular Gypsy myth that they are the descendants of the sons of Cain, condemned in Genesis to the life of 'a fugitive and a vagabond'. The credibility of this myth is enhanced by the fact that Jabal, Jubal and Tubal-cain were employed in the typically Gypsy trades of nomadic herdsman, musician and metalworker and that Cain is the Hebrew and Aramaic word for blacksmith.

Another myth devised to explain the Gypsies' wanderings is reminiscent of the medieval tale of the Wandering Jew who, because he insulted Christ as he carried the cross up Calvary, was condemned to roam the earth until the Day of Judgement. In this myth a Gypsy blacksmith forges the nails for the crucifixion but the Roman soldiers are too impatient to wait for the fourth nail to cool and leave it behind at the smithy. The Gypsies, it's claimed, have been running from this nail ever since. On the other hand, it's said that they're blessed because they forged only three nails, thus minimizing the Redeemer's suffering. As there is no reason to believe that there were any Gypsies in Palestine at the time of the crucifixion it's more likely that their religious persecution stems from the long association between blacksmiths and the devil.

In Isabel Fonseca's *Bury Me Standing*, a study of east European Gypsies, she cites two stories that 'explain' why the Gypsies have no 'book' or religion of their own. In one story, from Bulgaria, they say that when God was handing out religions they wrote theirs down on cabbage leaves which, in a careless moment, were eaten by a donkey. A Romanian version has it that the Gypsies built a stone church while the Romanians built one of ham and bacon. The Gypsies haggled, did a swap, and promptly ate the church.

There's no such thing as 'bad language' in Romani. This isn't to say that nothing's taboo, far from it: the entire subject of sexual relations and bodily functions is heavily tabooed. But there are few euphemisms, except for some bodily functions, and if something is not to be mentioned it's generally not because the word itself is 'bad' but because the subject should not be raised. For example, *minge* is neither a good nor a bad word, but the only word. However, it's extremely difficult to establish how much Gypsies swear. The problem is that most of those who are interested in such matters tend to be *gadje*, that is to say outsiders. Gypsies, who have good reason to be suspicious of outsiders, don't feel under any obligation to tell *gadje* the truth. So attempts to find out how Gypsies really behave seem to be governed by Heisenberg's uncertainty principal, only applied to people rather than electrons, in that it's impossible to tell what influence the investigation is having on the subject's behaviour.

Gypsy men, as we've seen, will say *Ha miro kar* (Suck my dick) and might also say *Dav ti dakery minge*, literally, 'I take your mother's cunt', both of which locate them in the main-stream of male European swearing. But sexual taboos and ritual purity make sexual swearing a perilous pursuit. In a manner redolent of some Indian castes and of Orthodox Jews, many groups of Gypsies have a strict and elaborate code of purity and the worst thing that can befall a Gypsy is to become *marimé* (unclean). Taboos attach to people, food and topics of conversation. But the real threat comes from the uncleanness of women. Everything associated with a woman's lower body is considered *marimé* and potentially defiling. These include genitalia, bodily functions, underwear, skirts and allusions to sex and pregnancy. Basins, towels and soaps for the two body zones should be kept separate and clothing may not be washed in the same bowl as cooking utensils and crockery. These restrictions are even more strictly applied, among some Romany groups, to a woman during puberty, menstruation, pregnancy and immediately after childbirth. In a strict house-hold she may not cook or serve food to men at such times.

But although the sexes are segregated in public and women have little prestige, for some groups of Gypsies the mere threat of defilement confers a certain power on them. Angus Fraser says in his book *The Gypsies*: 'For a Gypsy to be declared polluted is the greatest shame a man can suffer, and along with him his household. It is social death, for the condition can be passed on: anything he wears or touches or uses is polluted for others.' No wonder, then, that Gypsies have always eschewed intimate contact with *gadje*, who are almost certainly *marimé*, when such contact could result in ostracism or even banishment. This code of purity, therefore, informs all interaction between the sexes and between Gypsy and *gadje* and must certainly influence the degree and type of swearing among Romany people.

This tendency to keep to their own is true even among those Gypsies who have stayed in the same place for generations. Greek, Spanish and Portuguese Gypsies, for example, have shown little enthusiasm for the nomadic life and have stayed put, though not without some encouragement. In the eighteenth century, in Habsburg Europe, Spain and Portugal, legislation forced Gypsies into a more sedentary life and the Gitanos of Spain and Portugal have scarcely moved since. Something similar happened in the 1950s in the then Eastern Bloc countries which, starting with Poland, began forcing Gypsies to follow a settled lifestyle in what has become known as the Great Halt. Worse was to come, however, with the collapse of the Eastern Bloc governments in 1989, since when Gypsies have increasingly been subjected to arson attacks, violence and even murder. Attacks on Gypsies in Hungary, Romania and other eastern European countries have become commonplace as people unnerved by political instability take comfort in the ancient hatred of Gypsies. And they've dragged down from the attic that other trusty scapegoat: the Jews.

In 1516 the Venetian Senate ruled that Jews, previously forbidden to spend the night in the city, could live together on an island within the Laguna Veneta. The name of the island was Ghetto Nuovo, meaning 'new foundry'. In due course the term 'ghetto' was applied to the Jewish quarter in Rome. Ghettos, real and of the mind, have marked the road travelled by European Jewry, a journey that has been conjugated as: 'You shall not live among us as Jews. You shall not live among us. You shall not live.'

Jews have been called just about everything but no one calls them quitters. From the flight from Egypt to the scattering of the Twelve tribes it's been wall-to-wall trouble. Expelled en masse from Britain in the thirteenth century; from Spain at the end of the fifteenth; subjected to waves of pogroms in Russia and Poland in the nineteenth; and then, just when they had become integrated into all levels of central European life, the normally sensible Germans become convinced by some piss-and-wind son of an Austrian customs official that the Jews are the cause of all their troubles. And the sky fell in. All this and still the Jews go on being Jews, even though these days only a minority believe in the Jewish raison d'être, that they are God's chosen.

Leaders of Europe's Jewish communities regularly sound the alarm that through secularism and intermarriage Jews are close to succeeding where Hitler failed and are bringing about their own extinction. I doubt it. If the Basques and the Bretons can't be persuaded to forget who they are, why should the Jews? Of course it would be logical to assimilate, but when wasn't it? It's been clear from the first page of this book that Europeans are very assertive about their identity and in this respect Jews – who, heaven knows, have had every incentive to renounce theirs – are no different. Take this story. In 1917, entirely by chance, a community of marranos (converted Jews) was discovered in the village of Belmonte in a remote region of northern Portugal. They knew no Hebrew, said prayers in Portuguese and had adopted as their 'patron saint' Esther, the Biblical figure who had concealed her true (Jewish) identity in order to save the Jews from being massacred by the Persians. These Belmonte Jews had been practising their religion, or what they could remember of it, in secret since 1536, when forced conversion began under the Portuguese Inquisition, and believed they were the last Jews left on earth. Some people just can't seem to forget who they are.

Like the Gypsies, the Jews have been cast alternately as Europe's devils or its thieves, often both at once. And if a Gypsy forged the nails for the crucifixion, no one seems to be in any doubt that it was a Jew who hammered them in. Christ, of course, was a Jew. You have to laugh; Jesus, the great Christian icon, the 'anarchist who succeeded', in Malraux's words, a Jew. There's a church in northern Italy, in Lucca, whose pride and joy is a life-size wooden figure of Christ allegedly carved by an eyewitness to the crucifixion. And there he is, Christ the Redeemer, as Jewish as pastrami on rye, the spit of Dustin Hoffman in fact, only taller.

Jews are a barrel of laughs. In between pogroms there's nothing a Jew likes better than to crack a few jokes. They've produced a few funny guys in their time: the Marx Brothers, Mel Brooks, Woody Allen, Billy Crystal, Ben Elton, Alexei Sayle, Bette Midler, Phil Silvers, Zero Mostel, Marty Feldman, Danny Kaye and Lenny Bruce all make the short list. Surely at least one of them must have made just about everyone laugh at least once. So you might imagine that there would be some expression like 'funny as a Jew' or 'Jew wit'. Afraid not, they're all about money, money-lending and money-grubbing. Forget the funny guys. Forget, for that matter, Mahler, Mendelssohn, Pissarro and Chagall; never mind Gershwin, Rodgers and Hart, Bob Dylan or Carol King; who cares about Chomsky, Einstein, Mendeleyev or Marx? Europe is agreed, a Jew is wedded to his wallet. The Rothschilds, the Reichmann brothers, Goldman Sachs – these are the real Jews.

Even in Ireland, hardly a Jewish stronghold, they say of someone from Co. Cavan, whose citizens are allegedly tight with money, that 'When a Cavan man goes to Dublin, two Jews leave'. Jews are tight, Jews are mean, Jews drive the hardest bargains on earth, Jews are shysters. Speaking of which, a number of etymologists have gone to considerable lengths to show that 'shyster', an American term for a crooked lawyer, is of Yiddish or even Romani origin. One even resorted to inventing new Jewish names to strengthen his case. Now it's true that Jewish lawyers aren't exactly thin on the ground, especially in the US, and undoubtedly some of them are shysters. They are well able to defend themselves and don't need nor in many cases deserve any help from me. But for the record, the word shyster derives not from Yiddish, nor from Romani, but from the German *Scheißer*, a worthless, unpleasant person – a shit, to be precise.

This correlation between Jews and meanness hasn't exactly overtaxed the imagination. If you travel by Jewish airlines, you walk, people who are very close are 'as thick as two Jews on payday', while 'Jewish foreplay' is where one partner pleads for sex and the other refuses. In 1995 the Broadcasting Standards Council rebuked Henry Blofeld, a BBC cricket commentator, for referring to spectators watching the Test match for free from a vantage point outside the ground as being in the 'Jewish stand'.

The French have gone to the trouble of making a verb out of juif (Jew) so they can say *juivolver* (overcharge), although this is falling into disuse, and the Italian *truffare* (to cheat) is interchangeable with 'to Jew'. The Germans still say *Nur keine jüdische Hast* (There's no Jewish hurry i.e. no big rush), whatever that's supposed to mean, and why the French should call the funny bone *le petit juif* is beyond me. As for the Spanish, you'll find *judías* (Jewesses) on any menu, and what you'll get is a plate of beans. In Portuguese *judiação* means ill-treatment and *Que judiaria!* means 'How cruel!', both of which are echoed in the Spanish *una judiada*, an act of extreme cruelty. That's unless the *judiada* occurs in the world of finance, where it means – what else? – extortion. Spain's Jews were banished en masse in 1492, and the edict denying them right of residence had been in force for nearly five hundred years when Franco finally revoked it. But by then the double meaning of *marrano*, a converted Jew and a pig, had taken root in the language.

Ladino, the language that was spoken by Spain's Jews, is close to extinction, although with languages it's best never to say die. Irish was all but dead until the late nineteenth century, and until a few years ago Romani was thought to be in grave danger. And Hebrew, revived as the national language of Israel, was already virtually defunct at the time of Christ. But Ladino – a Castilian-Hebrew hybrid – has left little trace in Spanish, although the word for an informer, *malsín*, comes from the Hebrew via Ladino *malshin*. As for Yiddish, a blend of German, Hebrew and Aramaic, it was spoken by more than ten million Europeans before 1939. Now there are perhaps two million worldwide. Even this is a vague figure as the majority of today's Yiddish speakers are Hasidic Jews who obey the Biblical proscription on census-taking and whose numbers can therefore only be guessed at.

Yiddish had a considerable influence on European languages, especially German. The Nazis didn't manage, or didn't get round to, purging German of Yiddish, of which numerous traces remain. One of the most striking is that in parts of what was East Germany people refer to a stuck-up, haughty woman as a *shiksa*, apparently unaware that it's the Yiddish pejorative for a non-Jewish woman. In Bavaria they call empty talk *Schmuser*, from the Yiddish *schmouss* (chatter, now *shmooz* in Amero-Yiddish) and call a snug bar a *Beisel*, from *bajis*, Yiddish for a little house. These and many other words survive in the language, the talkative ghosts of German Jewry.

Yiddish surfaces in French slang in words such as *schpileur* (from *spieler*) for a gambler, *teuche* (cunt) from *tochis* (buttocks). It's also the source of the international argot for heroin, 'smack', from the Yiddish *shmeck* (sniff). But Yiddish has left little trace on English on this side of the Atlantic. It's possible that the cockney slang 'put the mockers' on something, meaning to upset a plan, comes from *makkes* (plagues) or that the east London habit of calling someone 'mush' derives from the common Jewish name Moshe, the way the generic Scot or Irishman is called Jock or Paddy. More likely this is a direct borrowing from the Romani *mush* (a man). 'Drack', Australian slang for an unattractive woman, probably comes from the Yiddish *dreck*, literally excrement but more generally 'trash'. But otherwise Yiddish has made its greatest impact on American English. Some of this vocabulary, like most things American, has started making the return voyage to Britain.

Thanks to Jewish-American comedians Yiddish terms such as *shmuck* or *shlock* have become household words, indeed *shmuck* has provided non-Jewish Americans with an acceptable euphemism for 'prick'. But the American idiom has also absorbed a manner of speaking that is characteristically Yiddish. Whenever someone says 'get lost', 'who needs it?' 'you should be so lucky' or 'excuse the expression', they are speaking Yiddish in translation, or Yinglish if you like. As they are when they say 'it shouldn't happen to a dog', 'I should worry', 'so what else is new?', 'I should have such luck', or 'I need it like a hole in the head'. More clearly Yiddish are heavily ironic idioms such as 'him you like?' or 'I should care'. So, too, such forms as 'may God strike me down' as an assurance that one is telling the truth, reflecting Jews' superstition about both naming the deity and wishing death on anyone. Telling a Jew to fuck off is rude; telling them to drop dead is unforgivable.

That other ancient Jewish tendency, of answering one question with another, evidently rubbed off on New York's Italians when the two were living cheek-by-jowl on Manhattan's Lower East Side. The sort of improvised dialogue spoken by actors such as Al Pacino and Robert De Niro is as Yiddish as it's Italian. You know the routine, it goes something like: 'You wanna eat?' 'Do I wanna eat?' 'Yeah, that's what I'm asking you, you wanna eat?' 'I hear you, hey, am I deaf?' 'Are you deaf? I dunno are you deaf. All I'm asking is do you wanna eat?' 'You're asking me, at a time like this, for Christ's sake, do I wanna eat?' 'Well, do you?' 'Well, hey, do *you*?' The protagonists will then proceed to argue loudly and pointlessly until the one who was originally asked the question will wrap up the scene with the line: 'What the hell, let's eat.' Brilliant. Hey, who needs scriptwriters already?

The handful of feckless Jewish immigrants who failed to become America's slum landlords or merchant bankers went on instead to invent Hollywood, Broadway, Tin Pan Alley and, let's face it, American show business. This has lately been revealed as a Jewish-Masonic plot to insinuate Yiddish words into the American vernacular, because you can't possibly succeed in show business if you don't have a vocabulary that includes to *kibbitz* (comment) or *kvetch* (whine). You have to be able to distinguish between sentimental *shmaltz* (literally chicken fat), which generally sells well, give or take the odd *glitch* (slide), and out and out *shlock* (rubbish), which is more risky. And the real art in showbiz is knowing how to *shmooz*, because if you can't, no one's going to pay any attention to your *shtik* (performance). Above all you've got to have *chutzpah*, pronounced 'hootzpah', a specialized variety of barefaced cheek. *Chutzpah* has been defined as the quality shown by a man who, having murdered both his parents, throws himself upon the mercy of the court because he's an orphan.

Jews appear to have been assimilated into American society along with all the other European immigrants. No political party is poised to sweep to power on a platform built on the assertion that Debra Winger or Barry Manilow is polluting the race or poisoning the water supply, for example. Nor, for all the sleazy tales of casting couches and cocaine binges, have there been any rumours of Hollywood moguls baking the blood of McCauley Culkin or any other Christian child star into their matzos. But then this was the level of integration and acceptance many Jews thought they'd achieved in Germany, France and Poland before the rise of the Nazis. Things change and, as they like to say in America, shit happens. While it may not have a large constituency in America, anti-Semitism didn't get left behind in the old country. As for America's Gypsies, the old stereotype of dirty, thieving and untrustworthy has followed them across the Atlantic like a lousy, unwanted dog.

And what of the old country? For the time being western European racism has focused its attention on the new 'strangers in our midst' – Turks, Arabs and Afro-Europeans. But in the East it's a different story. Unsure of what to expect under the new regimes after the Cold War's simple fare, eastern Europe is reheating its leftover hatreds and smacking its thin lips on the old certainties. Among them, Gypsies and Jews, Europe's bad blood brothers and favourite scapegoats. The old prejudices are still proving the best. Bohemians, vagabonds, bloodsuckers, rootless cosmopolitans. Plus ça change. As the Yiddish saying goes: 'Fear God, beware of people.'

14 ★ A Common Currency

> The poor have to labour in the face of the majestic equality
> of the law, which forbids rich and poor alike from sleep-
> ing under bridges, begging in the streets and stealing
> bread.
>
> Anatole France

Money, James Baldwin concluded, is like sex – having it leaves
you free to think about something else. Those who do have
it never tire of assuring us that love and happiness are not
among the things money can buy. A European, and an Englishman in particular, will add that another thing it can't buy is
class. In America, where Mammon is God, success is everything and no one gives a hoot about class. The main thing in
America is to make sure you're white. Class is just a pretentious
bauble worn by a handful of old families on the East Coast.
But for many Europeans, breeding counts for more than
wealth, even if this means being banished to the shallow end
of the gene pool. Better, they say, to be well-bred and down
at heel than vulgar but rich. You can always spot the real *crème
de la crème* because they manage to be well-bred, vulgar and
rich all at once.

It's hardly surprising that this obsession with class cuts little
ice in America. It was precisely to escape this mentality and its
consequences that so many Europeans, those 'huddled masses
yearning to breathe free, the wretched refuse of your teeming
shore' to whom the Statue of Liberty beckons, said 'no thank
you' to poverty, genteel or otherwise, and washed up on Ellis
Island. The rags to riches story is the essence of the American

dream. It is the confirmation that America remains an open society, the land of the brave and the home of the free – whatever the evidence to the contrary. When someone makes good in America everyone cheers. But in Europe we sneer at upstarts and parvenus. Even the Italians, who love money so much they deliberately retain a worthless currency so that street sweepers can call themselves millionaires, dismiss someone nouveau riche as *un pidocchio rifatto*, a reconstructed louse. But in Italy, where appearance is considerably more important than reality (some would say it is reality), the line between wealth and class is often blurred.

Among those Europeans who spurned America's charms and stayed behind to mind the monuments, the English and the French are probably the most class conscious, the Scandinavians the least. For Germans and citizens of the Benelux countries, poverty tends to be either denied or ignored, ostentation disdained, and a stolid burgherdom extolled as the cardinal social virtue. Some of us still have monarchies and this tends to provide a life support system for the sort of aristocratic remnants who fill the pages of *Hello!* magazine. In the Netherlands and Belgium the monarch is little more than a cake decoration; in Denmark, for God's sake, the royal family ride bicycles, while in Spain, where democracy is still a novelty, the king acts as its unofficial custodian. But in Britain, a nation that managed to transform itself into a social democracy and come through an industrial revolution with its feudal aristocracy unscathed, class is everything.

Every interaction between English people is informed by class. When English people open their mouths, both accent and grammar say where, economically, educationally and geographically, they're from – or pretend or aspire to come from. This is a peculiarly English trait. With, say, a French or Spanish person, their accent might betray what region they come from but it says relatively little about their class or level of education.

This is because most Europeans, regardless of their circumstances, speak their own language more or less correctly
whereas the overwhelming majority of native English speakers
speak what is technically 'bad' English. For example, thanks
to edicts laid down arbitrarily by some eighteenth-century
grammarians, the double negative is a no-no in English. But
the fact is that from Altrincham to Alabama the double negative
comes naturally to the English tongue.

In Italy, where nearly everyone speaks a regional dialect in
addition to the national language, accents vary enormously.
But wherever they come from, Italians share the same preoccupation with *la bella figura* which, while it means 'cutting a good
figure', has as much to do with saving face. Italians will go
to great lengths and considerable sacrifice to avoid the *brutta
figura* that results from being either *scaciato* (badly dressed, a
loser) or worse still, perceived as *miserabile* or *poveracci* (dirt
poor). In Italy, if you don't belong among i *ricchi* (the rich),
you are expected to have the decency to look as though you
do. Italians suffer from an almost Japanese dread of losing
face. Like the Japanese they will agree to arrange or provide
things that they know perfectly well they can't arrange or
provide. They do so not because they're congenital liars but
because to admit the truth is to make the dreaded *brutta figura*.
This is also what lies behind the national resistance to admitting errors. The words 'I'm sorry, I made a mistake' are rarely
uttered, whether in regard to taking a wrong turning or
accepting a bribe of a few *miliardi*.

It appears that there are two ways to get on in Italy. One
is to have *molto culo* (a lot of arse), that is, to be very lucky,
and maybe a bit *furbo* (roguish). There's always a chance that
through *una culata bestiale*, a great stroke of luck, but literally a
colossal (bestial) arseful, you will find yourself up among the
elect, i *pezzi grossi* (big shots). The other way to succeed is to
be *un figlio di papa* (a daddy's boy), a much-used expression to

indicate a person who doesn't really have to make an effort because they will in due course move into their father's business or profession. The fact that a *figlio di papa* is effectively guaranteed his place in the sun is part of what lies behind the tales of professional incompetence, all those horror stories of patients entering Italian hospitals for routine surgery and emerging as quadriplegics. But then you couldn't expect qualified surgeons to admit they were unsure of a medical procedure. *Che brutta figura!*

The drawback to being a *figlio di papa* is that you still have to go out to work. Much better to be born with a silver spoon in your mouth or *con una flor en el culo* (with a flower up your arse), as they say in Spain. Then you don't have to do a damn thing because you have a *Ph.G.*, an ironic Yiddish abbreviation of *papa hot gelt* (daddy has money). The French call such a man *un fils d'archevêque* (an archbishop's son), someone whose father *a du piston* (has influence). As they say in Sicily: *Comandare è meglio di fottere* (Ruling is better than fucking). But you won't find such expressions among the doggedly egalitarian Swedes and Danes. Two things Swedes and Danes will tell you: 1. They live in a classless society. 2. In general only uneducated people resort to swearing. There seems to be a contradiction here; if the society is classless there must be equality of opportunity, including equality of educational opportunity. So who are all these foul-mouthed, ill-educated people? Did they drop out of school simply in order to pursue a vernacular career?

Young Danes are schooled not just in the law of the land but in a moral code known as the *janteloven*. What this amounts to is a series of ten homilies designed to remind anyone who's getting a bit big for their boots that one Dane is as good as another. The first states *Du skal ikke tro, du er noget* (You shouldn't think that you are something). They proceed in this vein to number four which reminds you that *Du skal ikke bilde dig ind, at du er bedre end os* (Don't get it into your head that you're better than us) and so on until the tenth wraps it up with the encouraging *Du skal ikke tro, du kan laere os noget* (Don't imagine you can teach us anything). Discouraging arrogance and social distinction is a worthy project, but the side effect of the *jante-loven* is a pressure to conform which many young Danes understandably find rather stifling.

Dubliners ironically dub the toffs 'the quality' but the Germans are more precise and call them *die oberen Zehntausend* (the top ten thousand). Inevitably the French, who never stray far from the kitchen, call them *le gratin* (the topping). These people, *les grosses légumes* (the fat vegetables), don't have to *travailler pour les haricots* (work for beans), and just watch the world go by as they're driven around in their *légumiers* (limousines). Say what you like about what money can't buy, life seems a lot easier for those who *ont de la galette* (have got the pancake, i.e. are loaded) than for the rest of us who can only dream of finding *un gentil petit fromage* (a nice little earner). We've seen that the Greek *malakas* is related to the winnowing of grain, but in France when you're *fauché comme les blés* (winnowed like the corn), you're well and truly skint. When you're that poor the Spanish would say *no tienes ni mierda en las tripas*, you haven't even got shit in your guts. But even in the direst straits the French follow their stomachs and if they have to *prendre le café du pauvre* (drink poor man's coffee), so be it. This expression has very little to do with coffee, indeed coffee doesn't come into it at all. You drink poor man's coffee when you're too broke to go out to a restaurant and have to stay at home and make your own entertainment. This is how it's done: cook dinner at home, eat it, make love. *Et voilà!* That's what is meant by poor man's coffee.

No one likes a skinflint, a *Geldarsch* (gold arse); even the Danes hate a *fedte røv* (sticky arse), the sort of person of whom B. B. King sang that 'if he had a doughnut he wouldn't give you the hole'. You know the sort, a real *pisse-vinaigre* (vinegar pisser), someone who has *les poches plus longues que les bras* (pockets longer than his arms). Corsicans say *Hà i zini in istacca* (He's got sea urchins in his pocket), a nice way of explaining his reluctance to put his hand in there. Thrift isn't a great virtue in Spain, either, where the tightfisted are mocked these days as *gastar menos que Tarzán en corbatas* (spending less than Tarzan does on neckties).

There's a Yiddish saying that *Got hot lib dem oreman un helft dem nogid* (God loves the poor and helps the rich), but irony aside, mystics from Buddha to John the Baptist have extolled the virtues of poverty. The Bible is at pains to point out how tough it is for a rich man to get past the bouncers on heaven's gate and that the meek will inherit the earth, though presumably not before the assertive have made themselves comfortable elsewhere. And if fortune hasn't smiled on you, you should not, as the fatalistic Irish are fond of saying, make a *béal bocht* (poor mouth) about it. This making a virtue of poverty is encapsulated in a Basque expression, one of those sayings that reminds you that you can never really understand someone else's culture: *Aberatsa, aberatsa infernuko legatza; pobre, pobrea zeruko lorea* (A rich man is a hake from hell; the poor, the flower of heaven). The Basques are very dependent on fishing so a hake from hell is probably no laughing matter. Big fish, fat fish, more than any other beast the rich are associated with fish; the poor with lambs. These are just two of the many creatures in the European bestiary. If it's all right with you, I'll begin with the camels.

15 ★ Inside the Beast

> To God I speak Spanish, to women Italian, to men French,
> and to my horse – German.
>
> Charles V, King of Spain 1516–56

At no time did camels roam where Stockholm now stands. Nor have fossil remains been found under the vaulted cellars of Heidelberg, nor even in the sandy soil of the Portuguese Algarve. There is no evidence whatsoever that camels have ever run wild anywhere in Europe. So why does a German say *Ich Kamel!* to mean 'Silly me!', when the French *Quel chameau!* means 'What a bitch!'? How did a camel, this beast that's never lived here outside a zoo, become Gitano slang for a con artist, Spanish for a drug dealer, Italian for ugly, Portuguese for henpecked and Swedish for a waiter?

If we've managed to get ourselves into a state of confusion over camels at least we're of one mind when it comes to pigs. Winston Churchill said he liked pigs because, unlike dogs who look up to us and cats who look down on us, pigs treat us as equals. But as a rule no one has a good word to say about them. Call someone a pig anywhere in Europe and it means the same thing: a vulgar, dirty and generally unpleasant person. In Italy they are also associated with excessive or unusual sexual appetites, and with shameful acts, or *porcate*. An Italian says *mi ha fatto una gran porcata* (I've committed a huge *porcata*) when they've made some terrible gaffe. Second-rate or badly made things are also *porcate*. When Germans aren't eating pigs they're talking about them. Pigs form a staple part of the

German vernacular. If you're stumbling home at four in the morning in Manchester there's 'not a soul' about, in Bordeaux *il n'y a pas un chat* (there isn't a cat), but in Düsseldorf there's *kein Schwein* (not a pig); not even a *doofes Schwein* (fool), a *linkes Schwein* (left pig, i.e. a traitor) or a *schwules Schwein* (gay pig, in the homosexual sense). In Germany you read about scandals in a *Schweineblatt* (pig sheet) and might well comment that *das Buch besteht nur aus Schweinen* (this book is utter filth) if presented with a volume of *Schweinefotos* (pornographic photos). And if you can *den inneren Schweinehund überwinden* (overcome that inner pig-dog, i.e. weakness) you might just *Schwein haben* (have some pig, that is, some luck). Everyone knows that pigs aren't kosher but that didn't stop medieval Germans decorating their churches with a motif known as the *Judensau* (Jew pig) depicting a sow suckling Jews, which pretty well speaks for itself. Germans don't call the cops pigs but the English have for at least two hundred years, not just since Flower Power and the Black Panthers. The Finns call them pigs (*sika*), too.

There's a Yiddish expression for a shifty person who is trying to pass themself off as honest, *Chazer kosher fissel*, the pig shows off its kosher foot, but perhaps pigs don't deserve the bad press they've had. God denounces the pig as unclean in both Genesis and Leviticus and 1,500 years later Allah gives Mohammed the same message, although why has never been satisfactorily explained. The discovery in the nineteenth century that undercooked pork caused trichinosis (a sometimes fatal condition caused by larvae living in the meat) led to claims that the ancient prohibition had a sound medical basis. But this seems to overlook the fact that undercooked beef or poultry can be just as injurious and, bearing in mind the shortage of refrigerators in Biblical times, a health-conscious deity surely would have gone the whole hog and preached vegetarianism.

Pigs, you see, have a problem, not just a personal hygiene problem, but a design fault. Contrary to the popular saying, they don't sweat. So in order to save their bacon they need to cover themselves in whatever comes to trotter to protect their highly photosensitive and relatively hairless skin. In the hot sun and dry earth of the Middle East they would have found little with which to protect themselves except their own faeces. This unattractive garb might well have put God and Allah off pork for life.

Probably through a reluctance to cast any more of His pearls before swine, the Almighty hasn't shared His thoughts or recipes with anyone for some time, so until further notice Muslims and Jews continue to avoid the pig while everyone else badmouths the beast but eats it just the same. In Ireland there's an expression for when some irritating person has just left the room: *Nár chasfaidh tú, a sclíteach* (May you not turn round, o castrated pig!) though in Germany *Haksch* (castrated pig) is what you call a cheeky young boy. But not everyone hates pigs. In New Guinea they are revered and are the subject of extravagant cult rituals. But as New Guinea hasn't applied to join the EU, you'll have to read about that somewhere else.

There is some consensus elsewhere in the European farmyard. Anyone craving a white horse, for example, is understood to be a heroin addict in most of the Union. Goats, as we've seen, have a reputation for promiscuity but a Greek goat, a *trayos*, also signifies a priest or indeed any bearded man, while an unattractive woman is a *katsika* (nanny goat). However, while we all agree that donkeys are stubborn beasts, the assertion that *home casat burro espatllat* (a married man is a fucked donkey) seems to be a uniquely Catalan point of view. Cow-like insults for women were reviewed in an earlier chapter and cocks have been studied at some length but the rest of the farmyard has received less attention. Hens aren't invoked nearly as often as cocks. Swedes tend to call women *höna* (hens) and Germans take a dim view of a *Hühnerficker* (chicken fucker). But having congress with a Corsican hen must be linked to good fortune because they say that *fiddolu di a ghjaddina bianca* (the child of the white hen) is a lucky child. As for ducks, lame or otherwise, a naive Portuguese is *um patinho*, a duckling, while a Spanish duck is clumsy and uncouth. To an Austrian a duck is a Citroën 2CV and the French view of the Press is nicely summed up in *canard*, meaning both a newspaper and a piece of hearsay. A really preposterous *canard* might provoke the sarcastic Yiddish response to an unbelievable story, *Deriber geyen di genz borves un di katshkes in royte shichelach* (Hence the geese go barefoot and the ducks in little red shoes).

Trying to get one's ducks in a row when it's raining cats and dogs is another matter. A Dane who wishes to avoid mentioning the devil will say *Av for katten!* (For cat's sake!) but in a Madrid bar *el gato* is the person whose turn it is to pay. When something's amiss a Spaniard, rather than smell a rat, discovers either that *aquí hay gato encerrado* (the cat's shut in) or *se sube la mosca a la nariz* (a fly's got up their nose). I don't know about cats but a half-way polite way of telling someone to get lost in Portuguese is *Vai lavar o cão!* (Go wash your dog!).

In France they have a lot of trouble with *mouches* (flies, but also police informers), although with some people it's hard to know *quelle mouche les pique?* (what's eating them?). Sex isn't always as good as it's painted by French cinema but *les femmes* get through the more tedious encounters by *compter les mouches*, counting flies, that is, by thinking about something else. But if she takes a fancy to you, any Frenchwoman who likes to *appeler un chat un chat* (call a spade a spade) will let you know that *t'as du chien* (you've got some dog, that is, some charm). Before you know it she'll be calling you her *petit chien-chien*. But, *revenons à nos moutons* (let's get back to our sheep, i.e. to the point), keep an eye on your genders because in France and Italy a female cat (*chatte, gatta*) signifies a woman's genitals. But beware, should you ever be playing cat and mouse in Sweden or Germany, because in those countries a *mus* or *Maus* (mouse) is apparently what a woman has between her legs, which must cause havoc in the local cathouses.

Cats have always been objects of superstition. In Egypt they were sacred, in Rome a symbol of liberty, while in medieval Europe the cat was Satan's sidekick and no self-respecting witch would go out without one. Cats are haughty beasts; they make it plain that they're not really domestic animals, just feral animals that have opted for an easy life. They don't belong to you; a cat would never fetch your slippers. They also hate water, which is why the Basques coined the neat term *katubuzti* (wet cat) to describe an arrogant person who is putting on a show of humility.

But although cats have been associated with the forces of darkness, they've never been persecuted like the hated wolf, a creature that aroused such irrational loathing it had already been hunted to extinction in Britain by the sixteenth century. Across Europe the wolf has long been a symbol of evil and, metaphorically, of a vicious and predatory person, usually a man. The dog-loving French have extended their affections to the wilder version and call their lovers *mon petit loup* (my little wolf), and at dusk they say it's *entre chien et loup* (between a dog and a wolf). It was believed that to become a werewolf you only needed to don a wolfskin in the full moon but in Italy they say *il lupo perde il pelo ma non il vizio* (the wolf sheds its skin, but not its vices). The werewolf's Jekyll and Hyde existence is reflected in another Basque expression, *kanpoan uso etxean otso* (a dove in the street, a wolf at home). As Little Red Riding Hood can testify, it's not easy keeping the wolf from the door, especially if the wolf in question is an *Italiano allupato* (a wolfish Italian), the archetypal predatory male. And if you're still puzzling over how a French femme can have une chatte where a German Frau has eine Maus, ponder this: the Frau doesn't just have a cleavage, she has eine Wolfsgrube, a wolf's lair. Scary, huh?

We all seem to share this idea of inanimate things – the weather, a job, a situation – being beastly, bestiale, tierisch and so forth, though for the French une bêtise is a folly, not something unpleasant as such. And yet we seem to enlist beasts to our idiomatic army almost at random. For example, John may well drink like a fish and get pissed as a newt on snakebite but Johann wakes up with a Katzenjammer (a hangover, literally the wailing of cats), and Jean tries to get rid of it with un rince-cochon (a pig rinse). There are no flies on John, who naturally opts for a hair of the dog, based on the old belief that rabies could be cured by the hair of the dog that bit you.

It's a queer fish that falls for that old pesce d'aprile (April fool), though it's better than, as a Dane would put it, winding up død som en sild (dead as a herring) on la ruta del bacalao (the cod road). This was the two-hundred-mile stretch of road between Madrid and Valencia which gained notoriety in the early 1990s for fatal accidents as young Madrileños, high as kites, shuttled between Madrid and the Valencia club scene which had produced the form of dance music dubbed bacalao. Why bacalao? Why not? In Spain you don't say 'Who wears the trousers in this household?' but ¿Quién corta el bacalao en esta casa? (Who cuts the cod?), even though bacalao is yet another word for a woman's cat, or mouse, or mussel or what have you. But that's another kettle of fish.

If you get a bit above yourself and start running off at the mouth a Spaniard might suggest que te folle un pez (may you be fucked by a fish). While this presents an interesting challenge for the bestially inclined, it seems an unnecessarily harsh figure of speech. Preferable by far is the Irish put-down for a smart-arse which goes: *O muise, mustais frog ort, o bhitch!* (Oh indeed, a frog's moustache on you, o bitch). That should put a stop to the rabbit of any big fish who thinks they're the bee's knees or the cat's whiskers.

16 ★ A La Carte

You first parents of the human race . . . who ruined your-
selves for an apple, what might you not have done for a
truffled turkey?

Anthelme Brillat-Savarin

This could only happen in France. Bercy's been taken in by
les volailles, the poultry, the gendarmes, that is, and he's in the
soup. *Il a la cerise*, he's got the cherry, he's out of luck, and
they're trying to make him turn *casserole*, informer. Now Bercy
isn't *une poire*, you understand, not a pear, an idiot, and he
knows sure as eggs is eggs that the usual fate of the *casserole*
is, no pun intended, *passer à la casserole*, to get bumped off.
Which is no more than they deserve, but he's got *le chou farci*,
stuffed cabbage, worries enough without this. Really, this is
the last straw, *la fin des haricots*, the last bean. So he says to
Poulain, the detective:

'*Vous n'êtes pas à la flan*, Poulain, this flan isn't for real, you
can't be serious.'

Poulain, whose breath smells so foul you'd think he *se
lave ses crocs au Roquefort*, brushes his teeth with Roquefort, just
smirks.

'*Mais bien sûr, Bercy, mon petit chou en susucre*, my little sugared
cabbage, *vos carottes sont cuites*, your carrots are cooked. We know
that you're *un hareng*, a lousy herring, a pimp, who *aller va
épinards*, runs on spinach, lives off a prostitute. You'd better
wake up and smell the coffee or else you're going to *becqueter
les fagots*, live on kidney beans, you know, go to jail.'

Now the thought of a few years in *la grande marmite*, the big stewpot, of doing porridge, does not appeal to Bercy one bit and he can see that Poulain has him *dans le pastis*, in a bit of a fix. But he knows the cop is no milksop and has a reputation for being *très soupe au lait*, very bread and milk, that is to say, very quick to fly off the handle, so he tries to play *la gourde*, the dimwit.

'Is there some sort of *pomme de discorde*, some bone of contention? As for me, *je ne sais pas plus que de beurre aux fesses*, I don't know buttered buttocks, damn all, about anyone.'

'*Fais pas l'oeuf*,' Poulain snaps, don't play the fool. 'You're going to help us nail that bastard Rouille for *bouffer la grenouille*, for eating frogs, you see, for embezzlement. *La poire est mûre*, the time is ripe. Unfortunately it seems *il a changé d'épicerie*, he's changed his grocer, moved on, so you're here to tell us where he is.'

It so happens that Bercy knows a good deal about this Rouille, among other things that Rouille doesn't deal in *pain dur*, in hard bread or trifles, and that if he hears that Bercy's spilled the beans Rouille will see to it that he *passe à la moulinette*, gets put through the blender. Poulain interrupts his thoughts.

'Listen, *c'est bête comme chou*, it's as simple as cabbage, as easy as pie. I know you *esperto que nem um alho*, that you're as smart as garlic, as the Portuguese say, that you're very clever. So you tell us what we want and everything will be *aux pommes*, apples, just fine. But if you *tombe dans les choux*, if you let us down by falling in the cabbages, we'll tell Rouille that you sang for your supper, that you gave it to us *chou pour chou*, cabbage by cabbage, word for word, and he'll give you a *tisane*, a thrashing, that you won't forget. Now listen carefully, *je me suis cassé le chou*, I've bust my cabbage over this case, so you'd better not let me down.'

'OK, it's like this,' says Bercy, who can see he's cornered. 'Rouille is in partnership with Barila, a Milanese, who's *una pasta d'uomo*, as they say over there, a good-natured pasta of a man, although a real *pizza*, a terrible bore, when he's been drinking and he's *plein comme un boudin*, full as a sausage. Well these two are fine when it comes to business, but there's *mala leche*, as the Spanish say, bad milk between them. And with Barila being an Italian, of course *è sempre la stessa minestra*, it's the same old soup, the same old story – it's because of a woman.

'Rouille has this little *poulette*, this chick called Béarnaise. She's *très bien garnie*, really well garnished, well stacked you know, although if you want my opinion she overdoes the make-up, the way she *se sucre la gauffre*, sugars her waffle with all that powder and eyeliner. Now this Barila is *une bonne poire*, a good sort, but when it comes to women *è fatto d'altra pasta*, he's made of different pasta, and things between him and Rouille *essere el kiwi*, hit rock bottom, when Rouille came home to find Barila and Béarnaise getting down to some pretty serious *limonare*, no, not making lemonade, but heavy petting. Rouille gives him *un oeil au beurre noir*, a black eye, and tells him that if he doesn't keep his hands off the girl he's going to cut off and scramble his *huevos*, his balls, and he'll never get *un petit pain*, a hard-on, again.'

'So was it this Barila who fixed *les fromages*, the jurors, in that case involving all that Mafia *cavoli*, cabbages, all that business?' Poulain interrupts.

What does Poulain think he is, some kind of *huître*, an oyster, a complete idiot, that he's going to *piantare carote*, plant carrots, tell all these tall tales only for the cop to *chier du poivre*, leave him in the lurch, shitting pepper, with *une casserole au derrière*, his reputation in tatters? 'I don't know about that. I heard there was some German involved, an upstart by all accounts, what they call *Dreikäsehoch*, three cheeses tall, who fancied himself as *un gros poisson*, but I don't know what his connection was. He liked to *ramener les cerises*, lay on the cherries, put on airs, but he was probably just a *testa di rapa*, a sugar-beet head, an idiot.

'The thing about this Barila is that he's no stranger to *la brioche infernale*, the brioche from hell, the gay scene you understand. He's a two-footed player, ambidextrous, if you get my meaning, bisexual, and he had a crush on this little *finocchio*, a fennel, a young faggot from Modena called Lumache, a bit of a *gourmandise*, you know, a fellatio specialist, at least that's what I hear, with a record for petty theft, stealing *lasagne*, wallets, and that kind of stuff. Now Barila is so struck on this young *crevette*, the shrimp of a queer, that he drops his guard and one night when he's well *poivré*, well and truly peppered, the little *poulette* sets him up for blackmail. He pays *un homard*, a lobster, an Englishman, to take compromising pictures of the two of them together.'

'But how does Rouille fit into all this?' Poulain asks.

'I'm coming to that,' says Bercy. 'Now, of course, Barila knows all *les petites cuisines du métier*, all the little tricks of the trade, and he's no *andouille*, not a stupid sausage, so when Lumache tries to put the bite on over the pictures he tells him to *aller au fraises*, go pick strawberries, get lost. Lumache's a bit put out, he thought the whole thing would be *du sucre*, dead simple, and now he feels like he's been caught out in *salades*, some foolishness, so he goes off with his tail between his legs. Then, *au flan*, on the spur of the moment, he decides to visit Rouille, to cut him in on the deal. But Rouille pulls a gun and demands the photos. Lumache is out of his league, and hands over all the pictures *pour des prunes*, for plums, for nothing.'

'So what's the tie-in?' says Poulain. 'And this better not be *un poisson d'avril*, an April fool.'

'Well, it's a stand-off, isn't it? Rouille's got the photos of Barila, but Barila knows about Rouille's little problem with the *grenouille*, the frog, the embezzlement stuff. It's an impasse. As the Galicians say, *como as cereixas son as desgracias que unhas noutras se engarzan*, we are joined like cherries by our misfortunes or, to put it another way, sorrows never come one at a time.'

'And that's it? You call that a story? *Mon Dieu*, but you know how to *rallonger la sauce*, make the sauce go further, to spin out a tale.'

Bercy tries to laugh it off. '*Mais oui, mais ça ce boit comme du petit lait, non?* It slips down a treat, like a little whey, this story, doesn't it?'

'You think you're clever, Bercy, but *je cours sur le haricot*, I'm running on beans, I'm bored rigid by your story. I'm going to make you *poireauter*, be like a leek and kick your heels and dine *al fresco*, in the cells, until you think of a better tale. *Bon, changez de crémerie*, change dairies, piss off.'

17 ★ The Scatological Imperative

> I want loyalty. I want him to kiss my ass in Macy's window
> at high noon and tell me it smells like roses. I want his
> pecker in my pocket.
>
> Lyndon Baines Johnson, US President 1963–9

We have arrived at what the French would call the *cul*, in both
the sense of the arsehole and the end, the *cul de bouteille*, the
bottom of the bottle. We end where we began, in Catalonia,
in the Catalan capital of Barcelona. It's Christmas time and the
shops are full of holly and mistletoe and fairy lights and all
the other things you'd expect to find at Christmas anywhere
in the Christian world. But the shops and market stalls also
display two unusual items without which no Catalan Christmas
would be complete: the *caganer* (shitter) and the *caga tió* (shitting
log).

The *caganer* is a small, squatting figure, often sporting a red
barretina, the traditional Catalan cap; his trousers are around his
ankles and he's in the process of passing a large stool. Along
with the usual cast of angels, cribs and donkeys, the *caganer* is
a fixture of the *Belén* or nativity scene set up in most Catalan
homes at Christmas, although he is always placed a respectful
distance away from the religious figures. This figure, which
first appeared on tiles and other artefacts in the seventeenth
century, has been part of the *Belén* since the 1800s. But Catalans
are unable to explain why the figure of a man shitting on the
ground should be linked inextricably with Christmas. Even
the Amics del Caganer (Friends of the Shitter), a solemn organ-

ization with a fancy address in downtown Barcelona, doesn't know. They reject the popular theory that this defecating figure is a symbol of fertility and suggest that Catalans simply wanted to introduce something of their own culture into the nativity scene.

The treasurer of the Friends of the Shitter, who is a lawyer, assures me that he has collected similar figures as far afield as Indonesia and Puerto Rico but that only in Catalonia are they associated with Christmas. Every Christmas the *Generalitat*, the Catalan regional government, sponsors a number of exhibitions of *caganers*, and associated paraphernalia such as postcards, poems about shitting and so forth. Elsewhere in the world the little shitting figures are linked with good luck and there's a widespread belief that it's lucky to step in shit. Italians say *Montagna di merda!* (Mountain of shit!) when they hear of someone's good fortune, and in the Spanish theatre world you wish someone good luck on opening night with ¡*Mucha mierda!* (Lots of shit!), the way actors say 'Break a leg!' in England. In French *je te dis merde* (shit to you) is also a way of saying 'good luck'.

The *caganer*'s counterpart, the *caga tió*, is a split log, the Catalan version of the yule log. On Christmas day the family gather round the log and the parents cover it with a blanket, allegedly to keep the *tió* warm but really so that sweets and *torró* (a traditional fudge-like cake) can be hidden underneath. The children are sent out of the room to let the *tió* prepare for its great effort. When they return they beat the log with a stick and sing, always to the same tune: *Caga tió* (Shit log), *Neules i torró* (Sweets and cakes), *Si no cagues ben fort* (If you don't shit a lot), *Et donaré un cop de bastó* (I'll hit you with a stick). Then the blanket is pulled away, revealing the haul of sweets and *torró*.

The thrifty Catalans believe that if you dream of shit you'll make more money. This is the place where people say of a

cautious man that he *cagar molt prim* (shits thinly), and of someone careless with money that they *cagar molt gras* (shit fattily).
A Catalan with many mouths to feed *haver de fer cagar molts de
culs* (has to make a lot of bums shit). Catalonia's great artists,
Salvador Dalí and Joan Miró, shared this obsession and in 1935
the latter painted a picture entitled *Man and Woman in Front of a
Pile of Excrement*. The Catalan preoccupation with shit sets them
apart from other Mediterranean people and puts them in the
same anally fixated camp as the British and Germans. Well,
they've always insisted that by nature they're more northern
European than Spanish, although presumably they had something else in mind apart from an obsession with shit.

The British are renowned for their toilet humour and it
must say something about the culture that in an encounter
between a tenth-century English peasant and a twentieth-
century counterpart, three of the very few words they'd have
in common would be shit, fart and arse. Every British com-
edian knows that if they're beginning to lose their audience
they can be sure to win them back with a little scatology. The
merest mention of farts or turds, or failing that, bottoms and
knickers, is guaranteed to have the average British audience,
however sophisticated, falling in the aisles. The English generally regard anyone who doesn't find bottoms and underwear side-splittingly hilarious as a rather sad and repressed
individual.

The Germans would almost certainly agree. When it comes
to swearing, there can be no argument that they have nailed
their colours to *Scheiße* and *Arschloch*, shit and arsehole. So much
are these words the meat and drink of the German vernacular
that most Germans, when asked for examples of bad language,
draw a blank after these two and have to rack their brains for
more. Germans, and Bavarians in particular, have an even
greater appetite for toilet humour than the British. A typical
example: three executives – an American, a Japanese and a

Bavarian – are having a drink during a conference on telecommunications. From apparently nowhere, a phone rings. The American presses a button on his watch and has a brief conversation with it. Seeing the Bavarian's amazed expression he explains that his watch is a miniature satellite phone. Moments later another invisible phone rings and the Japanese starts talking, apparently to himself. At the end of his conversation he explains to the others that he's had a communications centre built into his teeth. The Bavarian, not to be outdone, stands up and farts loudly. 'Excuse me, gentlemen,' he says. 'I feel a fax coming on.'

Bavarians are uninhibited in these matters and wouldn't balk at using expressions that other Germans might consider too vulgar. In the south, for example, a heated discussion might close with the comment: Nix gibt's! Am Arsch kannst mi lecka! (Nothing doing! Go kiss my arse!). And the more perfunctory O leck! is equivalent to 'You're kidding!'. Throughout Germany Arschloch is a portmanteau word that does service for all species of unpleasantness and stupidity ranging from 'fool' to 'bastard' to 'dickhead', occasionally fortified as Oberarsch (chief arse) or Arsch mit Ohren (arse with ears). Despite its ubiquity, it's a strong insult that is not to be used lightly, unless among friends. In 1983 Joschka Fischer, the parliamentary leader of the Green party, was thrown out of parliament when he said to the president of the Bundestag, 'Mr President, you are an arsehole.'

In Romance languages cul or culo (arse) has an everyday use to mean the dregs or the end. The Spanish version of 'the neighbourhood's going downhill' is la ciudad va de culo (the town's going to arseholes), and more or less everyone has an expression like the German am Arsch dem Welt (the arsehole of the world) to indicate the middle of nowhere. Where the English use the toast 'Bottoms up!' the French say Cul sec! (dry arse). But you have to be careful with these things. When he was Soviet foreign minister, Andrei Gromyko decided to forgo the services of an interpreter and saluted the wife of Dean Rusk, the former US secretary of state, with the words, 'I offer a toast to this gracious lady. Up your bottom.'

The other *cul* the French have given us is *cul-de-sac* (the bottom of the bag), for a dead-end street, although in France such a street is more prissily labelled *une voie sans issue* (a street without exit). In Spain two people who are very close friends are said to be *culo y mierda* (arse and shit), which recalls the Yiddish saying about two people who are thick as thieves, that they are *azoy vi tsvey techeser in eyn por hoyzn* (like two bums in the one pair of trousers). The Spanish word for a soap opera, *culebrón*, is related to arseholes in that it *culea* (wriggles along) for ever like a *culebra* (snake). However, *culé* (arsehole in Catalan), the nickname for a fan of FC Barcelona, is not a reflection on the character or physique of the club's supporters. It records the fact that in their old stadium the hardcore Barça fans all stood at the open end of the ground. All a passerby would see if they looked up would be row upon row of Catalan backsides.

Not many Europeans go along with the Dutch in using *kuttelicker* (cunt-licker) as an insult but they are of one mind on the subject of arse-licking or arse-kissing. Sexual proclivities aside, nowhere is this considered anything other than a degrading activity and everyone has a pejorative word to describe it, although the Greek *kologliftis* (arse-licker) sounds like something you might find on a taverna menu. (The Irish folk-rock group the Pogues began their career under their full name Pogue Mahone, from *Póg mo hón*, kiss my arse, until someone told the BBC what it meant and they were taken off the playlist.)

Although everyone admires a sexy arse it's also reviled as an ugly part of the body that is better not exposed. W. B. Yeats expressed his apparent disgust at the propinquity of the organs of generation and elimination in the lines 'Love has pitched his mansion in / The place of excrement'. In Italian *fesso* (crack) means 'stupid' and when Italians make a particularly *brutta figura* and are suffering a terrible loss of face they say that they have *faccia di culo* (an arse-face). By no means incapable of irony, however, they describe someone deeply unpleasant as having *faccia di culo che incanta*, an enchanting arse-face.

Italians are proud people and will do almost anything to avoid finding themselves in the condition where they *avere le pezze al culo*, have a rag over their bum, a state of extreme poverty. With only a rag for clothing you would be very *malcagato* (badly shat), meaning badly dressed, indeed. The French agree that someone who *a du cul* (has arse) is lucky and that if they *a de la dossière* (have buttocks) they are enjoying truly amazing luck. But no one has much time for someone who thinks the sun shines out of theirs, or as they say in Paris, who *pense qu'il a chié la colonne Vendôme* (thinks he's shat the Vendôme column). Such people tend to be cantankerous, or as the Greeks say, *strimmeno antero* (a twisted bowel) and rather than argue with them it's better to *filer comme un pet sur une toile cirée* (slip away like a fart on an oilcloth), which is one way of making a discreet exit. The French *pet* (fart) is a diminutive of *pétard* (bomb or firecracker), a relationship that's unlikely to have escaped Shakespeare, the master word-player and devotee of the *double-entendre*, when he has Hamlet say, ' 'Tis the sport to have the engineer hoist with his own petar'. Why the French should call an absent-minded person *un pet-de-loup*, a wolf's fart, remains a mystery, however.

Despite the association between stepping in shit and good fortune, it's pretty well universally agreed that being in deep shit or up shit creek or anywhere else in the neighbourhood is to be avoided. No one wants to be dismissed as an Italian *stronzo* (a turd, but quite a strong insult nevertheless), an Irish *collach cíbe* (a male pig reared on bad grass), which is what they call a shithead, or a Swedish *skithög* (heap of shit). The Finns will tell you that you're *paskiainen* (made of shit), the Portuguese that you're a *cagalhão* and the Greeks will say that *te kanes skata*, you made a shit (mess) of something. But what could be more withering than the ironic Spanish title of *un don Mierda*, a Lord Shit, for a complete nobody, someone who talks poppycock (from the Low Dutch *pappa kak* meaning 'soft shit')? To such a person a German would say *Ach, du grüne Neune! Dir hat wohl jemand ins Gehirn geschissen.* Oh, you green nine! Someone must have shat in your brain. Why 'a green nine' should mean 'well, I'll be damned,' I couldn't say.

'Bad language' doesn't sustain itself by seeking out the unusual but by recycling the everyday, and nothing could be more everyday than shit. Yet its power to fascinate remains undimmed. *Scheiße* is on German lips almost as often as fuck is in foul English mouths. In its various permutations, *Scheiße* occupies page upon page of Küpper's vast dictionary of the German vernacular. For example, the German equivalent of 'it's got fuck all to do with you' is *das geht dich einen Scheiß an*. I have fought against this stereotype to the very end, to the *cul* you might say, but the fact is that Germans are raging scatophiles. Even their toilets are specially designed so that one's stool rests on a ledge, allowing *dem Volk* a thorough examination of the quality of the day's output before flushing it away.

A hundred and fifty years ago Stendhal commented that '*Il me semble que l'on fait plus de plaisanteries à Paris pendant une seule soirée que dans toute l'Allemagne en un mois*' ('It seems to me that one hears more witticisms in Paris during a single evening than during a month in all Germany'). This is a little unfair and it's not true that Germans have no sense of humour, but *jeux de mots* are not their forte. German is prized for its apparent ability to concretize the abstract, not for its playfulness. Germans eye metaphors with suspicion, as though such linguistic whimsy might undermine their sense of order. But now and then a little irony slips through the cordon, as in *scheißfreundlich*, shit-friendly, which means as nice as pie.

There is a poignant Italian expression of abject rejection, *no me caga*, he wouldn't even shit on me, but more common are curses involving shit. On the one hand these range from the Romany *Hlea ma ande ti bah* (I shit on your luck) to the more extreme Irish *Go bpléascfaidh do chac ort* (May your shit explode on you), or *Go raibh na seacht míle mbuinní ort* (May you suffer seven thousand torrents of diarrhoea). The French use the verb *chier* (shit) constantly, especially in reference to anything tedious or useless, which are invariably *chiant* (shitty) or *emmerdant*. *Tu me fais chier* (you make me shit) is a pretty crushing version of 'you're boring me stupid', but *il est chié* can mean either 'he's great' or 'he's the pits', depending on the context. Otherwise the French content themselves with frequent cries of *Merde!*, which remains their favourite expletive. It's also one of the most acceptable.

Outside of Germany the scatological curse thrives in Spain and Catalonia. Everyday Spanish expressions of surprise and disgust begin with *me cago en* (I shit on, or in) followed by anything ranging from *la hostia* (the host) through *la mar salada* (the salty sea) to *la leche de la puta madre que te parió* (the milk of the whoremother who bore you). The Catalans, for all their renown as the shock troops of the Counter-Reformation, manifest a blasphemous penchant for shitting on the sacrosanct in expressions such as ¡*Em cago en el cor de Deu!* or ¡*Em cago en l'ostia consagrada!* (I shit on God's heart or on the sacred host). If they can't open a door, a Catalan might vent their frustration by exclaiming ¡*Em cago en la porta de Déu!* (I shit on God's door). But the most extreme forms of such curses seem to issue from the lips of Spain's Gitanos, among whom such ferocious utterances as ¡*Me cago en tus muertos!* (I shit on your dead) or ¡*Me cago en tu descendencia!* (I shit on your entire family line) are not uncommon.

There's an Icelandic saying that 'everyone likes the smell of their own farts', but even if they do, no one else does, and on this at least we seem to be of one mind: with the exception of it being lucky to step in shit and those rare items that are 'hot shit', shit is worthless, literally and metaphorically. There is no corner of Europe, not even Catalonia, where talking shit, being full of shit or acting like a shit is regarded in a positive light. Nor is it particularly taboo. Of all the expletives that might slip past pure but unguarded lips, shit is the leading candidate – in a number of languages.

If shit isn't all that taboo, what is? Many people would complain that nothing is sacred any more, and anything goes. Plainly this isn't so, as we've seen that in every language there remains at least one thing that you simply must not say. And besides, these things aren't one-dimensional. For example, many English people, and many more Americans, don't mind saying shit but can't bring themselves to say toilet. They will go anywhere – the loo, John, rest-room, cloakroom, Ladies, Gents – anywhere but the toilet, and in Britain the word people choose will tell you immediately to which social class they belong or aspire to. Furthermore, even the most foul-mouthed people know, without being told, that they must moderate their speech in certain situations. No one, for example, would swear during a job interview, nor – unless they were very stupid – when they'd been pulled over by the police. And very few people swear in front of their mothers. So the taboos are still there, it's just that now they're not everywhere.

Taboos are also personal, depending on age and sex and class and, as I hope I've demonstrated, nationality. I had a few surprises researching this book, but nearly all of them made me smile. Although I accept that what I find amusing others might consider disgusting or shocking. The only thing that shocked me was discovering that the Dutch insult people by suggesting they are terminally ill. I'm assured that this is quite unconscious and as meaningless as calling someone a bastard or a *putain*. But it upsets me, which only goes to show that, in my case at least, the lid is still firmly screwed down on the death and disease taboo.

But lifting the lid off sexual and religious taboos isn't the same as lifting the taboos themselves; saying fuck every third word shouldn't be confused with sexual liberation. The truth is that 'bad language', rather than weakening taboos, serves to map out and perpetuate them. Rather than being liberating, it often trails in liberation's wake. For example, relatively few people in Europe these days believe that a woman who has had more than one lover is a slut or a whore but the pejoratives remain and, as we've seen, in many countries have lost none of their force. Gay liberation has been with us for twenty-five years but calling a man a 'faggot' or a 'poof' remains a dire insult anywhere in Europe. As for being born out of wedlock, nowadays an awful lot of us are, even in Catholic Europe, but bastard is still an insult, however mild it might have become in English. A day might come when no one knows what a bastard really is but when the insult still retains its force. Like a cuckold 'wearing the horns'; no one knows where it comes from but it rests on its semantic laurels, persistent as the light from a burnt-out star.

Some people complain that, now all the taboo cats are out of the bag, there is nowhere left to go, that overuse has blunted a vernacular that was honed for use in extremis, not for slashing at the everyday. But is this anything new? In those cultures where people swear a lot it's plain that they – or at least a section of people within that culture – have always done so, although the choice of words may have changed over time. I suspect that what lies behind this complaint is that swearing has over the past thirty or forty years spread to all social classes when for so long it had been confined to the working class. Now men swear in front of women and women swear right back. There's swearing in the movies, on television and on the stage, in literature, poetry even. Well, that's social democracy for you. But are the words really losing their impact? Perhaps, but if we tire of one set of particular words, we'll find others. Who knows, maybe they'll be words associated with death and disease.

But the source won't dry up, because 'bad language' is just another manifestation of our love of words and wordplay. As we look across Europe, we could take it as a rule of thumb that those who swear the most are also those who most enjoy a *jeux de mots* – the Irish, English, French and Spanish in particular. But it would be naive – not to say dishonest – to counterpose slang as some form of pure and unvarnished expression against the hypocrisy, cant and repression of conventional speech. Invective is pure mainly in the sense that so much of it is undiluted ideology. As I said at the beginning of this book, it's a distillate; it's for those who prefer to take their prejudice straight. Bingeing on the stuff isn't going to set us free, but then prohibition only increases its allure.

Bibliography

Allen, Irving Lewis, *The Language of Ethnic Conflict* (Columbia University Press, NYC, 1983)

Allen, Irving Lewis, *The City in Slang* (Oxford University Press, 1993)

A London Antiquary — A Dictionary of Modern Slang, Cant and Vulgar Words (John Camden Hotten, 1860)

Aman, Rheinhold, *The Best of Maledicta* (Running Press, Philadelphia, 1987)

Aman, Rheinhold, ed., 'Maledicta, The International Journal of Verbal Aggression', all vols (1977—89. Waukesha, Wisconsin)

Ayto, John and Simpson, John, *The Oxford Dictionary of Modern Slang* (Oxford University Press, 1992)

Barnett, Lincoln, *The Treasure of Our Tongue* (Knopf, NYC, 1964)

Beresford-Ellis, Peter, *Hell or Connaught! The Cromwellian Colonisation of Ireland 1652—1660* (Hamish Hamilton, 1975)

Borrow, George, *The Bible in Spain* (J. M. Dent & Co, 1907)

Brewer's Dictionary of Phrase and Fable (Cassell, 1970)

Brophy, John and Partridge, Eric, *The Long Trail. What the British Soldier Sang and Said in 1914—1918* (Andre Deutsch, 1965)

Bryson, Bill, *Mother Tongue: The English Language* (Penguin, 1990)

Bryson, Bill, *Made in America* (Secker & Warburg, 1994)

Bunyan, John, *Grace Abounding* and *The Life and Death of Mr Badman* (Everyman, 1928)

Burchfield, Robert, *The English Language* (Oxford University Press, 1986)

Burgess, Anthony, *A Mouthful of Air* (Vintage, 1993)

Caradec, François, *N'ayons pas Peur des Mots* (Larousse, 1988)

Cardinali, Mario, *Ambrogio Ha Trombato La Contessa: Dieci Anni Di Storia Italiana Nella Scandalosa Satira del Vernacoliere* (Ponte Alle Grazie, 1995)

Celdrán, Pancracio, *Inventario General de Insultos* (Ediciones del Prado, 1995)

Chadwick, Owen, *The Secularization of the European Mind in the 19th Century* (Cambridge University Press, 1975)

Chandler, Raymond, *Farewell My Lovely* (Penguin, 1982)

Chapman, Robert L., *The Dictionary of American Slang* (Pan, 1988)

Chapman, Robert L., *Thesaurus of American Slang* (Collins, 1989)

Cohn, Norman, The Pursuit of the Millennium (Paladin, 1970)

Collins, Roger, The Basques (Blackwell, 1990)

Collison, Robert and Mary, Dictionary of Foreign Quotations (Macmillan, 1980)

Dundes, Alan, et al, 'The Strategy of Turkish Boys' Verbal Duelling Rhymes. Directions in Sociolinguistics' (1972)

Enright, D. J., Fair of Speech: The Uses of Euphemism (Oxford University Press, 1985)

Enzensberger, Hans Magnus, Europe, Europe (Hutchinson, 1989)

Ettori, Fernand, Anthologie des Expressions Corses (Rivages, 1984)

Feinsilver, Lillian Mermin, The Taste of Yiddish (A. S. Barnes & Co, 1970)

Fernández-Armesto, Felipe, ed., The Times Guide to the Peoples of Europe (Times Books, 1994)

Fonseca, Isabel, Bury Me Standing – The Gypsies and their Journey (Chatto & Windus, 1995)

Forconi, Augusta, La Mala Lingua. Dizionario dello 'Slang' Italiano (SugarCo, 1988)

Fracastoro, Girolamo, Syphilis: or a Poetical History of the French Disease (trans. from Latin) (London, 1686)

Franklyn, Julian, A Dictionary of Rhyming Slang (Routledge & Kegan Paul, 1961)

Fraser, Angus, The Gypsies (Blackwell, 1995)

Funk, Charles Earle, A Hog on Ice and Other Curious Expressions (John Murray, 1950)

Ginsberg, Allen, Collected Poems 1947–85 (Penguin, 1987)

Giulianotti, Richard, Bonney, Norman and Hepworth, Mike, eds., Football, Violence and Social Identity (Routledge, 1994)

Gold, David L., Jewish Linguistic Studies (Association for the Study of Jewish Languages, Haifa, 1989)

Goldin, Hyman E., ed., Dictionary of American Underworld Lingo (Constable, 1950)

Grahn, Judy, Another Mother Tongue: Gay Words, Gay Worlds (Beacon Press, Boston, Mass, 1984)

Graves, Robert, Lars Porsena, or the Future of Swearing (Kegan Paul, Trench, Trubner & Co, 1936)

Green, Jonathon, The Macmillan Dictionary of Contemporary Quotations (Macmillan, 1996)

Green, Jonathon, A Dictionary of Contemporary Slang (Pan, 1992)

Green, Jonathon, Slang Down the Ages (Kyle Cathie, 1994)

Grose, Francis, The 1811 Dictionary of the Vulgar Tongue (Senate, 1994)

Hallam, Paul, The Book of Sodom (Verso, 1993)

Harris, Marvin, Cows, Pigs, Wars and Witches (Vintage, NYC, 1974)

Harvey, L. P., Islamic Spain 1250–1500 (University of Chicago Press, 1992)

Headley, Victor, Yardie (X Press, 1992)

Hietsch, Otto, Bavarian into English (Andreas Dick Verlag, 1994)

Higgins, Patrick, ed., The Queer Reader (Fourth Estate, 1994)

Hooper, John, The New Spaniards (Penguin, 1995)

Hornadge, Bill, The Australian Slanguage (Cassell, 1982)

Hourani, Albert, A History of the Arab Peoples (Faber, 1991)

Howard, Philip, A Word in Your Ear (Penguin, 1985)

Howard, Philip, The State of the Language (Penguin, 1986)

Hughes, Robert, Barcelona (Harvill, 1993)

Hughes, Geoffrey, Swearing. A Social History of Foul Language, Oaths and Profanity in English (Blackwell, 1993)

Jespersen, Otto, Growth and Structure of the English Language (Blackwell, 1930)

Jones, Ceri, Six Thousand Welsh Words (Gomer, 1995)

Kapuscinski, Ryszard, The Soccer War (Granta, 1991)

Katz, Dovid, 'A Thousand Years of Yiddish in the European Arena' (Paper delivered to the Conference on Yiddish Culture in Vilnius, 1995)

Kezwer, Gil,'Marranos Return to Judaism' (Published in The Month, July 1995)

Knox, Helen, et al, eds., Harrap's French/Anglais Slang Dictionary/Dictionnaire (Harrap, 1993)

Kofsky, Frank, Black Nationalism and the Revolution in Music (Pathfinder, 1978)

Kuper, Simon, Football Against the Enemy (Phoenix, 1994)

Küpper, Heinz, Wörterbuch der deutschen Umgangssprache (Klett, 1987)

Landau, David, Piety and Power: The World of Jewish Fundamentalism (Secker & Warburg, 1993)

Lawrence, D. H., Selected Essays (Penguin, 1950)

León, Victor, Diccionario de Argot Español (Alianza Editorial, 1992)

Leonard, Elmore, Glitz (Penguin, 1986)

Levy, Leonard W., Treason Against God: A History of the Offense of Blasphemy (Schocken, 1981)

Lewis, Nigel, The Book of Babel (Penguin, 1995)

Lupson, J. P. and Pelissier, M. L., Everyday French Idioms (Stanley Thornes, 1986)

Lotti, Gianfranco, Dizionario degli Insulti (Mondadori, 1990)

Lotti, Gianfranco, Le Parole Della Gente (Mondadori, 1992)

Lotti, Gianfranco, Insultopoli (Sonzogno, 1994)

McConville, Brigid and Shearlaw, John, The Slanguage of Sex (Macdonald, 1984)

MacQuarie Dictionary of Australian Colloquial Language (The MacQuarie Library, 1984)

Major, Clarence, Juba to Jive: A Dictionary of African–American Slang (Penguin, 1994)

Manzoni, Gian Ruggero and Dalmonte, Emilio, Pesta Dura e Vai Tranquilo: Dizionario del Linguaggio Giovanile (Economica Feltrinelli, 1980)

Mazzella, Léon, Le Parler Pied-Noir (Rivages, 1989)

Mencken, H. L., The American Language (Knopf, 1936)

Mills, Jane, Sexwords (Penguin, 1993)

Mills, Jane, Womanwords (Virago, 1991)

Miller, Casey and Swift, Kate, Words and Women: New Language in New Times (Pelican, 1979)

Montagu, Ashley, The Anatomy of Swearing (Rapp & Whiting, 1968)

Morton, James, Low Speak (Angus & Robertson, 1989)

Murray, Bill, The Old Firm: Sectarianism, Sport and Society in Scotland (John Donald, 1984)

Nash, Walter, Jargon: Its Uses and Abuses (Blackwell, 1993)

Nobre, Eduardo, Dicionário de Calão (Publicações Dom Quixote, 1986)

Núñez, Miguel Ropero, El Léxico Caló en Lenguaje del Cante Flamenco (Universidad de Sevilla, 1978)

Odean, Kathleen, High Steppers, Fallen Angels and Lollipops: Wall Street Slang (Dodd Mead, NYC, 1988)

Oliver, Juan Manuel, Diccionario de Argot (Sena, 1985)

Osborne, Lawrence, The Poisoned Embrace – a Brief History of Sexual Pessimism (Pantheon, 1993)

Paros, Lawrence, The Erotic Tongue (Arlington, 1988)

Parris, Matthew, Scorn: With Added Vitriol (Hamish Hamilton, 1995)

Partridge, Eric, A Dictionary of Slang and Unconventional English (Routledge & Kegan Paul, 1961)

Partridge, Eric, A Dictionary of the Underworld (Routledge & Kegan Paul, 1950)

Partridge, Eric, Shakespeare's Bawdy (Routledge & Kegan Paul, 1968)

Pepper, John, Ulster–English Dictionary (Appletree Press, 1981)

Pettifer, James, The Greeks (Penguin, 1994)

Pinker, Steven, The Language Instinct (Penguin, 1994)

Pinto, Neves B., Dicionário do Palavrão e Afins (Bicho da Noite, 1993)

Plato, The Symposium (Penguin, 1951)

Power, Patrick C., The Book of Irish Curses (Mercier Press, 1991)

Prager, Denis and Telushkin, Joseph, Why the Jews? The Reason for Antisemitism (Simon & Schuster, 1983)

Ranke-Heinemann, Uta, Eunuchs for the Kingdom of Heaven: the Catholic Church and Sexuality (Penguin, 1991)

Rawson, Hugh, A Dictionary of Invective (Hale, 1991)

Richards, Charles, The New Italians (Penguin, 1994)

Ricks, Christopher and Michaels, Leonard, *The State of the Language* (Faber, 1990)

Rosten, Leo, *The Joys of Yiddish* (Penguin, 1968)

Sagarin, Edward, *The Anatomy of Dirty Words* (Lyle Stuart, 1962)

Sage, Adam, 'Why white cheese is not cool-up in new Franco-Arab slanguage.' *Observer* (28.4.96.)

Sartre, Jean-Paul, *Being and Nothingness* (Methuen, 1969)

Sculatti, Gene, *Cool: A Hipster's Dictionary* (Vermilion, 1983)

Shaw, Duncan, 'The Politics of "Futbol": Spanish Football under Franco' *History Today* Vol. 35 (August, 1985)

Sheidlower, Jesse, *The F Word* (Random House, 1995)

Siguan, Miquel, 'La Europa de las Lenguas.' Series of articles in *La Vanguardia* (April–June, 1995)

Smitherman, Geneva, *Black Talk: Words and Phrases from the Hood to the Amen Corner* (Houghton Mifflin, 1994)

Spears, Richard A., *Dictionary of American Slang and Colloquial Expressions* (National Textbook Company, 1994)

Spears, Richard A., *Forbidden American English* (Passport Books, 1990)

Spender, Dale, *Man Made Language* (Routledge & Kegan Paul, 1980)

Teich, Mikulas and Porter, Roy, *The National Question in Europe* (Cambridge University Press, 1993)

Thorne, Tony, *Dictionary of Contemporary Slang* (Bloomsbury, 1990)

Tóibín, Colm, *The Sign of the Cross. Travels in Catholic Europe* (Vintage, 1995)

Warner, Marina, *Alone of All Her Sex: the Myth and Cult of the Virgin Mary* (Picador, 1990)

Wilkes, G. A., *A Dictionary of Australian Colloquialisms* (Sydney University Press, 1990)

Wistrich, Robert S., *Anti-Semitism: The Longest Hatred* (Thames Mandarin, 1992)

X, Malcolm, *By Any Means Necessary* (Pathfinder, 1970)

Out of the blue...
INDIGO
the best in modern writing

FICTION

Nick Hornby *High Fidelity*	£5.99	0 575 40018 8
Geoff Nicholson *Footsucker*	£5.99	0 575 40027 7
Joe R. Lansdale *Mucho Mojo*	£5.99	0 575 40001 3
Stephen Amidon *The Primitive*	£5.99	0 575 40017 x
Julian Rathbone *Intimacy*	£5.99	0 575 40019 6
Kurt Vonnegut *The Sirens of Titan*	£5.99	0 575 40023 4
D. M. Thomas *The White Hotel*	£5.99	0 575 40022 6

NON-FICTION

Nicholas Jones *Soundbites and Spin Doctors*	£8.99	0 575 40052 8
David Owen *Balkan Odyssey*	£8.99	0 575 40029 3
Peter Hennessy *The Hidden Wiring*	£7.99	0 575 40058 7
Elizabeth Jenkins *Jane Austen*	£7.99	0 575 40057 9
Jessica Mitford *Hons and Rebels*	£6.99	0 575 40004 8
Louis Heren *Growing Up Poor in London*	£6.99	0 575 40041 2
Stuart Nicholson *Ella Fitzgerald*	£6.99	0 575 40032 3
Nick Hornby *Fever Pitch*	£5.99	0 575 40015 3
Victor Lewis-Smith *Inside the Magic Rectangle*	£6.99	0 575 40014 5
Jim Rose *Freak Like Me*	£6.99	0 575 40033 1

INDIGO books are available from all good bookshops or from:

>Cassell C.S.
>Book Service By Post
>PO Box 29, Douglas I-O-M
>IM99 1BQ
>telephone: 01624 675137, fax: 01624 670923

While every effort is made to keep prices steady, it is sometimes necessary to increase prices at short notice. Cassell plc reserves the right to show on covers and charge new retail prices which may differ from those advertised in the text or elsewhere.